D0387265

ON THEIR OWN

ON THEIR OWN

*Creating an Independent Future
for Your Adult Child with
Learning Disabilities and ADHD*

A Family Guide

Anne Ford
with
John-Richard Thompson

Foreword by Sally Shaywitz, M. D.

Newmarket Press 🐩 *New York*

This book is published in the United States of America.

First Edition

ISBN: 978-1-55704-725-0 (paperback)
ISBN: 978-1-55704-759-5 (hardcover)

10 9 8 7 6 5 4 3 2 1

Library of Congress Cataloging-in-Publication Data

Ford, Anne
  On their own : creating an independent future for your adult child with learning disabilities and ADHD : a family guide / Anne Ford with John-Richard Thompson. — 1st ed.
     p. cm.
  Includes bibliographical references and index.
  ISBN 978-1-55704-725-0 (alk. paper) — ISBN 978-1-55704-759-5 1. People with disabilities—Education (Higher)—United States. 2.
Learning disabled—Education (Higher)—United States. I. Thompson, John-Richard. II. Title.
LC4813.F67 2007
371.9'0474—dc22
                          2006103008

QUANTITY PURCHASES
Companies, professional groups, clubs, and other organizations may qualify for special terms when ordering quantities of this title. For information or a catalog, write Special Sales Department, Newmarket Press, 18 East 48th Street, New York, NY 10017; call (212) 832-3575; fax (212) 832-3629; or e-mail info@newmarketpress.com.

www.newmarketpress.com

Manufactured in the United States of America.

CONTENTS

FOREWORD

SALLY SHAYWITZ, M.D.

W ith the shocking words, "No, I'm sorry, we can't take her, she doesn't belong here," five-year-old Allegra was rejected from kindergarten and her mother, Anne Ford, jolted onto the uncharted pathway those with learning disabilities (LD) must learn to navigate if they are to survive, much less thrive.

"What will become of my daughter? What kind of life will she have? What about her future? What can I do to help my child?" In my research at the Yale University School of Medicine, these are the universal questions that every parent of an LD child puts before me as I begin to evaluate her child. In *On Their Own*, Anne Ford has written the answer to these parents' prayers. Based on her own journey, and lessons learned along the way as a single mother of Allegra—an attractive, sweet, now thirtysomething woman diagnosed with severe, multiple learning disabilities at the age of five—*On Their Own* is intensely personal and at the same time highly informative.

Anne Ford is an extraordinary observer of the human condition. She knows and understands human nature and, at the same time, is a fierce protector of her daughter. Combining an unusual sensitivity with a dispassionate, no-nonsense examination of the range of life issues affecting an adult with LD, Anne provides an indispensable guide for families who are responsible for an adult LD son or daughter. She is every woman, vulnerable and yet tough; trusting and yet cautious; worried but ever hopeful; tenacious in her pursuit of any and all knowledge that could have a positive impact on Allegra's life. In *On Their Own*, she becomes our trusted companion, a wise, knowledgeable, and compassionate guide who gently takes our hand as she helps us find our way through the mysterious maze of letting go of adult children with disabilities. With a velvet glove and a sure hand, she illuminates the road ahead, always alerting the reader to potential roadblocks, suggesting the best direction to take, all the while giving practical, down-to-earth advice.

In her pursuit of the best possible adult life for her beloved Allegra, Anne Ford has had to dissect each of the small and large pieces that fit together to make a life whole and satisfying: how to protect and yet encourage independence; how to love and yet not smother; how to provide for and yet encourage self-reliance and choice; how to live in today's world and yet allow the natural feelings of a mature adult woman to express themselves safely; how to protect a vulnerable adult and yet give her confidence to make decisions and especially to make mistakes. Through discussions, anecdotes, and provision of hard data and extremely helpful but concise lists, Anne tackles each of these difficult dilemmas and provides the gift of experience.

All readers will learn something new here or, more likely, many new things that they can take and use to make life better for themselves and their adult child. Anne addresses each of the important, often challenging issues on the road to adulthood. Eventually most children with severe LD graduate from high school. What next? Is college a realistic possibility? Initially, based on her past experience with schooling, Anne viewed college for Allegra with equal amounts of skepticism and pessimism. But as she gathered new information she changed her perceptions to consider a new range of possibilities: community colleges, trade schools, and non-degree certificate programs. She emphasizes that this is about our child, not us, hard though it may be to come to terms with that reality.

On Their Own provides the cold, hard details, but always wrapped in the warm embrace of love and the practical ease of doing. Anne always has the long view in mind, the adult future of an LD child. This book is, after all, about life, and so each milestone is connected to what came before and what this will lead to in the future.

Anne Ford is tough—tough on others but also tough on herself; she spares no one and leaves no area uncovered in providing the most cutting-edge, research-based information filtered through the lens of practical personal experience. For example, in an intensely personal and brutally honest section on relationships, she touches on siblings, friendships, Internet dating, and marriage. A parent often may not be aware of how siblings are impacted when you, by necessity, have had to spend much, much more time with the LD child, nor of the jealousies and resentments it brews. Yet these siblings may have to take on the eventual lifelong responsibility for an adult LD sister or brother. Even readers who have never walked in the shoes of an LD parent will not put down *On Their Own* without being touched deeply by all that not only the LD child but her mother and/or father must endure. Anne Ford speaks poignantly of the responsibility that comes with the stark realization that your relationship as your child's caretaker may be the only real bond your adult child ever develops with another person; the pain of seeing your child rejected by so-called friends—a loner not by choice but by life circumstance.

More common than a parent overreaching in planning for the future, she explains, is underestimating or reaching too low. Seeing their children experience so much disappointment and frustration, the idea of their finding an interest or success may seem unattainable. Many parents as well as their adult LD children are too frightened to make a move, and so Anne provides concrete steps and friendly but firm advice on what to do next and how best to do it. Of course, the goal is eventual independence made possible by a job. And so, she tackles every aspect of employment, noting that learning-disabled men and women tend to be their own harshest judges.

Parents will find the section on business indispensable. To help ensure success in the business world, *On Their Own* provides just about everything they need to know about helping their children find and keep a job: writing a resume; what kinds of jobs the young adult might enjoy and be successful at; preparing for an interview, including a list of the kinds of questions to be prepared to respond to; and the types of organizations that tend to be a good fit for someone with LD. Included, too, is an important, well-articulated, and balanced discussion of the pros and cons of disclosing a learning disability to a potential employer; here, Anne's advice, showing her wisdom and awareness of human nature, may surprise some. Always honest, she does not avoid discussing the downside, often coming from those who resent the idea of anyone receiving so-called special treatment. She cautions against doing anything that may cause coworkers to resent and to isolate the LD worker. As someone who is pragmatic, never a Pollyanna, nor a Cassandra, Ford cautions against fooling ourselves, noting that resentment can be expressed by personal antagonism as well as by professional barriers.

She also brings to our attention the range of psychological and health issues that may impact an LD adult, especially anxiety and depression, often a reaction to a seemingly never-ending series of disappointments and frustrations. Never maudlin or self-pitying, experiences are shared for the lessons learned and to guide parents in avoiding hidden pitfalls and in facilitating good outcomes. Nothing that can make a difference to your child is overlooked, including suggestions on how to negotiate daily travel to and from work.

I found the chapter on estate planning easy to understand and brimming with information that was new to me and extremely relevant. This section is a must read and can make the difference in how your child lives once you are no longer here. It includes a frank discussion of the emotional side of estate planning—that is, how to introduce your adult LD child to the concept of your own mortality. Here, too, a light hand, humor, and a kind heart are evident throughout.

At the very heart of this book is the awareness of the universality of Anne Ford's experiences with her daughter, Allegra. Nowhere is the universal nature of LD more evident than in the wonderful concluding section, "Advice for Parents from Prominent People with LD."

The term "LD" encompasses a range of severity and types of learning disabilities. At one end are those, like Allegra, who have a severe LD encompassing multiple learning disabilities. On the opposite end are those with dyslexia, a disorder impacting reading but not other areas of cognition and reasoning. In her revealing and often touching interviews with five highly intelligent, extraordinarily accomplished and successful dyslexic men—Sir Richard Branson, Gaston Caperton, John Chambers, David Neeleman, and Charles Schwab—we learn about setbacks, worries, anxieties, and experiences that are more similar than different from those with more severe LD.

Together with Anne Ford, these CEO's and one former governor have tapped into the ofttimes painful experiences and the shared learned wisdom leading to success that reflect a universal bond among those who are learning-disabled and their parents. No matter the type or severity of a learning disability, it causes pain and anxiety that remains with, and helps define, that person. On the positive side, having experienced so much, the person with LD is often more understanding and sensitive to others. Similarly, the difficulties experienced by the full range of those with LD acts, in turn, as a positive stimulus for self-examination and exploration for other interests. The result is often a high level of self-awareness and the development of an array of compensatory strategies that allow the LD man or woman to bend and not break when faced with adversity.

As you read *On Their Own*, a feeling of comfort and trust sweeps over you. You nod to yourself and say, yes, this is the real thing; she really gets it; she knows what I am feeling and I can trust her advice. It provides the rare but wonderful feeling of having someone who truly understands and to whom you can always turn for guidance, for answers, and for direction. Every parent of an LD child will thank Anne Ford for her generosity of spirit in opening up her heart and soul and sharing all she has learned, which they can now apply to helping their own sons and daughters look to the future with hope. Thank you, Anne.

Sally Shaywitz, M.D.
Author, *Overcoming Dyslexia*
Co-Director, Yale Center for the Study of
Learning, Reading and Attention

INTRODUCTION
"Now What Do I Do?"

In my first book, *Laughing Allegra*, I recounted my experience as a young mother learning to cope with my daughter's diagnosis of learning disabilities. My journey from denial to acceptance was a long and painful one, with many lessons learned along the way. When I started writing about these lessons, my daughter, Allegra, had long since passed out of childhood and was approaching thirty years of age. I thought by then that I had left all the pain behind and that time had soothed the strong emotions of those early years; but when I began to relive those years as I wrote my first book, I realized that no, I hadn't left the pain behind at all.

Events from twenty years before replayed in my mind with such clarity they could have happened yesterday. I remembered what my daughter wore on a certain day. I heard again the words the teacher first used to tell me of Allegra's "problem," and once more saw the schoolbooks and colored paper I stared at when I turned from her, unable to look her in the eye for fear I might cry. It seemed I even felt the long-ago chill in the air when I stood at a pay phone in the rain and listened to the principal from the last school on my list say, "No, I'm sorry, we can't take her, she doesn't belong here."

The old feelings of helplessness and isolation, of frustration, anger, and disappointment, came rushing back, and I found myself sitting at my desk, thinking about them and once again hoping I might not cry. And yet...there is value in remembrance, even the most painful kind. By reliving these emotions and thinking them through, I felt their power slowly fade and realized that the past could be released. I could say goodbye to many pent-up emotions, and I could finally—*finally*—hang up that pay phone in the rain.

Soon after the publication of *Laughing Allegra*, I embarked on an extended book tour throughout the United States. I met hundreds of parents, mostly mothers, at bookstores, schools, and LD conferences. Many told me that the book "told their story" and that they related to every emotional twist and turn. I saw that my specific experience was in

fact a universal one and that every parent of an LD child is in many ways
the same, no matter who we are or where we're from.

I began to notice something else on the book tour. While some parents I spoke to had young children newly diagnosed with LD, many
more had children in high school or older. At LD conferences such as
those hosted by local chapters of the Learning Disabilities Association
of America or the International Dyslexia Association, I found that most
of the attendees were parents in a situation similar to my own. The challenges they faced when their children were young were long gone, but
rather than end their association with learning disabilities, they continued to participate and share their experiences with others.

But really, are these challenges ever gone? Do we still attend these
conferences, buy books about LD, and follow the latest research simply as
interested observers whose lives are no longer directly affected? After
Allegra went to school, I joined the National Center for Learning
Disabilities (NCLD), first as a member of the board of directors, and then
as chairman of the board. I hoped to devote my time and energy toward
helping as many parents and children as possible by providing information
on LD and directing them to the help they needed. But I wonder now, did
I do this as someone whose personal experiences with LD were wholly in
the past? I may have thought so at one time, but I now realize that, for
both the child and the parent, the challenges of LD never go away.

The parents I met during the book tour spoke not of the past, but of
the present and future. Their experiences did not end on graduation day,
but were ongoing daily experiences, with the same ups and downs of earlier years.

Was it the same for me? Putting aside my memories of hope and tri-
umph, real though they were, I took a good hard look at all that was
happening in my life and my daughter's life, and I realized that things
have evolved, but many of the issues we faced in Allegra's early years
remain. I never woke up one morning and said: "It's finally over, I no
longer have to worry!" Far from it. Every single day I worry about her. I
think about her. I call and talk to her. I deal with one situation after
another that is a direct result of her learning disabilities.

I began to listen more closely to the parents who approached me
after my presentations, and I heard more and more expressions of frustration and confusion—not about their young children in grade school,
but about their adult children with LD.

A few quick memories:

- A couple in Phoenix, at their wits' end, take me aside to tell me of their predicament. Their twenty-seven-year-old daughter is chronically unemployed and still lives at home. What can they do?
- A young woman in Texas comes to a book signing and hovers in the background. At the end of my presentation, she comes up to me and quietly says, "I have a friend whose brother is thirty-five. He has LD and has no friends. He wants a girlfriend but can't find one. What should I tell my friend to do?" I see the pained expression in her eyes and hear the tremble in her voice, and I realize there is no "friend." She is talking about herself and her own brother, yet still has trouble speaking openly about it.
- An elderly man in California shows me a picture of his adult daughter and says, "I'm worried about what is going to happen to her." He says no more, but I know what he means. I hear his unspoken words: "I am getting old, I won't be around forever. I don't know what to do about my daughter. What is going to happen to her after I am gone?"
- At a presentation in New York City, a woman begins to cry the moment I start to talk. I see her in the back row, her hands over her eyes. When I finish, I go to her and she unburdens herself. She has LD, and she's in way over her head in a job she is not qualified for. She knows she is going to be fired and doesn't know what to do, whom to talk to. She asks me, "What should I do? Where should I go?"

For some of us, the feelings of frustration and confusion arise because we cannot fully separate from our adult child with LD. To be an "independent adult" is a wonderful goal to strive for and hopefully achieve, but what do we mean by it? For Allegra, to be an "independent adult" means that she lives apart from me and is able to do most things on her own ... but not everything. It also means that I do not think of her as fully adult. She *is* an adult, of course, and on a surface, day-to-day, logical level I understand that. But I'm talking about something deeper now, something below the logical level. Allegra's older brother, Alessandro, is married with two children, a house, a career. I never think of Alessandro as an "independent adult." I think of him as an adult. Period.

That is not the case with Allegra. I still think of her as a child—not necessarily because she is immature, but because I have never been able to imagine her crossing that invisible line from dependent child to truly independent adult. Even so, the fact is there and unavoidable—she *is* an adult.

How much control can I, or should I, have in her life? When do I step in and when do I step back? How often should I offer my advice when I see that she is headed onto what I perceive is the wrong path. Should I just stay out of it, or throw my hands in the air and say, "Okay, do what you want, but don't come crying to me when it turns out wrong"? Most often I wonder: "What do I do now?"

These are questions I ask myself every day, especially the last one, and that is why I decided to write this new book. It is a search for answers, to find out what works and what doesn't.

Writing about adults with learning disabilities presents many challenges, especially when we consider the varying levels of severity of LD. Adults with LD range from CEOs of major corporations who have managed to compensate for mild dyslexia to young adults who struggle on a daily basis with every aspect of their lives, from reading a menu, to understanding a supervisor's instructions, to getting along with their coworkers. Some have the additional challenge of Attention Deficit Disorder (ADD) or Attention Deficit Hyperactivity Disorder (ADHD) added to the mix. (For the purposes of this book I will only use the abbreviation ADHD, with the understanding that it covers both forms.)

Covering the entire range of learning disabilities would seem to be impossible (and on a specific, detailed level it is), yet I am constantly surprised by how often an experience or feeling is shared in common by people whose lives appear vastly different. The CEO with mild dyslexia, when talking about reading a speech before a large audience, describes the feelings of inadequacy, the sweaty palms, the pounding heart, in nearly the same way that a young woman with severe LD describes her sensations when giving an oral report in school. The levels of LD may differ, but the feelings do not.

I hope parents will glean what they need from this book and gain a little insight from the experience of others, even if the situation appears to be different from their own. I ask parents not to compare their situation with mine or that of any others in the book, but to look for similarities in attitudes and actions, things they can relate to, identify with, and learn from, in the same way I have learned from so many of them.

PART I

The Adult with Learning Disabilities

1

"So What Is It?"

Recently I was called in for jury duty in New York City. There is no better way to find a cross section of people from all walks of life—different income levels, education levels, interests, different everything. It is true democracy in action, and it is often the only time such varied communities overlap. During one of the interminable breaks while waiting to see who would be called up to serve on a jury, a few of us sat around and began to talk about our lives. One man was a retired certified public accountant, a woman was a secretary in a law firm, and another was a young mother raising three small children at home. When they asked what I did, I told them of my advocacy work on behalf of learning disabilities, and immediately the conversation swerved into that lane.

First of all, as everyone with an LD child knows, it is nearly impossible to go anywhere without meeting someone who has a child or a relative with LD, or a friend who has a child with LD. Jury duty, airplanes, grocery stores, dinner parties, it doesn't matter where, chances are good that someone there knows or is related to someone with LD. From this we can assume it is a widespread condition and one that touches all levels of society. So why is it that this condition is met with a form of mass confusion?

"So what is it?" the retired accountant asked me. "I mean, I've heard the term 'learning disabilities' before, but what is it? Mental retardation? Autism?"

"It's neither one," I said. "It's a neurological disorder. Think of it as the brain being wired a little differently than most."

"It's dyslexia," said the young mother. "My son has it. He mixes up letters when he reads." From the way she said this, I knew that her son had a mild form of dyslexia, and that to ask her about issues such as independent living or classroom accommodations would result in an uncom-

3

prehending stare. I tried to make the point that not all LD is the same, and there are wide ranges of severity.

"So is it like mental retardation?" the man asked again, and once again I said, "No. Sometimes, in fact usually, you can't tell if someone has LD or not."

"Is it autism?" he asked.

"No, it's not autism, either."

"So what is it?"

I went into greater detail, this time talking about the really difficult challenges presented by social skills, and this time the man said, "You know, I have a friend whose daughter has all the things you said. She stands too close when she talks, she always talks in the same tone of voice, really loud...and even though she went to school, she just can't seem to *get* things. And I ask my friend all the time, 'So what is it?' and he doesn't know. But it sounds like what you're talking about."

"Yeah, I also have a friend," said the secretary. "Her son is, what, maybe twenty-three or four now, and he's the same way. Still lives at home, and he's lost job after job...but my friend never said he has dyslexia or anything. Maybe ADD." This added thought brought in a new twist to the story. "Is ADD the same as learning disabilities?"

"Not the same," I said, "though many people with LD also have ADD."

"So if he has ADD he doesn't have LD?"

"Not necessarily. He could have both. And there's also ADHD, which is Attention Deficit Hyperactivity Disorder."

"So...okay, so...," the man said, squinting behind his glasses in confusion. "So what's it all mean—that they can't learn?"

"It's more than that. It affects everything in their lives, not only schoolwork."

"So it's not mental retardation, right? You're sure of that?"

"I am."

"I still don't get it," he said after a short pause. "If it's not mental retardation, then what is it?"

He could have asked me four or five hundred more times and I'm not sure I could have explained LD in a way that would have made him understand. I did not get frustrated by his inability to get it right away, because I have had years of exposure to all the best and brightest in the LD field and still, when someone asks me outright, "So what is it?" my reaction is to try as hard as I can not to say the first thing that comes into my mind, which is usually: "I have no idea."

It is so hard to define learning disabilities. Dyslexia is the one most often grasped by the general public, not as a term for a condition that covers all forms of reading disability (which it is), but as a way to describe the reversal of letters or numbers. We can all visualize someone doing that. We may have done it ourselves, while taking down a phone number, for instance, and writing 489 instead of 498. We may even look at that simple error and think, "I wonder if I have dyslexia?"

But what about cognitive learning disabilities? How do you explain an inability to understand an abstract concept without leading the listener to the inevitable, "So is it mental retardation?"

The problem is that there is no single definition of a learning disability. LD is not any one thing, but rather an umbrella term used to describe any number of behaviors that are unexpected in individuals who are accomplished in learning in other ways. The only way to accurately define it is to explain the full range of problems encompassed by the term, but even then the possibility of accurately describing every specific combination of learning disabilities is next to impossible as every learning disability is unique.

Here is a broad description:

LD affects people's ability to interpret what they see and hear, or their ability to link information from different parts of the brain, because their brain is "wired" a little differently. These differences can show up as specific difficulties with spoken and written language, with coordination, with self-control, or with paying attention. People can have learning disabilities in reading, writing, and math, and in processing information (and they can have difficulties in one of these areas, two of them, or all of them). Most children and adults with LD can read words, but they may not always comprehend the meaning of the words. Learning disabilities can reach into personal relationships, since they often cause difficulty in common, everyday interactions with others.

Learning disabilities are not confined to childhood or to the classroom. They continue throughout people's lifetimes and touch upon every aspect of their lives, from school to jobs to relationships with family and friends. Even though they touch upon these aspects and influence them, however, they do not necessarily lead to failure in any of them.

THE TROUBLE WITH "LEARNING"

The term "learning disabilities" is itself a source of some controversy. Many experts and prominent educational specialists dislike the word "disabilities" and replace it with "differences." To them, saying that people have a disability means the same as saying they are flawed or that something is truly wrong with them, whereas saying that people learn differently means simply that—they learn things in a way that is different from that of most others. I understand the thinking behind this, though I still favor the word "disability," more for practical than for personal reasons. Through my work with the National Center for Learning Disabilities and its advocacy efforts in Washington, D.C., I have learned that government agencies in charge of funding and changes in the law are only interested in disabilities—not differences.

Now that my daughter is out of school and I am focused on the difficulties faced by adults with LD, I often find that of the two words in "learning disability," the first one causes the most problems when trying to explain what LD is.

The issue of disabilities vs. differences doesn't matter so much when talking about an adult, but the word "learning" is so tied to the classroom and images of homework, textbooks, chalk, and blackboards that you can't help but imagine rows of children seated at their desks, frustrated by their inability to solve a math problem. Few of us associate "learning" with the adult sitting in the front seat of his own car, frustrated by his inability to read a road map or figure out which direction to take.

I've never seen a survey or conducted a poll about this, but I would be willing to bet that most people when asked about learning disabilities assume they are a childhood issue, maybe one involving teenagers too, but soon after graduating from high school things settle down, and the issue is no longer relevant. Wrong. Oh, wrong, wrong, wrong.

"All right," they may say. "College, then. Sure, I suppose LD could cause some trouble in college, but after that...? No."

Wrong again.

There is no cut-off point. No statute of limitations. What caused trouble in second grade in school can still cause trouble on the second shift at work.

Learning may in the end be the only word that encompasses enough of the various manifestations of the disability to give some idea of what we're talking about, but even so, it is inadequate, especially when trying to explain or define the problem.

Another difficulty I have experienced, especially when it comes to those whose LD is severe, is that usually there are no outward signs of LD, no physical characteristics one can point to that give an immediate understanding of the situation. There are no wheelchairs, no crutches or braces. We have no way to tell if someone has LD until we are faced with a situation influenced by the LD, and this often comes as such a surprise or source of confusion and frustration that we meet the situation with something verging on total incomprehension. "Why would she *say* that?" we might think after a coworker has just uttered a completely inappropriate remark, or "Why on earth can't he understand this?" we wonder after explaining something five times.

During a phone conversation with a mother going through an unbelievable series of frustrations involving financial aid for her son's college education, I casually said, "Sometimes it seems like it would all be so much easier if they looked disabled." She gasped and fell silent, and I thought, "Uh-oh, maybe I shouldn't have said that," but she wasn't shocked or upset at all.

"I hate to say this," she whispered, "and I never, *never* imagined I'd tell anyone again, but I sometimes wish he was worse than he is. I said it to my sister once, and she thought I had gone crazy, but it's true. If he was worse than he is, things would be so much easier."

There is no need to feel guilty when such feelings arise. It's natural, especially when so much in life depends on outward appearances. I read an article in *The New York Times* in which a mother in Connecticut with two sons, one with physical disabilities and the other with LD, told how much easier things were with the physically disabled son.

Think about it: How many people do you know who would look at a young man in a wheelchair and say, "Come on, stand up. I know you can do it if you just *try*"?

No one would dream of saying such a thing to a person in a wheelchair, but that's exactly the sort of thing a child or adult with LD hears every day.

2
Signs and Symptoms

The effects of learning disabilities on a person's life are certainly difficult in the childhood years, but for many, these effects cause more problems as the person ages. LD in adults does not always remain confined to one specific area such as reading or spelling, but spreads into other areas of life. Even adults who have high intellectual strengths in most areas of learning can be affected by a disability that, in childhood, had been confined within one area of learning. As an example, we can picture someone who excels at all subjects except reading, or someone whose academic skills are outstanding, but who has poor social skills. Those single areas of disability don't expand, but the effects of the disability do, and they can prevent the adult from performing in certain life situations at a level equal to that of his or her peers.

The National Institute for Literacy has identified the following areas affected by learning disabilities in high school students and adults.

> **Self-Esteem** Being criticized, put down, teased, or rejected because of failures in academic, vocational, or social endeavors often leaves adults with learning disabilities with low self-esteem. Adults with low self-esteem tend not to take risks or strive to reach their potential. Also, adults with low self-esteem are less likely to advocate for themselves.

> **Education** Learning disabilities that may manifest themselves in difficulties in spoken or written language, arithmetic, reasoning, and organizational skills will affect adults in adult basic education, literacy, postsecondary, and vocational training settings. These students may perform at levels other than those expected of them. Adult educators are not always prepared to address the unique needs of learners with learning disabilities.

Vocation Errors are commonly found in filling out employment applications because of poor reading or spelling skills. Job-related problems frequently arise due to learning disabilities that cause difficulties in organization, planning, scheduling, monitoring, language comprehension and expression, social skills, and inattention. These individuals are often underemployed in jobs that are not challenging, and frequently move from one employment situation to another because of conflicts that result from misunderstanding LD and how to support these workers in a dignified and helpful way.

Social Interactions Adults with learning disabilities may demonstrate poor judgment of others' moods and attitudes and appear to be less sensitive to others' thoughts and feelings. In social settings these adults may do or say inappropriate things and may have problems discriminating response requirements in social situations. For example, they may have problems comprehending humor. These traits may result in difficulty finding and keeping a job or developing long-term relationships.

Independent Living Responsibilities such as writing checks, filling out tax forms, or taking phone messages may present problems for adults with learning disabilities. Adults with LD may find themselves without the support systems (parents, schools, social services, etc.) that they relied on as children and have to incorporate accommodation strategies on their own.

SIGNS OF LD IN ADULTS

Other things can have similar effects on the areas listed above, so how do we know if the trouble is caused by a learning disability? First we have to look beyond the general categories of LD toward the specific.

Learning disabilities often go undetected until high school or even later. For some, they never get detected at all. We have all kinds of statistics on the prevalence of LD in school-age children (currently an estimated 2.8 millon public-school children have been identified as having LD), but we have no statistics on the number of people who may have gone through school or dropped out without ever having been tested for LD. These former students, now adults, may have no clear idea of what LD is and therefore assume the usual—that they're stupid, dumb, lazy, or any number of negative words used by those with undetected LD to explain their inability to perform at a level equal to that of others their age.

The following is a checklist of problem signs associated with LD in adults. Very often people read such lists and think, "Hey, that sounds just like my brother," or "My niece has that problem, too." They sometimes even think, "Those symptoms describe *me!*" Bear in mind that *all* of us have one or more of these problem signs at some point in our lives, so don't assume that recognizing these behaviors in yourself or someone you know automatically indicates a learning disability. If there is no pattern or repetition of these problems over time, you may just be experiencing a normal range of difficulty—an occasional memory lapse, for example, or trouble organizing your desk during a particularly stressful time. But if the problems come up time and time again, or if they have a negative impact on everyday life, a formal evaluation for LD may be in order.

Checklist for LD in Adults

Problems with Language and/or Mathematical Skills

- Poor reading comprehension
- Reluctance to engage in reading and writing tasks
- Frequent misreading of information
- Difficulty summarizing
- Difficulty understanding textbooks or manuals
- Trouble with open-ended questions on tests
- Poor spelling, or spelling the same word differently in the same document
- Poor grasp of abstract concepts
- Trouble filling out applications or forms
- Poor skills in writing essays
- Difficulty learning a foreign language
- Poor ability to learn and apply math skills

Problems with Attention and Organizational Skills

- Poor organizational skills or difficulty staying organized
- Difficulty adapting skills from one setting to another
- Slow work pace in class or on the job
- Poor note-taking skills
- Inattention to details or excessive focus on them
- Poor ability to proofread or double-check work
- Weak memory skills
- Inability to focus during meetings

Problems with Social Skills

- Difficulty accepting criticism
- Difficulty seeking or giving feedback
- Inability to understand subtleties of humor
- Problems negotiating or advocating for oneself
- Difficulty resisting peer pressure
- Difficulty empathizing with others or understanding another person's perspective
- Difficulty with nonverbal social cues, such as a raised eyebrow or a frown
- Inability to detect irony or sarcasm; frequently "doesn't get it" when someone tells a joke

HOW TO GET TESTED FOR LD AND WHY

Assuming you recognize the signs of LD in someone you know, or in yourself, does this recognition alone indicate a definite learning disability? Possibly, but the only way to tell for sure is through a formal evaluation by a qualified professional who has training and direct experience in identifying learning disabilities *in adults*. Ideally, this person should also be up to date on the latest LD research and have a working knowledge of local, state, and federal guidelines for providing help in different settings. Most important, this person should be able to help adults with LD understand their needs as they relate to school, work, and everyday life.

These professionals may be clinical or school psychologists, learning disabilities specialists, or neuropsychologists. These words may frighten some, or conjure images of electrodes attached to the brain, or Rorschach tests, or doctors nodding and saying, "Hmmm, very interesting..." There certainly will be questions and testing, but it is a relaxed and informal process, and the benefits far outweigh any discomfort or trepidation the person being tested might have. For some, the relief upon discovering a *reason* behind all the years of difficulties is nearly indescribable. I know a woman who was not diagnosed until she was in her forties. She still says that the two happiest days in her life were her wedding day and the day she found out she had LD and ADHD. It came as a revelation that helped put to rest the self-doubt, the fears, and the terrible sense of never being good enough or smart enough that had plagued her since childhood.

Dr. Fred Epstein, in his book *If I Get to Five*, described the experience of finding out he had LD like this: "At the age of forty my view of myself opened up like an automatic convertible cover letting blue skies overhead for the first time in my life."

Those who undergo an evaluation end up learning a great deal about themselves, for it is not simply a matter of a professional saying, "Yes, you have LD" and sending you home again. The evaluation provides additional benefits such as:

- A detailed account of your areas of weakness and strength
- Specific strategies, including accommodations and modifications, to help you perform more effectively at work, in school, and in everyday life
- Recommendations for support services such as counseling, vocational assessment, and job training
- Recommendations for instructional strategies
- A documented learning disablility leads to civil-rights protection that ensures your right to accommodations at work and in school (learning disabilities are included in the Americans with Disabilities Act, or ADA)
- Documentation that will help you be an effective self-advocate

QUESTIONS TO ASK IN AN EVALUATION

When seeking an evaluation, it is important to be actively involved in the process. You also want to have confidence in the professional conducting the evaluation. To help with this, use the following questions before the evaluation takes place to determine the skill level and overall perspective of the professional:

I would like to know:

- What are your credentials?
- What training have you had in testing adults with LD?
- How long will the assessment take?
- Will you prepare a written report of the assessment results?
- Will you explain the results to me?
- Will the assessment give me information about why I am having trouble with my job, studies, or daily life?
- Will you give me ideas on how to work around my disability and improve my skills?
- How much will it cost? What does the cost cover?
- Can insurance cover the cost of the assessment? Are there other funding sources that can help? Can we work out a payment plan?
- What if I need additional consultation? Can I continue to come to you for help, or will you refer me to someone else?
- What is the cost for additional consultation?

Learning the answers to these questions will help build your confidence in the evaluator. If answers are not forthcoming, or if you have any doubts, you need to start looking for someone else.

HOW MUCH WILL IT COST?

Recent high-school graduates with up-to-date documentation of their LD from their school do not require additional testing to qualify for services as an adult with LD; but if the documentation is more than a year old, the person being tested may have to assume the cost of a re-evaluation. Consider the following to help pay for the evaluation.

Check with your health insurance company. Some policies will cover all, or part, of the cost of an evaluation. This is particularly so if other problems like emotional disorders or ADD/ADHD are listed as reasons for referral.

If you belong to an HMO, check to see if there is a psychologist or other professional on staff who can conduct an evaluation.

Look into Vocational Rehabilitation (VR) Services. VR may offer evaluation services if your learning difficulties have caused problems in getting or keeping a job. The key here is that you must be looking for employment.

Find out if any local universities with graduate programs in special education or psychology have clinics that conduct evaluations. These evaluations are frequently conducted by graduate students under direct supervision of highly trained faculty and are often offered at substantially reduced cost.

Check with your local county or state adult-education office. Sometimes that office will know of private practitioners who perform evaluations on a sliding scale or at reduced cost.

Ask prospective evaluators about sliding-scale fees, payment plans, and other payment options.

WHERE TO FIND A QUALIFIED PROFESSIONAL

The checklists, information, and advice on evaluations were compiled with the help of the National Center for Learning Disabilities. The free online Resource Locator on the NCLD website can help locate a source of help in your area.

NCLD Resource Locator—www.ld.org

In addition, you can find qualified professionals at these locations:

- Adult-education office of your local school system or community college
- Adult literacy programs or literacy councils
- Community mental health agencies
- Counseling or study-skills center at a local college or university
- Educational therapists or learning-disability specialists in private practice
- Guidance counselors in high schools

- Private schools or other institutions specializing in learning disabilities
- Special-education departments and/or disability support-services coordinators in colleges or universities
- Vocational Rehabilitation Services
- Local hospital-based evaluation and treatment programs

3

Allegra: A Portrait of My Daughter

How many times do we parents of children with LD think, "If *only* it would all go away"? The notion that someday my daughter Allegra, now thirty-four years old, might wake up suddenly free of learning disabilities is unrealistic; but after I've gotten off the phone for the fourth time in one day, trying to deal with one problem or another, I cannot keep such thoughts from entering my mind.

No matter what the situation, things always seem to be only halfway done, with LD standing in the way of full independence. The words *and yet* always enter the picture at some point.

Today, Allegra lives on her own, *and yet* she does not live entirely on her own.

She manages most day-to-day issues, *and yet*, because she cannot manage them all, she cannot be fully independent and in charge of her own affairs. Daily—and I do mean daily—I am confronted with one situation or another that requires my attention and continued involvement in her life.

She has been able to work, *and yet* finding and keeping a job has been a challenge.

She had a passionate interest in figure skating. It was the one activity that really gave her a sense of self-esteem and accomplishment, *and yet* even that has diminished.

Thankfully there are some positives without an *and yet* attached. She has real friends who love her and support her, and whom she thinks the world of. She has not wandered along paths that might have led her into problems with addiction or unhealthy relationships. Above all, she

17

is a genuinely happy person. These are all positives in her life and things I am so grateful for, *and yet*...

Many of the positive aspects of Allegra's life, especially her living situation and work history, come with a negative attached, as if the old cliché of the silver lining was reversed and every silver cloud has a dark lining lurking somewhere nearby. Sometimes I have no idea what to do about it. Sometimes I want to provide comfort and answers but do not know how.

This desire to help my daughter has never left me. The tears and desperation of the earlier days have evolved into frustration and feelings of being at my wits' end, but even in those moments when I am ready to throw in the towel, something always stops me and compels me to try one more time. My quest for answers continues. My hope that things will change for the better never disappears, though it does take a beating now and then.

Since the person I know best in this world happens to be one with a rather severe form of LD, I'd like to tell you a little more about her.

Allegra was born in January 1972 in New York City. There were no problems with her birth, no abnormalities, no sign of the troubles headed our way. As a toddler and then into early childhood, she was vivacious and fun—that's what anyone who knew her back then remembers most. She had no inhibitions. She sang and danced at the drop of a hat. She had a marvelous sense of humor, even in her youngest days, with an enormous capacity for silliness.

In her second year of nursery school, her teacher called and asked to speak with me. "Allegra's a fun-loving, happy child," she said, "and yet ... she is not able to keep up with the other children and seems more distracted than most." She thought she should be tested.

"For what?" I asked, and her response was the first time I heard the words "learning disabilities."

The first doctor I took her to see was a prominent pediatric psychologist in New York City. By the time we arrived at his office, I had convinced myself that he would examine her and tell me nothing was wrong, or that maybe he detected a small problem easily corrected if I spent a little more time helping her with homework or prevented her from watching too much television. Instead he examined her, took me into his office, closed the door, and said, "Your daughter is mentally retarded, and I think the best thing for you, for her, and for your family is to institutionalize her."

I stared at him, nearly paralyzed with shock, and almost missed his next statement. "I would like to help you out with this," he said, "but unfortunately, I'm simply too busy right now."

I could not accept that diagnosis. How could this five-year-old girl, so full of life and joy, be so mentally ill that the only realistic option was to send her to an institution? She wouldn't die if I followed his advice, but to lock her away for the rest of her life . . . was that so different from death? I vowed to work with her and try to find whatever help I could. I saw one doctor after another: pediatricians, psychiatrists, neurologists. One might say, "She'll grow out of it," and my hopes were lifted, only to be dashed when the next told me: "There's something wrong with her, but we don't know what it is."

The final diagnosis (final in that it was the only one agreed upon by more than one doctor) was that she had been born with severe multiple learning disabilities.

Much less was known about LD back then. Most pediatricians knew very little about it; one school after another rejected her; and even I was unable to be open and upfront about it. I was reluctant to speak about her disability to my closest friends or even to my family.

Allegra did not process information the way other children did. As she grew older she seemed unable to understand even the simplest concepts. For example, she had no idea that fifty dollars was more than five dollars. If I sent her to the store with a twenty-dollar bill to buy a three-dollar magazine, she would come back with no change. She couldn't follow the rules of the most basic childhood games.

I remember one sad day when she was about twelve and playing Chutes and Ladders with two much younger children. She came to me in tears after they accused her of cheating. When I looked into it, I discovered that she wasn't cheating—she simply couldn't move her game piece the correct number of spaces. If she was supposed to move it two spaces forward, she'd move it three. When one of the children pointed this out, she moved the piece back five spaces instead of the original three. Of course, the younger children couldn't imagine an older girl, almost a teenager, being unable to grasp what they so easily understood. As far as they were concerned, it had to be a matter of cheating. What else could it be?

There were no more games after that.

From her earliest years certain characteristics have defined Allegra. At her present age, thirty-four, she stands 5'8" tall and has dark auburn hair with blond streaks. She appears much younger than her age, and upon first meeting her, few would guess she has a disability of any kind. She goes to the gym nearly every day and is in great physical shape, especially when focused on her skating.

Much of her skill with conversation (which can be quite formidable at times) comes from reading *People* magazine or watching the *Today Show*. In the first minutes of conversation it would still be difficult to detect any kind of disability. She has very good social skills, based mostly on observation. She has an uncanny ability to mimic voices and mannerisms, and can often find her way around a problem by watching how others solve it. A little later in the conversation she might say something or respond to a question in a way that doesn't quite make sense. Or maybe she will not be able to understand a concept that, for you, is obvious and easily understood.

She has difficulties in all areas of learning, particularly in math, but also in reading. She also has difficulty with abstract concepts, though this has improved enormously. The problems she had understanding concepts as simple as "more" or "less" have disappeared, and she has no difficulty with such things now.

Through all of her childhood and most of her teenage years she was unsure of herself around her peers, especially those who did not have LD. She was spared some of the overtly cruel remarks made in classrooms because of the special schools she attended, and she never had to endure the terms "lazy" and "stupid" still favored by some unenlightened teachers. Allegra's patient and understanding teachers were immensely helpful, but they were not there for her during the summer months, and those were some of the roughest times, when children who should have been her friends dropped away, one by one, leaving her an isolated, lonely child, unable to understand the world around her or the rules of the game.

Because of these difficulties with children her own age, she has always attached herself to an older person, usually a teacher or a coach or someone in a position of authority. She did it in nursery school, in every school she attended after that, and still does it today. She doesn't drop these attachments when another comes along, but stays in touch for years after. (How many people do you know who are still in contact with their nursery school teacher? Allegra is.) These attachments are not the burdensome, clinging kind. If they were, I cannot imagine people putting up with them as long and as well as they do. The nursery school teacher, for instance, might eventually say, "Uh...listen, Allegra. You're thirty-four. Don't you think it's about time to move on?" But she doesn't say that. Allegra's long-lasting friendships from her school years are genuine ones. The main difference between her and most others is that instead of maintaining long friendships with classmates, she has done so with her teachers.

Allegra attended special schools from nursery school on. She stayed in high school for five years and graduated in June 1991. I was relieved that she made it all the way through, and extremely proud that she was able to accomplish so much, but my happiness and pride were tempered with a sense of foreboding. I remember watching her on the stage wearing her white cap and gown, receiving her diploma with a big smile on her face. My little girl was no longer a little girl. She was a young woman with as much hope for the future as every other graduate in every other school; and though I tried very hard to enjoy the spirit of the day and the celebration of true achievement, two words seemed to hover in the air around me: "Now what?"

Allegra had already applied to and been accepted at a program at Lesley University called the Threshold Program. Many of her classmates were going on to the same program, and I was confident that Allegra would thrive there for the next two, and hopefully, four years. My unease was not for the immediate future, but beyond her final graduation day at Threshold. What then?

There would be no more schools after that. No more structure. She would have to fall back on the skills and training she had already learned, and I could only hope they were enough.

ON THEIR OWN

In any compilation of lessons learned by a parent of an adult with LD, the first, and possibly most important, lesson of all is this: how to let go. All parents have faced (or soon will) the experience of sending their children off to college for the first time or helping them move into their first apartment. It is not necessary to be the parent of an adult with LD to feel the pain of separation, but in my admittedly biased opinion, this pain is magnified when the child has learning disabilities. That first separation can come with shocking force and with feelings so great they border on actual trauma or grief. Whenever Allegra and I separated for any meaningful amount of time, we did it with something close to hysterics.

This behavior is easily explained: you spend every day for however many years focused on the needs of this one child, often at the expense of your other children. You don't do this because you love the child with LD more, or favor her, or even because she consciously demands it of you. You do it because she *needs* the attention. Doctor's appointments, tutoring, endless hours going over homework again and again, figuring out ways to help her make and keep friends, finding activities she can excel in—these issues loom large in the lives of children with LD and their parents. It is a daily, demanding job that can be frustrating at times. It may even appear hopeless, but we don't give up. We have no alternative. When our children go away for the first extended period of time, no matter how old they are, the overwhelming responsibility is suddenly lifted—not completely, but enough so that it is no longer the first thing we encounter when getting up in the morning, nor the last when going to bed. Now a summer camp or school or college program has taken over some of our duties, and for some, this first taste of liberation can unexpectedly lead to a period of confusion and even grief.

I've long since gotten used to our separations, but even so, Allegra remains always in my mind, sometimes in the forefront, sometimes below the surface, but always there. Recently I returned to New York on a flight from Detroit. I am a terrible flyer, always nervous, and when something failed on the plane and we had to turn back to the airport to make an emergency landing, I was beside myself with fear. It was not fear for myself, though, or even for my son (knowing he would be fine no matter what happens). All I could think was, "What about Allegra? What's going to happen to Allegra?"

Will I ever be free of these thoughts and fears? I don't imagine so. They may be so deeply ingrained that I cannot shake them off even if I have firm proof that my daughter could live a truly independent life. And what about me? I am as bound to her as she is to me. For the last thirty-four years my life has been defined by her needs, her joys and sorrows, her challenges and triumphs, and I would be lost if I went to bed some night and realized I hadn't talked to her that day.

These are frustrations and restrictions in my life that my friends do not have, but would I trade my situation for theirs? Not in a million years.

PART II

Relationships

4

The Parent-Child Bond: Learning to Let Go

Most of us have a set of assumptions about the course our children's lives will take. We look at our tiny baby and can't help imagining the possibilities. Happy thoughts of school, marriage, and grandchildren come along to keep us company while we sit quietly beside the cradle. We have daydreams about our children's eventual careers and lives full of good fortune and adventure. Whatever shape these thoughts take, no parent envisions their child still living at home at age forty-one, unhappy in love and work and life in general.

For too many parents of adults with LD, this becomes the unexpected reality as they continue to bear the primary responsibility for their children's emotional needs, financial assistance, and desire for companionship.

For some parents, a stark realization creeps upon them when they begin to see evidence that this caretaker relationship may be the only real bond their adult children ever develop with another person. For them, the earlier pressures and tension felt when their children were young are greatly magnified by a sense that time is running out. You might hear, as I did, an exasperated mother say to a friend, "I'm seventy-five years old and I'm *still* taking care of this kid!" The things she didn't say, the unspoken concerns underlying her frustration, are the really big ones: "Who will take over when I am gone? And who will take over the role I now play as the most important person in my child's life?"

These may seem like rare and extreme cases (and thankfully they are), but nearly every parent faces similar feelings to one degree or another. Even if adult children live independently and have lots of friends or are married with children of their own, parents will still won-der and worry about the future.

The word I just used—worry—may be the dominating emotion most parents feel about an LD child. Yes, there is joy, happiness, fear, anger, guilt, pride, all the thousand-and-one positive and negative emotions that make themselves known at one time or another; but worry always seems to hang around and form an undercurrent to all the other emo-tions.

I found this quote attributed to Buddha: "The secret of health for both mind and body is not to mourn for the past, worry about the future, or anticipate troubles but to live in the present moment wisely and earnestly."

Obviously Buddha didn't have a child with LD.

THE PARENT OF THE DIAGNOSED CHILD VS. THE PARENT OF THE UNDIAGNOSED CHILD

Parents of LD adults fall into two categories. Well, no...they fall into all sorts of categories, but for now, I'll focus on two of the major ones. The first category is parents whose children are diagnosed with LD while still in school, maybe as early as first or second grade. The second is parents whose children may not have been diagnosed until well into adulthood. Of the two, the first group is more fortunate, and though these parents may not have an easier time than those in the second group, at least they understand the situation and can explain what is going on when the inevitable challenges associated with LD arise.

The parents of the children not diagnosed until adulthood may have had lives full of unexplained chaos and confusion, with their children behaving in incomprehensible ways. They may even have jumped on the "You're not trying, you're lazy, you're stupid" bandwagon along with frustrated teachers and the children's taunting classmates. The chil-dren's self-esteem plummets. Maybe they get involved with the "wrong crowd" and turn to alcohol or drugs as a means to escape. Often as adults, especially if they have mild forms of LD, they overcome these hurdles on their own.

When I interviewed successful adults with LD and asked what they thought was the most important thing parents could do, every single one of them came up with the same advice: show children unconditional love and help them find something they love to do.

"Everyone knows that!" you say, but the fact is, no—not everyone knows it. Even if they do know it in an abstract, generalized way, they may sometimes have difficulty putting it into practice. This is especially true for those whose children were not diagnosed until later in life. These parents may not have understood the needs of children with LD, and they may have made a few missteps along the way, all with the best of intentions. For those parents—and there are hundreds of thousands of them—the most important thing at this stage is not to wallow in guilt over past behavior. Instead, take that energy and direct it toward doing everything possible to get on the right track and make some positive steps now. One way to do this is to accept that the past cannot be changed and that *all* parents of children with LD, whether diagnosed or not, have made mistakes along the way

Parents who know everything there is to know about their children's LD and understand the importance of fostering self-esteem can still have as much difficulty as any other parent when it comes to certain issues involved with LD. Homework is a good example. I used to call it "The Battle Zone." I knew Allegra had learning disabilities, and yes, I knew she had been in a special school since she was a young child. I knew all those things, but that did not prevent me from sometimes wanting to scream when she forgot something she knew only a few minutes before. "Why can't you remember?" I'd ask. "We've been over it and over it, and you *knew* all of this ten minutes ago. Come on, Allegra, try."

"I am!" she'd say, obviously frustrated.

"Then I want you to try harder."

Inevitably she dissolved in tears, followed by me doing the same, and anyone walking into the kitchen would think we had just come from a funeral.

That's a scene from her school days, but what about now? I'd love to report that I've reached a level of saintly understanding and acceptance. I'd love to think so, but you should hear me on the phone sometimes. "Why haven't you sent out your resume? Come on, Allegra, you're not trying."

"I am!"

"Then you need to try harder."

I try to catch myself before I start hurling the same old accusations of years past, but it is difficult, especially in those moments when I really do believe that some issue might be resolved if only she would try a little harder.

By the time a child reaches the final years of high school, parental encouragement or the lack of it is a given fact. It has either been there and been effective, or it hasn't. Hopefully, the first applies to your situation, but if not, is it too late? If you have come to the party late and only now realize what you should have said or done to make things better, is there any action you can take to remedy the situation?

The first thing you can do, starting today, is to *stop* the behavior you now realize may have added to the problem. Let's say you have spent the last years wondering why on earth your son hasn't been able to find a job that you know he is qualified for, or if he does find one, why he always quits or gets fired within a couple of months. I can think of so many things this parent might have said to the son, pushing him, criticizing him, maybe even shaming him; all under the guise of "encouragement." Now he comes to you and says he's been diagnosed with ADHD or dyslexia and finally understands why he's had so much trouble over the years. What do you do now? Continue to push and criticize in exactly the same way as before? Of course not.

Genuine encouragement is not only desirable: it is critical. It is the most valuable thing you can give to your adult child. Let others in his world hand out the criticism and blame, as they invariably will. Your role should be that of encourager-in-chief and to be the one person your child feels understands him best. Even when you have an opinion that you feel you simply *must* express, you can do it in a way that helps rather than impedes.

This does not mean a parent should encourage and praise no matter what comes down the pike. Nor does it require acquiescence in everything, or accepting the status quo no matter how damaging. Opinions and advice are often necessary, especially when delivered in a calm, nonjudgmental way.

THE FINE ART OF BITING YOUR TONGUE

Your son or daughter has just done something to upset you. It doesn't matter what—choose from any number of things that have happened in the recent past (I know you can come up with at least one!). The question for us is always, "How do I handle this?" Tempting as they are, losing our temper and ranting and raving are rarely the best way of doing it.

Abraham Lincoln had a habit of writing critical, sometimes harsh letters to his adversaries. He then put them in a drawer and did not mail them. The act of writing down his feelings helped dispel his anger. It also helped him gather and organize his thoughts. When he finally got around to rewriting and sending the letters, they were far more conciliatory, and his criticism was viewed as fair and constructive.

Why can't we do the same? Before writing the letter or hitting the send button on the e-mail, it helps to step back, rethink, maybe rewrite, and only then make our feelings known. This works with the phone, too. If you feel a burning need to call and complain or criticize, you might consider taking a brisk walk or going to the movies instead. When you come home, hopefully a little calmer, then you can make the call.

Then there are those times when we just don't feel like being Abraham Lincoln. We have simply had it right up to *here*! We dial the number with great force, or hit the send button so hard the keyboard jolts, and we let our son or daughter know exactly what we think about some issue or another. Well, fine. We're all human, and we're all likely to do this at some time. We can still get a grip on the situation and stop it from spiraling into one of those awful family squabbles that can go on for days, weeks, or even years by doing one small, simple thing that at times seems quite impossible.

Apologize.

I know, I know, sometimes you would rather jump off a bridge than say "I'm sorry," but even an apology for the way you presented your case rather than the substance of the dispute can do a world of good. I am by no means advocating a full retreat. You shouldn't apologize for an honestly held opinion, only for relating it in a less than helpful way. Even then, you may ask, "Why should *I* always be the one who backs down and apologizes?"

You already know the reason. It's because your adult child, no matter how old, may not be able to apologize or may not have the social skills required to make the first move. Your apology is in itself a form of encouragement, especially if focused on the manner of the dispute rather than the substance. It says to your son or daughter, "You see? This is the way adults get around in the world. This is how you deal with similar issues with coworkers and friends."

Every action we take has the potential to teach and illustrate an effective way to handle the world around us.

HEART-TO-HEART

It's also possible to prevent apologies by heading them off at the pass through avoiding situations where they may be required. In a conversation with a friend about his college-aged daughter with LD, I asked about the daughter's boyfriend. His response was, "I have no idea. All my friends know more about my daughter than I do." He couldn't understand why, and I suggested the reason might be that "they ask and you don't."

If you already have the kind of relationship in which your child tells you everything, good for you. That can certainly make things easier, especially during difficult times. The ideal is to develop a relationship in which you talk about everything and feel comfortable asking any question, no matter how personal. This is not an easy thing, especially for those unused to such direct communication, but you want your child to be able to talk to you about anything at all. If you can't answer your child's questions, find someone who will. Don't get overwhelmed or embarrassed or bogged down in judging the situation, and don't let it go. If a sibling or another relative can give a better answer, by all means let them try. Maybe a psychiatrist or social worker can provide the answers. It doesn't matter who, so long as the child gets the needed answer.

What about those parents who don't have this type of relationship with their children and are constantly surprised by their own children's lives, always the last ones to know, the last ones to be told? These parents may recoil from the idea of asking personal questions of their adult children, or feel that such questions would be viewed as an unwelcome intrusion. Is it too late for them to develop a close, communicative relationship?

It's never too late. Of course, you don't want to sit down at the kitchen table some night and suddenly, out of the blue, start prying into subjects never touched on before. It's a slow process. You have to gain your child's trust, which implies that you somehow lost it to begin with. That's a difficult notion for many of us to accept. We love our children. We've always tried to provide for them and help them out as best we could. How could they possibly not trust us?

We're getting into "water under the bridge" territory here, but the fact is that you may have passed judgment on an issue years ago (wrongly in your child's eyes), or you may have scoffed at a particular concern or not taken your child seriously. That small incident may have resulted in a certain hesitation the next time something similar came up, followed by a reluctance to come to you for further advice. Before long it becomes a pattern—especially if a negative reaction has become the expected response—and sooner or later, you find that you have been shut out altogether.

You can't take back any of those long-ago actions or change the reactions. The best thing is to embark on a new and different course, and to work in small steps to show that you can accept and react in a positive way, no matter what the subject happens to be.

Regaining trust or keeping the trust you already have only requires two simple things: asking questions and listening.

The first can be tricky sometimes and may not even be necessary, especially in the beginning, but the second is critical. Listen, listen, listen—*especially* if you have asked a question and your child is giving a response. There is no one more aggravating than someone who asks you a question and then barrels over your answer, wholly intent on making sure that you know what *they* think that answer should be.

LESSONS LEARNED—A CHECKLIST OF REALITIES

Isn't it awful, reading a book to gain a measure of hope about your situation, only to be told that you have to be the one to apologize and that the main responsibility for developing a better relationship with your adult child falls upon you? It is awful, yes, but parents of LD children and adults have dealt with truths far more difficult than these. Here is a checklist of realities I have struggled to learn and accept:

I'm not alone, even though I think I am

This is an old standby left over from the earliest beginnings of my journey with Allegra and learning disabilities. I'm not sure why, but for some reason parents of LD children and adults all too easily believe they are the only ones going through something like this, that no one understands, and they are destined to go through it all alone. Even when such thinking is proven false, the idea lingers on and pops up at unexpected times. This can be especially difficult for single parents who have no one to take over once in a while or to bounce ideas off of or to help share in the frustrations.

The reality is that we *are* alone sometimes—even in two-parent households. Yes, there are hundreds of thousands of other parents undergoing similar trials, but right then, in the moment after you've hung up the phone after a heated argument or just learned of yet another unexpected difficulty, no amount of imagined camaraderie helps ease the situation. When I'm in the middle of trying to figure out how to handle something, it simply doesn't matter how many others are going through something like it. They're not with me *then*!

Once the situation settles and the smoke clears, it's true: the knowledge that others are experiencing similar challenges really does make you feel part of something larger than your own narrow experience. There's a sense of belonging to a club—maybe not one you wanted to join, but one that truly does give a measure of comfort.

If this sense of belonging and comfort has completely eluded you, or if you feel isolated and lost, you do have options. Parent support groups and LD organizations such as Learning Disabilities Association of America (LDAA) are filled with parents who feel exactly as you do now. (You'll find a list of these organizations in the Resource Guide.)

I don't know what I'm doing or if I'm doing the right thing

This is a feeling that hovers in the background all the time. Well, guess what? No one is perfect. You're not. I'm not. No one is, and not every decision we make will be the best one, or even all that good. The reality is that no one else in your situation could do a better job than you are doing right now.

Energy gets channeled

The amount of energy expended on a young child with LD is enormous. It lessens somewhat when a child becomes an adult and leaves home. Often this leaves a vacuum in a parent's life, especially one who has devoted every day, all day long, to the challenges of LD. That excess energy needs to go somewhere. Why not channel it into positive, outward directions? Become involved in local LD groups. Volunteer. Use your hard-earned knowledge to help other parents just starting out with a young LD child of their own. It helps so much. If nothing else, it relieves those feelings of isolation. Don't worry about feeling left out in these organizations and support groups, or think that you might be the only parent there with an adult child. Many parents who join these organizations do so when their child is young, but they remain on long after their child has reached adulthood. Younger parents want to hear your experiences. They want to know what to expect and how to prepare for it. To them, you are an invaluable source of wisdom and support.

If you need help, ask for it

Oh, what a hard lesson this was for me. I spent far too many years thinking I could handle things on my own without help from family, friends, or the professional community. Now it's quite the opposite, especially when it comes to professionals. If I don't know something, I ask. If I don't feel qualified to handle a situation or advise Allegra, I find someone who can. Don't be shy.

You don't need to know everything

This goes hand in hand with the previous lesson. When asking for help, try not to get tangled up in insecurities about your own lack of knowledge about LD. I spent twelve years as chairman of NCLD, I raised a daughter with LD and wrote a book about it, and I *still* have trouble explaining Allegra's disability when someone asks. I sometimes meet parents who understand every bit of obscure jargon and can expound at length on the very latest research findings. And me? A phrase like "Nonspecific nonverbal, global disabilities" leaves me standing still, blinking, trying like mad to appear as if I know what the heck it means. I am not denigrating these parents. Obviously, it is preferable to learn as much about your child's particular situation as possible; but if you *don't* know or can't quite understand it, have faith that there are professionals out there who can help you.

Not everyone will understand your experience

This is a reality that feeds our occasional sense of isolation, but it's a fact that sooner or later we all need to come to terms with. *Not everyone understands our situation.* Friends and relatives may nod and make sympathetic sounds, but it's almost impossible for anyone to *really* know what you're going through unless they have a child with LD of their own. Rather than waste emotional and intellectual energy on *wishing* they understood, follow my earlier advice and try to channel that energy in positive ways. You can start by trying to release any lingering resentments. Ask yourself this: Would you understand if the situation was reversed? (First, impulsive answer: "Of *course* I would!" Second, more honest answer: "Well, maybe not.") No matter how compassionate, no matter how sympathetic, only another parent in a similar situation truly knows what you are going through.

Wanting to rip someone's head off is normal, if not advisable

Now that you've followed my advice and become a serene and tranquil person free of all resentments, what about those times when someone says something so outrageous and hurtful that you feel you really have no alternative other than to kill them and bury them in the backyard? This is when your best friend hears that your son finally has a girlfriend and reacts with a shocked, "Really? But what would she see in *him*?" Another time was when the pediatric psychologist advised me "for the good of the family" to send five-year-old Allegra away to an institution where she would live out her days separated from everyone she knew and loved.

My personal pet peeve is when someone casually compares Allegra to someone much more disabled than she is, for example someone with severe mental retardation. This often comes with a bit of unwanted advice. "Have you thought about sending her to an assisted-living home?" asked one oh, so helpful friend, who *knows* Allegra has been doing quite well living on her own for the last ten years.

What do we do in such situations? Grit our teeth. Bear it. Try to remain calm and civil. Maybe try to explain the situation in a way that might help them understand, even if they are impervious to such explanations.

Then again, sometimes it's fun to just let them have it.

No matter how bad things get, someone else has it worse
You will *always* be able to find someone with a situation far worse than yours. I could list countless examples, but so could you. Think about it.

It doesn't end
This used to be something I refused to accept. I clung to the idea that a cure was just around the corner and someday all the difficulties would disappear. I still cling to a version of the idea in which Allegra's LD doesn't completely disappear, but we'll learn to accommodate the challenges and lessen their impact to a manageable and even negligible level. Wishful thinking? Maybe. But maybe not, which leads me to the next reality:

Don't give up the fight
Days, weeks, and even whole months will come along when you'll want to surrender, throw in the towel, and say, "I've had it, I quit!" This is how it happens for me. "I can't do this anymore," my interior voice says. "I'm tired—I'm really tired. I've been doing this every day for almost thirty-five years. I have a

child who has been hovered over all her life, and now I feel like I've created an adult who still expects to be hovered over and not challenged. It would be nice if someone else could take over some of this." And so it goes, mostly when I am physically tired, but it only lasts a little while, usually overnight. The urge to sur-render comes and goes. The pressures build, and with them comes fatigue, and then my mind wanders into self-pity or thoughts of escape, or I dwell on old resentments about Allegra's father and how awful it was that he never acted like a real father to her, and on and on.

Well, okay, fine—for a while. But sooner or later things set-tle down and the urge to surrender fades, and I once again face the daily challenges and continue to do so until the next time. Often, all it takes is for me to hear her voice.

It's a roller coaster, isn't it, this parenting thing we do? Ups, downs, unexpected curves, and sometimes unexpected heights.

Learn to laugh at it all

Remember in *Reader's Digest*, the section called "Laughter Is the Best Medicine"? How true that is. Humor has been a saving grace in my family, with Allegra's own sense of humor at the forefront. While all the rest of the uncaring, uncomprehending world swirls around us, we have learned to take refuge in a sim-ple laugh at our own foibles and difficulties. I truly don't know what life would be like for us if we didn't have this as a buffer.

5

Brothers and Sisters

Allegra is six years younger than her brother, Alessandro. In her school years, especially those soon after her diagnosis, I spent an inordinate amount of time focused on her needs: doctor's appointments, testing services, parent-teacher meetings, tutors, the list goes on and on. There was a psychological focus, too. Even when I wasn't actively engaged in one of the above activities, I was *thinking* about it. Worries, fears for the future, anxiety about whether I was doing enough or too much or the wrong thing . . . again, the list goes on and on.

During this time I saw my son through high school and off to college with never a thought that he might harbor resentments over what he might have perceived as favored treatment of his sister. I thought that my focus on Allegra was an obvious necessity and that Alessandro and everyone else would view it as such.

During his last year in college, I asked him to write an article for the annual magazine for the National Center for Learning Disabilities. I thought it might be nice to get a brother's perspective on LD, especially as I was sure he would go on at length about his mother's self-sacrifice and nobility.

Alas, no.

He let me have it. The whole article (thankfully written as "Anonymous") reprimanded me—not for the time I spent with Allegra, but for neglecting to explain my reasons for doing it. He used to complain, for instance, that Allegra was able to watch television while he had to do homework. I told him that was because she didn't have any homework, but the complaints kept coming. Finally, I solved the problem like this: "Then why don't you spend a day as Allegra," I snapped. "Why don't you go to her doctor's appointments, why don't you be the one without friends, and see how you like it?" I had only to add "Nyahnah-na-na-nah" at the end to make it a completely immature way to handle it.

I should have done what he suggested in his article. I should have sat down with him and explained in a calm, mature manner exactly what was wrong with his sister and why she required so much attention. Further, I should have taken him to one of her doctor's appointments so he could hear it from an expert. He might still have come to the conclusion that life is unfair, but at least he might have been spared the belief that Mom is unfair.

Does this situation hold true for adult siblings? Surely, once they pass the legal voting age, the old resentments have been laid to rest. For many they have, but for others . . .

I went out to dinner one night with two friends and their college-aged daughter, who also happened to be the older sibling of a brother with LD. The conversation turned to Alessandro's article and suddenly the floodgates opened. The daughter kept her cool and never raised her voice, but her resentments and lingering sense of anger and injustice poured out. Her parents sat there, stunned and speechless. They had absolutely no idea she felt this way.

The truth is, most adult siblings behave and act like adults. At thirty or forty years old they aren't likely to rant and rave about your spending more time doing homework with their brother or sister than you did with them. Chances are good that they perfectly understand your reasons for doing so and realize they would have done exactly the same thing if they had found themselves in your shoes. Most of this is realized at an intellectual level, but sometimes there is a deeper, unspoken emotional level where memories of the smallest and, to our eyes, most trivial incidents can linger for years. You missed one of their soccer games because you had to bring your child with LD to the pediatrician, or you didn't praise them when they got an A in math, but you went overboard in praise for the LD sibling who just squeaked by with a C.

As you read this, I imagine some of you might think, "Well, yes, that's the case for other families, but not in mine."

Are you sure about that?

No matter how old your children are, it's really not too late to take Alessandro's advice and explain to a sibling why you did the things you did (and may *still* do!). It's possible you will be met with a blank stare and an uncomprehending "Why are you telling me this now? Of course I understood." You may also be met with the opened floodgates. If so, I strongly suggest you handle it with respectful silence like my friends at the dinner table.

The point of the exercise is to clear the air. Yes, you will have endless justifications for what you did or did not do, and yes, you will be right. But give them this one chance. Even if their memories are faulty, try not to get defensive and say, "Yeah, but . . . ," and try not to remind them yet again what a selfless hero you've been to the child with LD. For now, let it be enough that *you* know you were and are a hero. When all is said and done, and the waters are calm again, these long-held resentments will usually disappear beneath that bridge they should have passed under years and years before.

THE PRODIGAL SON

I know a mother who has two sons, one thirty-six and the other thirty-two. She also has two girls, both older than the boys. The younger son, Glenn, has learning disabilities that were not diagnosed until he reached his early twenties. His older brother, Paul, does not have LD, and I asked if he would share his experiences with me.

In our first phone conversation, he was quite guarded about his feelings and memories of growing up. I wasn't getting what I suspected might be there, so I told him about others who had difficulties because of a sibling with LD. He thought it was all very interesting, but he couldn't really relate to it.

A week or so after this first phone call, I heard from him again. "I've been thinking about our conversation," he said. "I didn't think my experience matched the others you told me about, but now that I've had a little time to reflect, I think I fit right in . . . which is kind of a surprise."

I asked him why.

"I was four years older than my brother, Glenn," he said. "I always did well in school, never got in trouble. I was the 'good kid.' We grew up in rural Colorado, and I can't remember anyone talking about learning disabilities. I don't think I ever heard about it until years later, and even then I only knew about dyslexia, reversing letters and things. It never seemed very serious to me and certainly no one ever connected my brother's behavior to LD.

"My parents had all kinds of excuses for him. He didn't have the right teachers, or he was more interested in sports than in class. At one point they even considered the possibility that he might be mentally retarded, but that was when he was very young, before he could talk. They didn't understand why he didn't develop at the same rate as I did, or our sisters. Glenn certainly isn't retarded. I've never even believed he was 'stupid,' though that's something I'm sure he believes about himself. I always thought he just didn't care. For me, the trouble I had . . . I guess I should be honest and say the *resentments* I had began when I was in high school and Glenn was entering junior high. He was always good in sports. I was a fairly good athlete too, but my heart wasn't in it. For Glenn, sports were everything, and he became the captain of every team.

"My parents were thrilled by this, especially my father. I guess they saw it as an acceptable substitute for academic achievement. No matter how badly Glenn did in school, no matter how low his grades, it didn't seem to matter as long as he led his team to victory. When he got into high school he started getting into trouble, too. Nothing major, but he was definitely on a path toward juvenile delinquency.

"My parents were at their wits' end. They couldn't understand why he behaved the way he did. I think, like me, they believed he wasn't trying hard enough in school and just didn't care. They decided to enroll him in a private school outside of Denver, and that decision really changed my brother's life for the better.

"Now, I would never say I wished my brother hadn't gone to that school. He's very successful now. I also have a successful career in real estate, so I can't say I was hurt by the education I received. But the truth is, I *do* think I would have benefited tremendously from going to the private school my brother attended. And if I'm really honest, I have to admit that I harbored resentments about this situation for years—

resentments against my brother, against my parents, and against what I saw as favoritism.

"You know the Bible story of the Prodigal Son? A man has two sons. The oldest is a hard worker, stays at home, tends the flock, all the things expected of a dutiful son. The younger son is a gambler and a ne'er-do-well. He spends his father's money and leaves home to go on a wild spree. I always imagine he went to the biblical version of Las Vegas. When he finally comes home, broke, homeless, and hung-over, what does the father do? Kills the fatted calf and throws a party to celebrate. The older son says, 'Hey, what about me? I've been here all along, never got in trouble, didn't spend your money,' and the father says something about the younger son being lost but now he is found.

"It's a parable about the sinner returning to faith, but man! I've always hated that story. I think every sibling of a prodigal son or daughter hates it. Yeah, yeah, we understand, lost and now he's found, blah-blah-blah. But how can anyone expect us to sit down at the party and watch little brother carve the fatted calf and not steam with resentment?

"I don't know if things would have been different if I knew Glenn had a learning disability. Maybe, maybe not. Intellectually, I might have understood in the same way the older brother in the Bible story probably understood, but that doesn't make it easier on a deeper emotional level. People aren't always rational or selfless at that level.

"I can guarantee, one hundred percent, that my parents had no clue they were showing favoritism. They would never have admitted that's what it was, even if someone pointed it out to them. My two sisters and I did just fine in public school. As far as my parents were concerned, we didn't need a boost up the ladder. They directed all their thoughts and energy toward the child that needed the most help.

"It makes sense. I undoubtedly would do the exact same thing in their position, but like I said, it's not easy for the other kids in the family. I've never spoken to my sisters about it. In fact, I've never spoken to *anyone* about it until today, because I don't think I fully realized I had these feelings."

I asked Paul what advice he would give to parents, especially those with adult children with LD.

"My advice would be to talk to your other children about it. It doesn't matter how old they are. It doesn't even matter that it's all in the distant past. Nothing can be changed now. We all know that. But if my parents were to tell me they were aware of the disparity in their treatment of their children, it would mean a lot to me. They don't even have to say they're sorry. There's no point, especially since I'm not sure they have anything to apologize for. But just to say, 'Hey, I know you had to sit back and watch your brother get all the things you wish you had and that couldn't have been easy. If we had it to do all over again, we would probably do the exact same thing . . . but we would have explained things a little better to you along the way.'"

THE FUTURE AND THE NON-LD SIBLING

Siblings of an adult with LD often bear additional responsibilities toward their brother or sister, especially after a parent's death. Much of this depends upon the severity of the disability, but even for those with mild LD or ADHD, the benefits of an extended family cannot be overstated. Losing a parent is a difficult time for everyone, and there's no question the new responsibilities thrust upon the non-LD sibling can be burdensome or even threatening to someone who also has a spouse and children to worry about. Some may feel they have suddenly acquired another child, possibly at the very moment when their own children are finally out on their own. They may even find themselves in the position of trying to promote independence in their LD sibling while at the same time figuring out when to step in and assume control—the same dilemma their parents faced every day. The situation is even more difficult if latent feelings of resentment and jealousy resurface. That's why I advocate clearing the air of these old resentments long before it reaches this point.

Here are a few questions parents have asked about sibling relationships and what might be waiting for the non-LD sibling down the road.

"When should I talk to my son and daughter about their eventual responsibilities toward their brother with LD?"

This depends on how old they are now. If your children are adults, now is as good a time as any. Undoubtedly, they'll have already come to some conclusions on their own.

In general, eighteen is an appropriate age. They are mature enough to understand the situation and young enough to know it won't happen right away (we all remember at eighteen how anything beyond a four- or five-year time frame seemed part of a distant future we need not worry about). Discussing future responsibilities at an earlier age works if parents believe their non-LD children have the maturity to understand.

I told Alessandro when he was quite young, around age thirteen. He handled it all well. Even so, I didn't burden him with it all at once or in a way that might have caused worry or fear about the immediate future. "I think you should know that eventually, long after you and Allegra are grown, there will come a time when I won't be able to take care of her anymore. You'll have to be the big brother then and take over for me. Can you do that for me?"

Of course he could. I knew that then and I still do, but in my mind, I knew he would also have to be her guardian, her friend, and even a father figure. I didn't say all those additional words then for fear it would all be too much for a thirteen-year-old to understand.

"What can we do as a family to help ease the burden on the siblings?"

Information is vital. The worst thing to do is to put things off until it's too late. I will go into estate planning in depth in a later chapter, but would like to touch upon a few items here that have less to do with lawyers and wills than with simple common sense and consideration.

Plan for emergencies by creating a master file with all relevant information about the LD sibling. This file should be kept in a place known by all family members and, depending on the severity of the LD and the nature of the sibling's dependence on family and others, should include things like the following:

Master File

- Names and numbers of the LD sibling's doctors, dentists, and mental health professionals and the location of all medical records
- Copy of health insurance card and policy number

- Information on relevant government programs, such as Supplemental Social Security (SSI) or Vocational Rehabilitation Services
- If the LD sibling lives in an independent living center, be sure to include all relevant information
- Copy of Social Security number, passport, and driver's license
- Employment-related information, such as the name and address of the employer so the sibling will have it in case of an emergency

Including so much information may seem a bit overdone, but it's surprising how many small details of a person's life remain unknown to their siblings.

A MESSAGE FOR BROTHERS AND SISTERS

With all this talk of resentments and prodigal sons and eventual burdens placed on the non-LD sibling, we can easily lose sight of the positive effect of learning disabilities in the life of a family. I wrote of Alessandro's lingering resentments, but when I look back on the years when he and Allegra lived with me in New York, I do not remember a sibling relationship based on jealousy or rivalry. Oh, sure, Alessandro harbored a degree of resentment, but this must be considered in light of his overall feelings toward his sister. They were always close and remain so to this day.

A disability of any kind brings an element of compassion and acceptance into a family, and I have a special message for the siblings. You, as brothers and sisters of an LD sibling, grow up seeing that not all people have an easy path in life and that some must struggle on a daily basis, often without much result. You may feel anger at times, resentment, jealousy, or even guilt, and that is all completely normal; but in addition, it is quite possible that you feel a surge of pride when your disabled sibling achieves something, or sympathy when they fail, and over all, feelings of love and devotion.

I have seen you countless times . . .

You are the sister with a family of her own still taking the time to escort her brother to a social gathering.

You are the brother who makes room for his older sister at his own family's table during holidays to make sure she will not spend them alone.

You are the one looked to by your parents, even though they may not always thank you for it, or even say so directly—but trust me, they do indeed look to you. You are as much a part of their thoughts as your disabled sibling, and in many ways your presence alone is the thing that most allays your parents' fears for the future and allows them to sleep at night.

6

Friends

Many adults with LD or ADHD have exciting social lives, but I have spoken to many parents whose adult children do not. I have been a longtime member of that less fortunate group of parents who have fretted and worried about our children's lack of friends and their increasingly lonely lives, even when there was no apparent reason for doing so. Let me explain that little paradox: Allegra has alternated throughout the years from periods of loneliness and isolation to periods of friendships and a full social life. Much of this has depended on outside circumstances such as her particular geographical location, her routine daily activities, and most of all, the people around her. For example, in her years in New York, her friends dwindled down to only one or two, and she did not go out very much at all. When she was in school in Massachusetts, she had lots of friends and was always out having fun with them. They were mostly classmates with LD, and they formed quite a close-knit little group. Even so, the earlier years of her isolation were difficult—not so much for Allegra, but for me. I still feel my heart tighten when I think of how she was ignored by girls her own age who should have been her friends but decided not to be, and I am forever worrying that she isn't spending enough time with those few she has befriended.

If we could distill all the problems associated with LD and analyze them to discover the most worrisome of all, I think we would find that difficulty in making and keeping friends causes the most mental anguish. One of the best quotes I've ever heard about this came from Rick Lavoie, former headmaster of the Riverview School and author of *It's So Much Work to Be Your Friend*. Rick said, "No parent has ever come into my office crying because of low math scores. It is the lack of friends, the isolation, the loneliness of the child that breaks our hearts."

Our hearts do break for our young children, yes; but those same hearts do not harden and become unbreakable once our children become adults.

THE MYTH OF THE LONER

Most of us know someone we think of as a loner. Often this person wears the label as a source of pride or a mark of defiance. True loners thrive on solitude and love nothing better than spending hour upon hour by themselves, but I believe many adults with LD who bear the loner label do so for the wrong reasons. They have followed the "if you can't beat them, join them" line of thinking in which they tell themselves, "If everyone else thinks of me that way, I suppose I really am a loner, so that's what I'll claim to be."

In reality, most of their isolation is a reaction to a lifetime of difficulties in social settings. Even those who were considered happy, outgoing children can grow into semireclusive adults when most of their social interactions have resulted in a degree of embarrassment, frustration, or ridicule. They become guarded and defensive. They withdraw into a narrow life, convinced that solitude is an easier, more comfortable way to live, free of confrontations and awkward interactions with others. Before long they acquire the reputation of being a loner, but is this an accurate characterization? Are they truly happy or, in their case, is loner simply another name for a deeply lonely person? All parents ponder these questions when calling their adult children on a Saturday night, only to find them home alone, the same as the Saturday before, and the Saturday before that.

"Are you going out tonight?" you ask.

"No, I don't feel like it," your daughter might say in a dull, weary tone, or maybe your twenty-two-year-old son claims to be "too tired" to go out. You think back to the days when you were twenty-two and try to remember if you were ever too tired to go out on a Saturday night.

It's embarrassing for adult children to admit they have no one to go out with and no invitations, so there's no point in parents attempting to solve the dilemma by insisting they just "go out and find friends." Blanket statements like that imply that you, and quite possibly the rest of the world, suppose it's as easy as all that—just step out the door and voilà! You've found a friend! If making friends were that easy, chances are you would have reached your child's answering machine on Saturday night.

The superficial encouragement to just go out and find friends only enhances a sense of frustration and even bitterness in those who cannot easily do so. The way to help is through first understanding the problems and then offering constructive and specific ways to deal with them.

THE NUANCES OF FRIENDSHIP

Family members are held together by natural bonds. Tough times come and go, but the majority of parent-child and sibling relationships endure. Friendships also weather such storms, especially close ones. Casual friendships and acquaintances are another matter. In these relationships, a code of manners comes into play. By this I don't mean etiquette of the "please and thank you" school, but the consideration we must extend to others if we hope to get along in the world. For most of us, these things come naturally, as though a part of our genetic makeup or the result of a long evolutionary process. Think that's too broad a statement? Consider this: Why do we instinctively know when we or someone else is standing even an inch or two too close when talking to us and therefore violating our space? No one taught us that. My mother never said, "Anne, you're standing an inch and a half too close when you talk. Stop it." It simply *feels* wrong and even mildly threatening when someone can't judge the proper distance.

For many with LD or ADHD, the hard-wired aspects of social interaction have become tangled and short-circuited, and seemingly minor problems in the way they interact with others add up over time to an inability to connect in any meaningful way with anyone.

Let's look at some of the difficulties involving social skills.

Physicality
Some adults with LD act in physical ways that give others an impression that something is wrong. They may stand too close, for instance, or overreact to noises or other stimuli that don't bother anyone else. I know of one young woman with ADHD, a friend of Allegra's, who becomes so distracted by the slightest touch or noise that she finds it nearly impossible to sit still in a movie theater. If someone behind her

lightly touches the back of her seat with a knee or foot, or makes the smallest noise, she leaps with such startled fright you'd think someone had dropped a tarantula in her lap. At other times she might suddenly turn around to look behind her even though the person never did a thing. If she did this only once, it would be fine, but it happens so frequently during the course of a two-hour movie that it distracts everyone around her and quickly becomes annoying.

Some adults with LD talk too fast or too slowly, or especially too loudly. They don't know how to judge the distance between themselves and the person they are talking to, and so they may use a tone of voice more suited to a soccer stadium than an intimate conversation. Others have trouble with eye contact. They stare so intently that they make others uncomfortable, or they make little or no eye contact. They look at the floor, the walls, the ceiling, your shoulder, everywhere but into your eyes.

Their response to touch can also cause some awkward moments. The woman distracted in the movie theater also has a difficult time with physical contact, especially with strangers. A handshake or a hug can be a deeply unpleasant experience for her. She's never told me this, but when I once tried to hug her goodbye, she stiffened and dropped her arms to her sides, giving me the impression that my embrace was not welcome. You see how this can cause an acquaintance to pull away and cool down any progress toward a deeper friendship? If I hadn't known she had LD, I might have wondered if I had done something to offend her or thought she didn't like me, when in fact that was simply the way she reacts to physical touch.

Visual and Auditory Perception

Tied in with an inability to judge the proper physical and audible distance in a conversation is an inability to understand subtleties in communication. Everyone uses nonverbal communication techniques, and most of us can conduct an entire conversation without saying a word. When traveling to a foreign country or trying to talk to someone who doesn't understand English, we can make ourselves understood in a broad sense through a combination of gestures and facial expressions. Many adults with LD have trouble doing this, even when speaking a language they understand. They cannot interpret a raised eyebrow or a frown or a wink. Similarly, they may be at a loss when it comes to vocal cues. Someone may use a certain inflection or tone of voice to indicate he or she is telling a joke or being sarcastic, but those who cannot read such cues take the words literally.

Adults with LD may also have a tendency to say the wrong thing at the wrong time or ask inappropriate questions of a stranger. I knew a young man who had an unerring ability to alienate everyone around him within a matter of minutes, usually by making insulting remarks meant as friendly jokes. I still cringe when I remember introducing an insecure, overweight young woman to him. His first statement was a question directed to me: "Where did you find her, in the dump?"

For some reason he thought this a charming pleasantry that the young woman would find amusing. Needless to say, she didn't. Whenever he appeared, the social scene deteriorated into one of anger, red-faced embarrassment, awkward explanations, and attempts to smooth ruffled feathers. At the time, I thought he was simply an insensitive boor, but one night at a party I saw him recoil in confusion when something he truly meant as a casual joke caused an uproar and a biting response from a young woman he had met only a half hour before. I don't know what he said. It may have been another witticism about a landfill. Whatever it was, I knew when I saw his expression that he did not have a clue as to why she reacted as she did, or why the small group he had joined now moved away from him, effectively cutting him off. This was long before I knew the signs of learning disabilities in adults. I'm quite sure this young man had undiagnosed LD, and I now wish I had been able to take him aside and suggest he get tested for a learning disability. Some might imagine that would be a difficult subject to bring up, with the person becoming indignant and insulted. Possibly. But what a relief it would be for someone in that situation to finally discover why his social interactions inevitably led to disaster.

Adults with ADHD have their own set of difficulties with visual and auditory perception. They may understand all the social nuances and yet find themselves at a loss when surrounded at a party by too many people talking at the same time. The stimuli from all sides overwhelm them, and they can't follow the thread of any single conversation, so guess what happens the next time they are invited to a party? They decline, preferring instead the quiet of home.

Language

How many times have I had a conversation with Allegra only to find out she had absolutely no idea what I was talking about, or missed the point of the conversation entirely? I might start talking about redecorating the bathroom and her first response could be, "What's going to happen with the refrigerator?"

My own first response to such a comment (though I rarely voice it aloud) is: "Where did *that* come from?" It seems so arbitrary, so out of touch with the moment, but in Allegra's mind she may be looking ahead to the possibility of redecorating the kitchen at a later time, or reaching back to some remembered renovation in years past when the refrigerator did indeed get moved or replaced. I have no doubt that she is following an internal logic in these seemingly incoherent statements, but they never seem to be fully thought through. She seems to say whatever pops into her mind, no matter how far removed it may be from the subject of the conversation. Alessandro calls it the "loose cannon" effect. I never know what she might say or where she'll say it or to whom, and it can be quite unnerving at times.

Egocentrism

Many adults with LD are unduly self-absorbed. I never really thought of this as an issue until I spoke at Eagle Hill, a school for students with LD in Connecticut. During the question-and-answer session one of the teachers asked me if I had seen a lot of egotism in the LD population. I could tell by the way he asked the question that he not only saw a great deal of it but found it difficult to handle. As far as Allegra goes, I have to say that egotism has never been a major problem. Yes, she enjoys being in the limelight at times, but that's usually when she actually is in the limelight during a skating competition. A healthy ego is something every parent should strive to instill in a child with LD, but even so there is a fine line between a healthy ego and self-centeredness.

The egotism referred to by the teacher at Eagle Hill was not the boasting of a preening braggart but something quite different. Nearly all the adults with LD I have met have a degree of self-centeredness, as if everything they encounter must first be filtered through their own sense of self. This is partly owing to an overall difficulty with social skills (someone incapable of listening to someone else, for example) and partly because, in fact, many *were* the center of everything while growing up, or at least they were the center of their parents' worries and fears.

Egocentrism or self-absorption can damage any relationship and is particularly hard on friendships. Sometimes adults with LD or ADHD may be so caught up in their own world that things like showing up on time, returning phone calls, or remembering important events simply fall by the wayside. They may see these as minor matters, but when you are on the receiving end, they matter a great deal.

One former classmate of Allegra's had a deep interest in motorcycles—how to fix them, how to restore them, every detail about a motorcycle's design. Each and every conversation with this young man became a nonstop drone about motorcycles. Even for those with an interest in the subject, the experience of listening to someone turn every single topic of conversation back to Harley-Davidsons can be trying at best. He couldn't see this. His interest so consumed him that he couldn't imagine others did not share it, and so he went on and on, with no fluctuation in his tone of voice and no awareness of the effect of this on others.

In such cases, a parent should step in (but not in front of others) and say something like this: "Last night I noticed that you didn't stop talking about motorcycles. It's great that you're so interested in them, but you have to remember that not everyone else is, and you have to learn to give others a chance to talk." If this doesn't sink in—and it most assuredly won't the first time around—point it out to him again the next time he does it. You may think you are being a nag, but if you say things in a calm and easy way, you might as well run the risk, since it may eventually work.

Some of you have already tried this to no avail. It's true that sometimes we cannot change behaviors like this no matter how hard we try. In that case, we can do little more than sit with a frozen smile and watch while everyone else strives mightily to pretend they are interested in motorcycles.

A Need to Control

An unexpected by-product of egocentrism is controlling behavior. When a person's needs come first and are the only ones considered, it's a short step toward that person becoming impatient and frustrated when those needs are not met, even if it means trampling over or disregarding the needs of others. Adults with LD can become irritated and impatient when things do not go their way, and sometimes they do not hesitate to make their feelings known. Imagine you are the friend of a young man with this need to control and you show up late for a planned meeting at a restaurant. This has happened many times before, but in reverse, with you arriving on time and him showing up fifteen, twenty minutes, maybe a half hour late each and every time, and always with a lame excuse. Now you show up ten minutes late because of traffic, and there he is, impatient and angry that you made him wait. Makes you want to walk out of the restaurant, doesn't it? If not that, it certainly might make you hesitate before agreeing to go out on another date.

Low Self-Esteem

The opposite of egocentrism is low self-esteem. Sometimes these opposites occur together in the same person and we find someone who is self-centered, yet at the same time takes a dim view of that self. Uncertainty, lack of confidence, even self-hatred: all of these cause great problems with a social life. Adults with LD may feel unworthy to be someone's friend or so ill at ease about themselves and how others perceive them that they avoid all situations likely to make them uncomfortable.

Perseveration

This is a fancy way of saying "harping on the same subject." It's close to the situation with the young man who goes on and on about motorcycles, but in this form, the person focuses on specific phrases or ideas and repeats and repeats them until whatever humor and interest they once held have long since flown the coop. But do they stop? No. After a while you as the listener get into a routine of nodding and saying the occasional "uh-huh, uh-huh," which gives an appearance of rapt attention while allowing your mind to move on to other things. Allegra has sayings that she repeats over and over, and nicknames for everyone she meets. Most of the time this is harmless, and often it is extremely funny. Others play along with it, so she has no reason to stop, but once in a while I get the sense that she wouldn't know when to stop, even if she wanted to.

Memory Problems

We all have occasions when we cannot remember a person's face or name, but some adults with LD have enormous difficulty with this. They may meet someone repeatedly and act each time as if they are meeting for the first time, with no memory of the person's face or name. Landmarks or specific locations may be impossible to remember. They'll agree to meet at the Pizza Hut, but forget where it is, or they'll drive in circles for an hour trying to figure out where they are (this can be especially frustrating for those unable to interpret a road map).

Memory problems can also come into play with social situations. Some adults with LD make the same social errors over and over again. They approach these situations as if they've never experienced them before, when in fact, they're something they do all the time. Let's imagine an initial meeting between two businessmen, one with LD and one without. The one without holds out his hand for a handshake, but the adult with LD fails to notice. The other now must go through that awkward hand-in-the-air ordeal, trying to figure out how to lower his hand without calling too much attention to his embarrassment.

A woman with LD named Paula had an equally small but very unnerving trait. Whenever I called and she picked up the phone, she never said "Hello" first. Never. I would wait, wondering if I had been disconnected, and then venture a tentative "Hello?" only to hear her say it back to me, startling me every time. I'm not sure this falls under memory problems or social skills (and it should probably be pointed out that apparently I, too, forgot she would answer the phone this way), but the result was that every single phone call began on an unsure footing.

Presumptions of Friendship

Over and over I have seen adults with LD who take the merest show of kindness or attention from someone and inflate it into proof of a fully formed relationship. They'll impose demands or expectations upon this newfound "friend," expecting to go out to dinner or on a date or even a sleepover. There is an octopuslike quality to this, where you as the victim feel unable to escape the phone calls, the sudden appearances, the inappropriate remarks and interruptions of conversations with others, and you eventually resort to outright rudeness in an effort to escape. Of course, the person with LD who somehow thought you were a good friend is now hurt and confused, and if through guilt or kindness you try to ease things a bit, you invariably start the whole thing all over again.

Our world is full of pleasantries and pseudo-invitations said more out of social custom than sincerity—"Let's do lunch sometime" comes to mind—but for those with LD, any offer or invitation is taken at face value, and "Let's do lunch" leads directly to a message on your voicemail by the time you return to your office, with reservations already made and dates suggested for a follow-up lunch. A business card casually handed out is viewed as a request to call the same day or several times a day, even if there is nothing to talk about.

Some adults with LD have no ability to judge the timing of a friendship. Rick Lavoie, when speaking about the students at Riverview School, called it "putting out the candle of friendship." Just when the student managed to befriend someone, or met someone with the potential to become a friend, he or she went all out, full-steam ahead, smothering the person with attention and putting out the candle before it ever had a chance to shed its light.

A PARENT'S ROLE IN FRIENDSHIP

As with all relationships, a friendship requires work, and the responsibility for this lies with both parties. Allegra has been blessed with some wonderful, long-term friendships, but some she has allowed to fall by the wayside owing to now-forgotten grudges. (I have often seen grudges play a damaging role in friendships where one or both friends have a learning disability.) We all can relate to this. Some friendships turn out to be too much work to continue, yet because of the difficulties adults with LD have with making friends in the first place, many simply cannot afford the luxury of turning friends away. This is especially true when the reasons for the breakup of a friendship have more to do with their own perceptions than with reality.

Have you ever found yourself in this situation? Two friends have an argument over something. Both come to you at separate times to tell you what the other has done, and it soon becomes clear that both parties have misunderstood the original situation and are actually arguing over nothing. It may also be that each would like to reconcile with the other but pride will not allow either one to make the first move. If you find yourself in the middle of a situation like this and one of the parties is your LD adult child, throw caution to the wind and get involved.

It happened to me recently.

Hilary is a woman with LD in her mid-thirties, married with two young children. When she was a young girl, her mother, Judy, brought her to a tiny ice studio in Manhattan in the hope that skating might interest her daughter. I did the same thing with Allegra, and she took to the ice right away. She stuck with it for years, filled with enthusiasm and confidence, and Hilary was one of the main reasons for this.

They connected through a shared love of an activity. Learning disabilities did not matter on the ice. No one cared if they could read as well as anyone else, or if their math skills were up to par. They skated together. They grew up together. Allegra spent her first sleepover away from me at Hilary's apartment.

Childhood friendships sometimes last and sometimes don't. A family may move, new interests replace old, or maybe former friends simply no longer click. Allegra has a long history of making and maintaining friendships with older people but not with people her own age, so I suppose it's not that surprising she and Hilary went their separate ways. In this case, the friendship drifted apart because Hilary got married. Allegra and Hilary hadn't lived in the same city for many years, and with a husband and then children, Hilary had moved in new directions.

Whenever I asked Allegra about the situation, she answered with a breezy, "I don't know," which sounded more in tone like "I don't care." I sensed the presence of a grudge, a resentment built upon . . . what? A feeling of abandonment because Hilary got married? Some real or perceived slight from years before? I didn't know, and I'm not sure Allegra herself knew, or if she did know, that she could explain it to me or anyone else. It made me sad, since I felt they were natural friends with the bond of LD between them and many long years of companionship and memories behind them.

Hilary's mother, Judy, became one of my very best friends during the time of our daughters' association. She died of cancer several years ago. I still feel her loss to this day, for remember, it is not only the adult with LD who needs understanding friends but parents, too. We each knew exactly what the other was going through, and that is not easy to find.

Because we were so close, I still have occasion to be in touch with her family. I called Hilary recently to ask how things were going. All mothers of young children go through tough times, and having a learning disability only adds to the difficulty, but when I asked how she was coping, the first thing she said was, "I miss Allegra."

For much of my daughter's life I worried over her lack of friends, especially when she was younger. I spent an inordinate amount of time trying out strategies and tactics to bring as many other children into our lives as possible, often without much success. Now here was someone reaching out to her through me, hoping to restart an old relationship. It's so natural when we go through hard times to look to the comfort of old friends, but many adults with LD don't have the skills to renew a friendship in an active, "I'll-call-first" way.

I considered Hilary's words "I miss Allegra" as the first move and felt I needed to step in and approach Allegra for a response.

I told her Hilary missed her and needed her, and Allegra said she would call. In my heart, I knew she said this to placate me. "I really hope you do," I said and left it at that . . . or rather, I tried to leave it at that. I had a small internal flare-up of anger—unexpressed thankfully—that went along these lines: "I really hope you do call her, because you need to *stop* thinking about yourself and realize that someone is having a difficult time and needs you."

Instead I closed my eyes and, after a moment to calm myself, said, "You know Allegra . . . I was just thinking how lucky you are to have someone who feels that way about you."

THE CARE AND MAINTENANCE OF A FRIENDSHIP

A social life is made up of the bright threads we call our special friends, but among them are the many lesser threads of neighbors, acquaintances, members of clubs or organizations we belong to, and coworkers. Woven together, these threads help create the full and varied fabric of a life. For some, this fabric is a little thin and worn in places, and may not have many threads at all. These people live with isolation and loneliness, often by choice (the loner again), preferring those to the difficulties of making and keeping friends.

Parents may want to consider the following suggestions and strategies when trying to help their adult child create a friendship or keep one together.

1. Is Your Adult Child Capable of Becoming Someone's Friend?

"Of course!" you say. "Anyone can become a friend to someone!" I agree, and believe that every person has the capacity to become someone's friend, and that certainly includes anyone with LD, no matter how severe. But we're not talking here about what *we* believe—it's our adult children's belief about themselves that matters.

Of all the challenges and difficulties I listed earlier, low self-esteem, that ever-present shadow in the lives of those with LD, can and does have an enormous influence in your son's or daughter's ability to create and keep friendships. Very simply put, they may not believe themselves worthy or capable of friendship, feeling that they are somehow undeserving. These attitudes are left over from long years of struggle and frequent failure. Those with challenges in social skills are especially susceptible.

Don't fall into the trap of believing this yourself.

If you are reading this now on that Saturday night we spoke of before, and your son or daughter is home alone or in the next room watching television instead of being out with friends, don't view this with resignation as if this is the way things *must be*. Hold on to your belief in your adult child and your *certain* knowledge of all the good and positive things your adult child can bring to a friendship. Parents should point out to their adult children the positive elements of their personalities, their interests, their strengths. These are the tools parents can use when they try to help their children reach a similar understanding about themselves.

2. Debunking the Myth of the Loner

In other words—stop it! Even if your adult child truly is a loner, don't use the word, even if he or she does. A parent's job in this is as challenging as the child's: sometimes it seems all but impossible to maintain an optimistic view of our child's potential, especially after year upon year of disappointment. The trouble is that we end up falling into our own myths created through disappointment and defeat, myths that tell us things will *always* lead to disappointment and defeat. This is simply not the case. Always expecting the worst nearly always guarantees the worst and blinds us to small, hopeful signs that could lead to something greater.

I am not advocating a flight from reality or a sudden transformation into a chirpy optimist who comes up with ludicrous insights that are simply not true. I am saying to look for the good. Look for the silver lining, the rainbow, or whatever other image best helps you avoid sinking into a wholly negative view of your child's prospects, whether for a job, further schooling, or making friends.

3. Find Supportive Friends

Easier said than done but certainly not impossible. As a parent, you can encourage friendships when you see that someone genuinely has your child's best interests at heart. I would also encourage my child to consider divulging the presence of LD if it hasn't already been done. There is a world of difference in people's reactions when they understand that occasional difficulties arise as a result of their friend's disability and not because their friend doesn't care.

4. Unsupportive Friends

Is there a parent alive who hasn't at some time or other looked askance at one of our son's or daughter's friends, worried this so-called friend might lead our child down the wrong path or into the wrong crowd? This is a legitimate fear for parents, since children and young adults with LD are often far too eager to belong and may not always be able to discriminate between supportive friends and those who might take advantage of them.

We sometimes come across a perplexing situation when we discover that some friends who take advantage can be supportive at the same time. As an example, let's imagine your LD son has a friend named George who never seems to have enough money to pay for dinner and relies on your son to pick up the tab. Obviously George is taking advantage of the friendship. But what if George also happens to be the most supportive, most fun, and most interesting person your son knows? In such a case, a parent should weigh the pros and cons. Yes, on the down side George is a hanger-on, a freeloader, a so-called friend who uses people, but all that is outweighed by the positive things he brings to the relationship. What possible good would it do to convince your son to drop George from his life when it may be his most valued friendship?

5. Maintaining Contact with Friends and Acquaintances

Maintaining ties with friends is one aspect of modern life that challenges everyone, especially those who do not live in small, close-knit communities. We get so busy with jobs, families, marriages, and relationships. We move to different cities in different states. We get wrapped up in our own world and no longer have the time to spend in long relaxing conversations with friends of old. The trick is to keep the spark of friendship alive long after the vibrant fire has gone out. Some with a learning disability may see the natural dimming of an old friendship owing to distance or changing circumstances as a catastrophic end. "She moved away!" your daughter might cry, often with a touch of anger in her voice, as if her friend's departure was an act of personal betrayal and not the result of a job transfer. I sense a bit of this in the situation with Allegra and Hilary: life intervened to separate them, but not forever, and not irrevocably, and it is always important to point this out.

We have built-in systems to combat this loss. One of the best is holiday or birthday cards. They are an ideal way for young adults with LD or ADHD to reach out to someone on a yearly basis, just to say, "Hi, I'm thinking of you." Many old friendships have been rekindled because someone lifted a pen one early December day and scribbled a few lines.

Maybe you could sit down with your son or daughter and think through friends and acquaintances from the past. Don't let age become a limiting factor in this: a person who was an adult in a position of authority when your child was small, such as a teacher or neighbor, could conceivably become a friend. Age differences diminish as the years go by.

E-mail is also a great way to keep in touch with friends and family, and has done wonders for many friendships, especially for those people who have trouble writing a letter or card.

6. Parent as Coach

Take a good look at your son or daughter in a social situation or even in private conversation with you. Do you notice any of the traits listed earlier—standing too close, trouble with eye contact, maybe talking too loudly? Sometimes there isn't anything we can do to change this. You may know that from personal experience, having tried for many years to change or at least lessen something you feel has caused trouble in your child's social life.

How, for instance, could you possibly change the fact that your son misinterprets jokes or cannot understand certain abstract concepts? If we could do that, we could market the technique as a cure for one troubling aspect of LD.

Other traits might be easier to influence. Don't think of it as eliminating the trait but as helping your adult child compensate for it, the same way note-taking in class might help compensate for an auditory processing disability.

Let's take listening as an example. This touches upon so many issues with LD: language comprehension, social skills (interrupting others), ability to form a response, and even egocentricity (people who don't listen are perceived as being interested only in themselves). If your adult child has difficulties due to problems with listening, maybe you could sit down with him or her for a coaching session.

Assuming your adult child would accept this (and granted, that is a big if), you might first describe the problem as you see it: "You know, sometimes I notice when you're having a conversation, you constantly interrupt the speaker. I'm sure it's because you have a hundred ideas you'd love to tell them, but it's better to let them finish before you start. Listening is as much an art as it is a social skill. If you look at the person when they speak and concentrate on hearing what they say, it really helps with relationships. Look at President Clinton—that's what made people like him, the ability he had to listen ... and even if he wasn't listening, he made it *look* as though he was. The act of listening says to people that you think they are worthy of your attention and that you take them seriously."

7. Support Groups

One terrific way to find friends is through LD support groups. For a further discussion of this we turn to the next chapter in Relationships ... the scary and exciting world called Dating.

7

Dating

In adding to my already long list of challenges the adult with LD or ADHD faces in friendships, I now continue with some involved in the dating game.

IMMATURITY

I start off with immaturity because I have yet to meet an adult of any age with severe learning disabilities who comes across as a fully mature individual. Bear in mind that I know some adults with severe LD who are married with children of their own, but the way they handle the complications of life has a childlike ring to it.

All people can find love and fulfillment in their lives, no matter how disabled they are, but I can't help feeling that the best match is one that takes these disabilities into account. The most successful dates or boyfriend-girlfriend relationships I have seen in the LD community are between two adults with similar levels of disability who act more like best friends than lovers. Such relationships appear almost chaste, like something out of a Victorian novel, where companionship, laughter, and symbolic gestures and phrases like exchanging rings or "going steady" still loom large, even in adults who are well beyond their teenage years.

Of course, all this comes with the usual caveat regarding the severity of the disability. Adults with milder forms of ADHD or LD conduct their dating and romantic relationships much like everyone else, with all the attendant joys and heartaches. I do not find immaturity to be a major factor in their relationships. Their main challenges come from the things listed in the chapter on friendship: poor social skills or difficulties with time management.

Immaturity in those with the more severe forms of LD can create barriers, but it can also be an equalizer. It puts a distance between severely LD adults and others in their age group with more maturity, yet it also brings them closer to those with a similarly immature outlook on life and can help balance out some of the other difficulties associated with LD. Think of it this way: If you are thirty-five and you laugh hysterically at jokes only a twelve-year-old might find funny, it is a relief to find someone else who feels the same. When you do find someone like that, other quirks and oddities of behavior don't matter so much. Still, there are those times when an LD adult falls in love with someone who is not learning disabled, and though at first things appear to go smoothly, it isn't long before the immaturity comes into play. When it does, the relationship can continue, especially if the non-LD partner accepts and understands the situation. If not, it comes to an end.

A young woman I met through the National Center for Learning Disabilities has severe LD but is as charming as anyone could wish. She is vivacious and funny and makes a real effort to get along with everyone, but alas, has the emotional maturity level of a young teenager. She is now in her late twenties but appears much younger, mostly due to her giggly schoolgirl demeanor and an outlook on life that is still quite innocent and naive.

She met a man her own age who did not have LD. Their first few dates went well, but then they came to a disagreement of some kind. I don't know what it was, and she was not able to tell me. She used to come into my office in tears, but no matter how many times I asked her what happened, she could never give me any specifics. I am quite sure that he said some innocuous thing and she blew it way out of proportion. In any other relationship, such small matters would have no effect, but she took his mild expression of disapproval as a serious reproach and fell into a state of extreme anxiety over the relationship. At first she spoke only to her friends and coworkers about it. Her perspective was so out of kilter, so far from the reality of the situation, that we all had a difficult time getting to the heart of the matter. When we finally realized her anxiety was a response to something that seemed rather trivial, we tried to comfort her and give her advice. "Just don't worry about it so much," we said, or "I'm sure everything will work out."

Things might have worked out, but she took her anxiety to a new level and began to call the boyfriend several times a day, usually to voice her unfounded fears. He reacted as most would. Up to this point they had only been out on a couple of casual dates, and certainly had not reached a level of intimacy where one might expect this kind of thing. He began to pull away and asked her not to call so often. This only added fuel to her imaginary fire. No matter how many times we advised her not to call or not to send him an e-mail, she would turn right around and do it anyway. It was terrible, like watching someone walk toward a cliff, and no matter how much you wave and shout, she just keeps walking.

Needless to say, the boyfriend became so alarmed by her overreactions that he put an end to the relationship. A few months later she met another young man, and after only two dates she began to do the exact same thing. Once again, we tried to advise and warn her, but with a little less enthusiasm, as we all expected that she probably wouldn't listen. We were right.

All anyone can do in such cases is give the advice you would give to anyone else. And believe me, there are plenty of people without LD who would behave in a similar fashion. If the advice is not taken, you cannot be faulted. The sad truth is that there are times when someone will keep on walking toward the cliff no matter what you do or say. Hopefully, experience will be a teacher and they can learn from their mistakes. Most do, though the maturity gained is hard won.

INTERNET DATING

I'm sure there are many parents whose hearts stop at the sight of the two words "Internet" and "dating" in the same phrase, and undoubtedly will disagree with my views. I wondered if this topic had any relevance for parents of adults with LD, but after talking with a few parents who voiced their concerns—their *strong* concerns—I realized that yes, indeed, it does have relevance, if only to address those strong concerns.

Those of us in the generations before the widespread use of the Internet tend to view it with alarm and suspicion, but it really won't do us or our children any good at all to bury our heads in the sand and pretend it isn't there. It *is* there, and many young adults have chosen this strange new form of communication as a way of meeting.

"Internet dating" conjures images of predatory men surfing the web for vulnerable young women, and yes, unfortunately that does happen. But predatory men also hang out in bars and nightclubs, and patrol quiet streets in vans. We can come up with all kinds of dreadful scenarios involving predators, but unless we plan on locking our adult children in their rooms for the rest of their lives, we'll have to bravely assume they will end up like the majority of us who have never had a problem.

Like so many of you, I was initially disturbed by the idea of Internet dating. It seemed to have unending potential for trouble. It also seemed so impersonal: as someone who doesn't type very well, I couldn't imagine how someone could get beyond the mechanical aspects of the process and get to the personal.

I decided to look into it and was a bit surprised by what I found. First of all, we should all understand that there are various ways to initiate an online relationship. Just as elegant nightclubs and low dives can be generally classified as "bars," a wide range of Internet venues can be classified as "Internet dating."

Let's start with the low-dive version first. These are the infamous chat rooms we have all heard of, unsupervised, unmonitored, with all sorts of opportunities for a young person to get into trouble. I know of one young woman with LD who went off to college and immediately immersed herself in this murky online world. She created a profile for herself so far from the truth that we might as well say she created an alternate personality for herself. Think of how alluring this could be for a young person who has a history of social awkwardness—you can become who you want, with as many friends as you care to name, with no labels of "disability" or "special ed" in your background. Who is to know the truth?

Well, eventually others did learn the truth because this young woman got into all sorts of trouble. She had no experience with boundaries, no ability to differentiate between intimacy and promiscuity. This became such a problem so quickly that her parents took her out of school before she'd completed even one term.

That is the first type of Internet dating, and I don't care how many success stories there are—I can't imagine a time will ever come when I will tell parents that it is a good thing.

The second type of Internet dating involves the use of reputable online dating services. I looked into these with the same wariness I had for the more casual ones, but once the newness wore off, I saw something rather more comforting than frightening.

First of all, the safety factor. This is by far the largest worry for most parents, but all the major sites have very specific rules and protocols. There are rules against giving out phone numbers or home addresses. All of them strongly suggest that any first meeting occur in a public place such as a coffee shop or diner, and not close to where you live. Candidates are matched through various means, though most are based in large part upon a profile created by each person. This profile lists their interests and hobbies, their likes and dislikes, and how they see themselves as people—all aspects of their personal character that are rarely, if ever, given much prominence in a casual meeting in a bar. In addition, some of these dating services conduct background checks and provide the option of creating a video to go along with the profile.

I've now come around to the view that Internet dating through these reliable agencies could actually be safer than a casual meeting in a bar or dance club. We don't know people we talk to in a dance club; we don't know anything about their lives, their interests, or the baggage they carry with them. We know nothing beyond the initial physical appearance, which we may or may not find attractive. This too is handled well in the Internet dating services. Pictures and videos allow people to see potential dates long before they actually meet in person.

We may not like Internet dating, but what can we do about it? It's the future, so we might as well accept it. If you walk into your son's or daughter's apartment and see a computer on the desk, don't panic. Sit down and explain your concerns in a way that lets him or her know you mean it. Ironically, this new form of technological communication has led to a need for that most ancient form of communication: the serious talk. You know your child best. If you can't dissuade him or her from abandoning the casual chat rooms, at least you can give the same advice offered by those who run the more reputable ones:

- Do not give out your phone number or home address.
- Always meet for the first time in a public place such as a coffee shop or diner, and not one that is too close to home.

- Understand that not everything said in a chat room is necessarily true.
- And finally, suggest they enroll in an online dating service with the characteristics I outlined earlier. It may not eliminate all of your fears, but it could alleviate them just a little.

I sometimes wish there were a supervised online dating service for the LD community. I haven't found one yet, though I have found something close and will turn to it now.

SUPPORT GROUPS AND SOCIAL CLUBS

Many state chapters of membership organizations such as the International Dyslexia Association (IDA) and Learning Disabilities Association of America (LDAA) host events specifically designed for adults with LD. This is a terrific way for our children to meet and form friendships. Children and Adults with Attention Deficit Disorder (ChADD) also hosts support groups for young adults with ADD and ADHD in many locations throughout the country.

These organizations not only offer support groups for young adults, they also (and primarily) provide support for parents of both children and adults with LD. Parents come together from all across the country to counsel one another and give one another encouragement and support. You may find others in a similar predicament, wondering where their son or daughter might have a chance of meeting someone to befriend or go out on a date with. If your local chapter doesn't host get-togethers for young adults, I see no reason why you and the other parents can't organize one. It doesn't have to be a big expensive event—maybe a movie or a picnic in a local park, anything to bring together disabled individuals with similar experiences and backgrounds.

Another possibility for your son or daughter is a local social club unrelated to disabilities. Think of your adult child's interests, passions, and even potential interests (we don't always know what we might be interested in until we've tried something new). Look for a club or membership organization that coincides with those interests through bulletin boards, word-of-mouth, or local newspapers. Another possibility is your local church or synagogue. Many host gatherings for single adults,

and while it's true that your son or daughter may run into the same difficulties as always when trying to meet new people, it's worth a try.

If your son or daughter happens to live in rural Idaho or Alaska or
some other place with no LD-related social events, they still have ways
to connect with others.

I direct your attention once again to the Internet. Many of the
main search engines such as Yahoo or Google host what they call
"groups." You can think of these as clubs that bring together people
from all over the world according to their interests, no matter how
obscure. Believe me, if more than one person is interested in something, there will be a club devoted to it. Victrolas made in the 1890s?
Ball bearings? Obscure tractor parts from the Soviet Union? Go online
and I'm sure you'll find a group or club devoted to it. There are bird-
watching clubs, fishing clubs, literary clubs, fan clubs, endless numbers
of sports clubs. There is no cost to join, and though membership in an
online club probably falls more into the category of friendship than of
dating, you never know what can happen!

If you read this and scratch your head and think, "But he doesn't
have any interests at all," you are still not out of luck. How about learning disabilities as a topic?

As an experiment I went online to both the Yahoo and Google sites
and went into their "Groups" sections. In Yahoo, in the place called
"Find a Group" I typed in "Adults with Learning Disabilities" and 24
specific groups came up (when I typed in "Learning Disabilities" alone,
299 groups came up). Included were groups such as ADDadults, with
421 members; Developmentally Disabled Dating, with 312 members;
and ldpride with 134 members.

The last one, ldpride, described itself this way: "A support/social
group for youth and adults with learning disabilities and/or Attention
Deficit Disorder to share their thoughts, ideals, frustrations and get the
support they need. The main purpose of the group is to provide peer
support while also providing a means for social connection and information sharing."

When I went onto Google, I found listings for over nine thousand
groups and forums. The reason there are so many is that Google also
includes mailing list sites, e-mail newsletter sites, and forums where

individuals can post information about LD and how it affects adults. These groups are not only devoted to social issues; many also focus on LD in the workplace or on college issues.

In addition to joining a Yahoo or Google group, you can also start one. "LD Adults in Alaska" might be the ideal way for that LD adult living outside Fairbanks to discover others with the same challenges, goals, setbacks, and triumphs.

8

Marriage and Parenting

If parents were to rate their fondest hopes for their adult child with LD, I have no doubt that most would put marriage at the top of the list. A happy marriage takes care of many of our concerns, at least in theory. Loneliness, lack of friends and companionship, security in later years; all the nagging fears for the future that beset us on a daily basis fade when we think of our adult child in a stable, long-term relationship.

Reality—that word again—intrudes upon these daydreams as it does upon so many others. The same challenges that cause problems in friendships and dating relationships continue on into marriages as well. I know of marriages between two adults with LD that have thus far succeeded, and others that haven't. I also know of marriages in which only one partner has LD, and likewise, some have worked, some have not. As always with LD, much depends on the severity of the disability, the person's ability to compensate (especially for poor social skills), and the ability of the partner to accept and understand the challenges that come their way.

When we talk about someone with severe LD, we might expect that a partnership with another person with a similar level of LD would be most likely to succeed. Several students from Allegra's schools fell in love and married, and as far as I know, they have made it work. I suspect they have a strong support system at home and are able to talk about various problems and work them out before they become too serious.

Discussion is a great idea for any marriage where LD is part of the mix, even when there are no obvious or serious problems. Sometimes an objective eye is all it takes to keep a relationship on track. I know of one couple, both with severe LD, who probably could have made a go of it, but they ended up separating due to disagreements and misunderstandings that spiraled out of control. Neither had the emotional maturity required to cool things down. By the time their parents noticed, it was too late for anyone to step in and keep them together.

I am not advocating parental involvement or interference in marital squabbles. That can make things worse, as we all know. A parent's suggestion of marriage counseling isn't out of place, however, and can truly be helpful, especially for those who might never consider such a thing on their own.

Marriages between a partner with LD or ADHD and one without also can work. I know of one extremely successful marriage between a woman with severe LD and a man who has no disability at all. After close to ten years of marriage, they are still very much in love. I once heard the husband tell a story of his wife and a difficult situation clearly caused by her learning disabilities. They were on a trip and his wife's problems with time management resulted in the delay of an entire busload of fellow tourists. The husband described how his wife eventually showed up, completely unaware of the turmoil and fury she had caused. He told the story without a hint of reproach or embarrassment—indeed, his overall verdict came down to these words: "It was so cute." So there. For every person whose LD presents challenges, there is someone out there prepared to meet them.

As much as parents would like to see their adult children with LD enter into happy, long-term relationships, parents may view the subject of grandchildren with concern.

There is no question that people with LD can and do make wonderful parents. We all have our own views regarding our adult children's abilities as parents. Will having LD matter on a day-to-day basis? Will they be able to cope with the pressures of a child, especially a newborn? Will they need additional help? Most of us can come up with a satisfying answer and ways to help if needed, but the one question very few of us can answer is this: "Will my grandchildren have LD, too?"

This is a matter of importance, not only for you but for the person marrying your son or daughter, and for new family members about to encounter LD or ADHD for the first time. If *you* are wondering if your LD son might pass on learning disabilities to his children, you can safely bet that the family of the non-LD woman he is engaged to marry will be wondering the same.

I had never thought about it in any serious way, mostly because marriage was not on the radar screen as far as Allegra was concerned. I suppose I did what I often do, which is decide to deal with the situation if and when it came up. Then Alessandro came to me shortly before his own wedding to ask if there was a possibility that *he* might end up having a child with disabilities. That thought had never occurred to me. As soon as he said it, I thought, "If LD is genetic and passed down through families, then of course there is a possibility my son carries the gene. Just because he doesn't have LD himself doesn't mean he can't carry the gene for it."

We contacted a geneticist who tested Allegra to see if her LD was in fact genetically based. I had always assumed it was hereditary and was therefore flabbergasted to learn that her LD was a result of a chromosomal abnormality very specific to Allegra. What this meant in essence is that while Allegra has a fifty-fifty chance of passing on the abnormality, Alessandro cannot pass it on at all.

THE GENETICS OF LD

In some ways, all unexplained learning disabilities within families are genetically based. By unexplained, I mean those cases of LD not caused by outside factors such as environmental hazards (lead paint poisoning), substance abuse (fetal alcohol effects), or low birth weight. An article in the *British Medical Journal* estimates that 40 percent of all moderate to severe learning disabilities and 70 percent of mild developmental delay cannot be traced to a specific cause. The *Journal* further estimates that between 30 percent and 50 percent of undiagnosed learning disabilities are genetic in origin.

Most of us involved with LD know of families with rampant LD. I know of one in which every family member in three generations has ADHD—and those are the only generations who have been tested. I have no doubt it goes much further back along the family tree. In this case, the hereditary genetic component is obvious. The chances are slim that every single member of a family since the time of great-granddad has been eating lead paint. For many of these families, the cause may be small chromosomal abnormalities. A recent study of 400 children with unexplained LD found that 7.4 percent of them had small chromosomal abnormalities. The parents of these children were also tested, and many were found to have the same abnormality. This may not appear to be a large number, but remember, this means 7.4 percent of *all* causes of LD, including environmental, accidents, and other health problems. Within this context, at 7.4 percent, chromosomal abnormalities are the second most common cause of LD. (The first is Down's syndrome, which itself is caused by another chromosomal abnormality.)

About one in every 200 babies is born with a chromosomal abnormality. Many, but certainly not all, have LD, mental retardation, or behavioral problems.

WHAT IS A CHROMOSOME?

Our bodies are made up of millions of cells. Each cell contains a complete copy of our specific genetic plan or blueprint. This genetic plan is packaged within the cells in tiny stringlike structures called chromosomes.

Every cell has forty-six chromosomes. Of these, twenty-three come from our mother's egg and twenty-three come from our father's sperm. When the egg and sperm meet at conception, the two pairs of twenty-three chromosomes join together to form the forty-six chromosomes needed to start the development of a new person through cell division. Each new cell contains the new combination of forty-six chromosomes.

If a chromosome were to be stretched out, it would look like a string of beads. Each one of these beads, about thirty thousand for each chromosome, is a gene. These make up our genetic blueprint and determine things like our hair and eye color, how tall we are, and the shape of our nose. They also direct the growth and development of our bodies. Genes are made of a chemical substance known as DNA—the same DNA used in court cases to determine someone's guilt or innocence. It is so effective because each person's DNA or genetic plan is unique to that person. No one else on the planet has DNA like yours.

CHROMOSOMAL ABNORMALITIES

All of us are born with several faulty genes. Usually these faulty, or mutated, genes cause no problems at all, but when they are found within the egg or sperm cells, they can be passed on to children. These mutations may be within the egg or sperm cell because that person received them from one or both of his or her parents. In this case, the mutations would cause the type of genetic conditions we think of as "passed on through the family." Not all mutations are passed on this way. Sometimes a mutation occurs for unknown reasons in an egg or sperm cell and can cause a genetic condition. The person created from that particular egg or sperm cell will be the first in the family to have the condition. This does not mean the person is necessarily the last, however, as this new mutated gene may then be passed down to the person's children and future generations.

No one knows why these mutations occur. We do know that nothing a parent does or does not do before or during pregnancy can cause a chromosomal abnormality in a child. In other words, you can have the healthiest pregnancy in the world and still be unable to prevent the chromosomal abnormality that occurred during and right after conception when the egg or sperm cell was developing.

THE EGG AND SPERM CELLS

Unlike the rest of our cells, egg and sperm cells do not have forty-six chromosomes. They have only twenty-three. When they come together to form forty-six, a pregnancy begins. Once in a while something goes wrong before this happens. When the egg or sperm cell is dividing on its own, an error can leave one or the other with too many or too few chromosomes. When this cell with the wrong number of chromosomes joins with a cell with a normal number of chromosomes, the result is a chromosomal abnormality in the developing embryo. In most cases, an embryo with the wrong number of chromosomes will not survive. Up to 70 percent of first trimester miscarriages are caused by chromosomal abnormalities.

Some of the most common chromosomal abnormalities are those involving the sex chromosomes, or the X and Y chromosomes. We all have them. Two of our forty-six chromosomes (or one from each of our twenty-three pairs of chromosomes) are the sex chromosomes. These determined our sex at conception, with females receiving two X chromosomes and males receiving one X and one Y chromosome. Most people affected by abnormalities involving the X or Y chromosome lead normal lives, though sometimes these abnormalities can lead to problems with sexual development or infertility. They can also result in behavioral problems and LD.

A GRANDPARENT'S CONCERN

As we reach the end of this chapter on marriage and parenting, at the end of the larger section on relationships, it makes sense to look at a role most people hope to play someday—the role of grandparent. Those whose adult children have severe LD may view the possibility of becoming a grandparent with trepidation or even alarm. It does happen that two people with severe LD find each other and fall in love, and based on our understanding of genetics, it's quite possible their children could be born with disabilities similar to those of one or both of the parents. What choice do we have in this situation? No court will allow you to step in to prevent the marriage once your child is an adult, nor will you have any legal control over your child's decision to have a child.

All sorts of dreadful situations may come to mind. You'll wonder if your daughter has the capacity to be a good mother or if your son has the maturity to provide for his family. It's more than likely you'll be struck by the thought that your own "golden years" are going to be taken up by your duties as a caretaker, because *surely* the actual job of raising the grandchildren will fall to you. I wish I had a clear-cut answer to address these concerns. All your fears may indeed come to pass, but then again, they may not.

That's not much comfort, I know. No one can tell what the future holds, but we can reflect upon some lessons learned in the past. I think of a woman I heard at a conference involving the administrators of a special school and parents of children with severe LD. I can't remember the issues, nor the reason the meeting was called, but in the middle of a heated discussion, a woman stood and took the microphone. "I have a son with Down's syndrome," she said, "and I can honestly say that every single day has been a struggle. It's been really hard, and I'm sure every parent in this room who has a disabled child can say the same." She then asked a simple, yet profound question. "But even though it's been so difficult, is there anyone in this room who would give up your kid, or turn them in for a new one?"

No one raised a hand.

So, yes, grandchildren could bring all sorts of new difficulties into your life, but if marriage and parenting become a part of your adult child's life, you cannot change it, nor should you. Accept it, as you've learned to accept so many other things. It's one more curve life has thrown your way, but sometimes a curve can lead you to deeper satisfaction and moments of unexpected joy.

PART III

After High-School Graduation Day: The College Student with LD and ADHD

9

Is College an Option?

Some parents already have an answer when asked, "Is college an option for your child with learning disabilities?"

"No," they say, "it's not an option and never was."

These parents (whom I will call the nay-sayers) are not being entirely truthful when they claim college "never was" an option. College may once have burned brightly in their dreams, but they have been so defeated by their perceptions of their child's failures in high school that they no longer think of college as an option, and they may even deny that those long-gone dreams ever existed at all. For other parents, the dream still burns. They never entertain thoughts that college *isn't* an option, and they remain determined that their child will go on from high school into a college or university. Good for them . . . as long as their dream is tempered by reality. Too often parents have dreams that are anything *but* realistic. I'll call them the deluded optimists. Like the nay-sayers, they veer off into realities of their own making, based on flawed perceptions of their child's abilities.

Of the two types of parents, I am more familiar with the nay-sayers because I was one, at least in the beginning. Like them, I too tried to close the door to all possibility before it had time to open more than a crack. My earliest hopes for Allegra centered in large part around a college experience that would propel her into life as a professional of some kind. When learning disabilities entered the picture and I finally accepted reality for what it was (or *appeared* to be), those hopes faded. "She'll never be able to go to college," I said, and I firmly believed it, even though Allegra had not yet turned ten. Over the years I learned more about children with LD and their potential, and I saw that hopes for college did not have to be abandoned, only revised. My notions of "college" needed revising as well.

I had fixated on a classic idea of college or university and never went beyond it. Community colleges, non-degree certificate programs, trade schools—none of these entered my thinking, though each falls squarely into the category of higher education. In years past, when we left high school we had two straight paths we could follow. One was work. The second was college, which eventually merged into work—hopefully at a higher level of pay and position due to the expertise developed in college. Nowadays there are many trails and sidetracks that crisscross the two paths, with all sorts of educational opportunities after high school, even for those who do not receive a high-school diploma. These opportunities also apply to students with all levels of LD and ADHD, from mild to severe.

Degree programs and non-degree certificate programs are usually classified as postsecondary options. (For the purposes of this book, I prefer to use the generic terms "college" or "trade school," even when they don't strictly apply, since all the different terms can get a little confusing. We all do this. Have you ever heard anyone refer to a college classmate as "my higher-education friend," or has anyone ever told you she just sent her child off to postsecondary? No. They say college, even when they really mean something else.)

Now let's look at the second type of parent, the deluded optimist. These parents never come to grips with the fact that their child has LD and may not be equipped to attend the college that they, the parents, choose. Some are so determined to see their child enter a high-powered college that they resort to extreme measures.

I call them "deluded" optimists, but that's a bit misleading since they are not completely deluded. If they were, they would simply send their child with severe LD off to college, blithely expecting a 4.0 grade average and an eventual Ph.D. in molecular biology. But they don't do this. They make what I view as reckless and drastic attempts to force success where there is no reasonable expectation of finding it, and in doing so, they often ensure that their child's college career ends in failure.

Once I was to be interviewed on a morning talk show in Washington, D.C. Before the interview, a gentleman connected with the show sat with me in the green room and we talked in a general way about learning disabilities. He told me that his girlfriend had a son with severe LD who had been accepted into a prestigious college in Boston. "He can hardly read at all," he said, and when I wondered aloud how the young man got into such a high-powered school, he told me that the boy's mother wrote the essays for his college application. I then asked how the young man was doing, and he told me things were beginning to spiral out of control. He was in way over his head, but rather than allow him to transfer to a college more appropriate to his level, the mother chose instead to pack up everything and *move* to the college town, not only to keep an eye on her son, but to do all his homework for him! We can already see the eventual outcome, can't we? We envision the day when a professor asks the young man to explain something, and he looks around, helpless, unable to respond, because the one who actually did the work is not there. She's home, possibly writing an essay for his next class or, more likely, fretting and worrying about her son becoming ensnared in the tangled web she has woven, which is indeed the very thing that is taking place.

I understand the impulse. When Alessandro applied to Boston University, I wanted so much to say, "This admissions essay is too important. Let me help you, or better yet, go out with your friends. I'll do it for you." I didn't follow through, and he did just fine on his own. But what if I had tried something similar for Allegra? What if I had chosen to ignore her learning disabilities and had tried to get her into a college far beyond her abilities? How long would it have taken before reality hit us both squarely in the face?

I met another deluded optimist who was not so hands-on as the first but was equally myopic in her thinking. This mother told me her LD daughter applied to and got into Yale University, where, at her parents' suggestion, she majored in Business Administration. I am not going to question the application process in this case because I don't know the circumstances. She may have gotten in without any help from her parents. I simply don't know. However, I *do* know that she had absolutely no interest in or aptitude for Business Administration. None. She floundered in her classes. Her self-esteem plummeted. She had serious trouble with roommates. She had no friends, no one she could relate to. In short, she had no business being in Business.

She dropped out. When her parents came around and finally gave in to reality, they approached her with the possibility of attending a smaller liberal-arts college closer to home, but her experience at Yale had so traumatized her that she had no desire and no intention of giving college another try. She had been defeated and remains defeated. She had dreams of being an artist, not a businesswoman. Now she is neither.

Don't do this, parents—just don't do it. Don't step in and do the work, and don't ignore obvious eventualities for the sake of short-term satisfactions. As painful as it may be, we must try as hard as we can to keep our own fantasies and daydreams to a minimum, or at least out of sight, when it comes to finding the right school. Stand back, encourage from afar, put the pen down or, better, hand it to your child. These are all part of the letting-go process, and a particularly difficult part at that, especially when getting into a specific college looms with such importance in a parent's mind. Yes, fine, dream of Harvard and Yale; but look with clear eyes at your child's abilities. Your most cherished words in the English language may be "I have a son at Harvard," but really, is it going to help your son to be there? At the same time, it is extremely important not to go overboard and shortchange him by thinking he can't go to any school at all. Some people I know could have looked at Allegra (and probably did) and never imagined she could have gone on to any school or program after high school, when in fact she attended the Threshold Program at Lesley University. Threshold gave her a solid grounding in the life skills that have enabled her to live on her own.

The line is thin between the parents who can't conceive of college for their child and those who conceive only of the college most out of reach. In between lies the realistic and optimistic possibility of enhancing a life through education best suited to the child's ability and interests. Those two things—ability and interest—are the ones to focus on. What *can* your child do? What does your child *want* to do?

Some form of higher education is not beyond the realm of possibility. It all comes down to planning and preparing so that you can help your hopeful young student find the school best attuned to his or her abilities. This planning and preparation are most effective when started in the years before the student graduates from high school, and that's where we'll start.

10

Before Graduation Day: Transitions from High School

Most parents begin the process of preparing their child for life after high school long before graduation day. Some start as early as middle school. For parents of a young child with LD, especially one recently diagnosed, looking so far into the future may seem an impossible feat, especially when his or her present problems are so overwhelming.

In the years following Allegra's diagnosis, I was weighed down by all the doctor's appointments, tutors, school meetings, and most of all, by the realization that my child's life had taken a drastic and unexpected turn. I went through the same phases of denial and anger and sorrow we all experience, and I could barely think about the coming year, much less a future far down the road.

But the future came, and soon after reaching a level of acceptance about having a young child with LD, I faced the new reality of having a teenager with LD. I could no longer focus only from day to day. I had to start thinking of things much further down the road, and the early years that I once thought were so traumatic and difficult now began to take on a glow of nostalgia. I didn't have to worry about college or careers or marriage back then, because things were going to change, everything would be different, and I had plenty of time.

Allegra spent many years of her childhood in a special elementary school for LD students. I still remember the moment the principal called me in to tell me that they had done all they could for her and that it was time for my daughter to "move on." Amazing how such simple words can instill uncertainty and even dread.

Every parent goes through it to some degree. Some mothers tell me how it saddens them to see their son or daughter pass from twelve to thirteen years of age, knowing childhood is at an end. Others look upon this as a hopeful time, a new phase in their continuing adventure as a parent. Those of us with children with LD rarely view the transition from childhood to young adulthood as an exciting adventure. For us, this time is so fraught with emotion that Kristy Baxter, the head of The Churchill School in New York City, calls it a "second grieving process." "At Churchill," she told me, "we have a meeting with the parents of every student to discuss the child's future after graduation. We meet at the end of 10th grade if the parents are anxious, or the beginning of the 11th grade if they're not. Some students already know they want to apply to college, get accepted, and then take a year off. Some know they want to go to an art school. Some know they want to work for a year and then go back to school. Some know they want to go directly to work and not go to college at all."

Regardless of their children's plans, this time of transition is stressful for all parents. For those with a child with LD, the issue of letting go looms larger than it does for other parents. The anxiety usually starts when the child is in middle school, in seventh and eighth grades in particular, when adolescent issues come into play. According to Kristy, the grieving process that parents go through when they find out they have a child struggling with a learning disability now resurfaces. "The parent ends up going through that process all over again," she says. "Much of this comes about through a bit of fantasy. When a parent first learns that they have a small child with LD, the initial sadness and grieving process eventually leads to a final stage of acceptance. But within that acceptance we can usually find an element of wishful thinking, that somehow everything is going to change and go away when the child grows older. And then when the child does grow older and enters seventh or eighth grade, the parents see them still struggling and see that it's not going away. That's when the grieving process resurfaces, and that's when they say, 'Well, we still have middle school and high school ahead of us.' Then in ninth and tenth grade it happens all over again, and the fear that high school is ending hits them."

Anxieties about college or work are real, but lurking beneath them is the greater anxiety about the fact that child will soon be on his or her own. It is the ever-present question that looms in our minds: "Can my child ever take care of himself?"

Leaving childhood behind to start down the road toward adulthood is a process. No one becomes a fully formed adult in one giant leap, wearing a cap and gown on graduation day, without having given a single prior thought to goals in life or some idea of how to attain those goals. It all comes about through a system of decisions and plans called transition.

All students make a transition when high school ends. Their world changes, and how they make their way through the world changes, too. Until now, the parents have made all the major decisions. In school, the demands were teacher-based. Very soon, the students themselves will need to make decisions and choices. If students don't show up for classes in college, what happens? A truant officer doesn't come looking for them. The school doesn't call their mothers to find out where they are. Overslept? Too bad. They get an F.

The same goes for work. Yes, an employer might give a warning or two, but ultimately the responsibility for showing up and performing a job rests on the shoulders of the employee.

Transitions, no matter what the ultimate goal may be, are simply a way to help students ease into their new reality as young adults.

It's an anxious new reality for parents, too. Your child is older now, and the time of looking beyond those day-to-day childhood worries to the broader worries of adulthood has arrived. Makes you want to crawl back into bed and pull the covers over your head, doesn't it? I remember the feelings well, but I'm now on the other side of the forest, and I can tell you that even though things might appear bleak from where you now stand, it's not as bad as you might expect.

THE IEP: A PLAN OF ACTION

All high-school students with LD are covered by the Individuals with Disabilities Education Act (IDEA), until they leave high school. After high school they are covered by the Americans with Disabilities Act (ADA). The greatest difference between the two laws is that IDEA guarantees the *right* to an education while ADA guarantees the *right to equal access* to education. IDEA also has direct bearing on the transition to college because part of its stated purpose is to "prepare [students] for further education, employment, and independent living."

The way this is done is through the use of an Individualized Education Plan, or IEP. I can hear it now: "Oh, no, not *this* again!" Most parents whose children have been diagnosed with LD are more than familiar with the IEP, but those whose young adult children have only been recently diagnosed (and are still in high school) may not yet understand the importance of this document.

Every school-age child with a diagnosed learning disability has the *legal right* to get evaluated. This evaluation can be done within the school or by an independent testing center. If the evaluation team determines that the student qualifies as having a learning disability, then all the data, test scores, recommendations, and anecdotal information from the evaluation are collapsed into a working document that stands at the core of the educational experience of a high-school student with LD.

This document, the Individualized Education Plan, summarizes all the collected data in order to come up with an operational plan. The information by itself isn't all that helpful. To say that a student is two years below grade level or scores at the 6th percentile is all well and good, but it doesn't tell us what to *do* about it. The IEP takes that next step and leads to action—and that's the best way to think of the IEP, as a plan of action. Now let's look at some of the things that go into this plan.

THE IEP DIPLOMA OBJECTIVE

When a student is fourteen (or even younger if appropriate), it's important to start looking at long-term goals based on the student's preferences, needs, and interests. At the beginning of high school, the school has to formally recognize and plan for eventual transition out of high school. This begins with a "diploma objective," which reflects the overall plans for the student's life after high school.

There are several types of diplomas offered at the end of high school, depending on which state you are from. New York State, for example, offers you:

    1. IEP Diploma. This is for students with more severe LD who are not focused on academics as much as on learning skills

for daily living. If they have accomplished the goals in their IEP, they graduate with this diploma.

2. Local Diploma. This diploma is local to the school and is the school's way of saying the student has attended.

3. Regular Diploma. The majority of students end up with this type of diploma (in some states it is called the Regents Diploma).

4. Advanced Regents Diploma. This diploma shows that the students have taken Advanced Placement classes. They may also get college credit while in high school.

Once the diploma objective is decided upon, the IEP then determines the best Transition Services to help meet that objective.

THE IEP: TRANSITION SERVICES

The Individuals with Disabilities Education Act (IDEA) states that a student's IEP must begin to address the issue of transition to life after high school when the student reaches age sixteen. Once the diploma objective and transition goals are established in the IEP, the next step is to identify the Transition Services that will help meet those goals. Essentially, Transition Services help the student move from high school to post–high school. For the college-bound student, the Transition Services plan could include collecting information on colleges' learning disability services and documentation requirements, and developing the student's ability to talk about the impact of the learning disability and which accommodations are helpful. It's important to note that high schools are required to identify only the student's *current* educational needs—not to provide the actual documentation for college. Some colleges may require new or supplemental testing such as a psycho-educational test. Parents may need to look outside the high school for this.

In addition, Transition Services include actual steps that the school will take with the student. For example, community integration is considered a part of Transition Services. Has the student learned how to function in the community? The school may suggest that the student volunteer in the community to gain some experience of what it's like to be working outside the school. Other opportunities in community integration could be internships, part-time jobs, or any other activities that help the child integrate into the community.

Transition Services include a section on preparing students for careers. This helps students relate their chosen school subjects to possible careers through determining their strengths and interests, and then thinking about realistic career options.

Transition Services also include sections on preparing for independent living and daily living skills, such as personal grooming and hygiene, shopping, and banking. We might not normally associate these skills with school, but they are vital for students with the more severe forms of learning disability.

USING THE IEP

Once a student leaves the public education system after twelfth grade, there is no IEP, and the responsibility for requesting and arranging for services falls completely on the individual. If students need documentation of a learning disability, it is now up to them to get it. This means that students need to have some understanding of their own high school IEP. Parents can help with this.

Dr. Sheldon Horowitz of the National Center for Learning Disabilities talked with me about how parents and students can prepare for Life After IEP. "When talking about transition," he told me, "students need to take ownership of their IEPs. They should be asking questions like, 'What information is provided in my IEP? How has this information made a discernible impact on the quality of my life in high school? What do I need to do during this transition time to preserve the benefits provided by my IEP until I graduate, and how do I arrange for the same type of support when I leave high school and head off to college, work, or a combination of both?'"

I asked him how a parent is supposed to get a rowdy teenager to focus on these questions, or even how to ask them in the first place.

"This is where parents must play a role within transition planning. Together with the school personnel, they need to initiate an honest and ongoing dialogue, ideally during the middle school years, but surely no later than tenth or eleventh grade. Begin by setting the stage for this conversation, provide some background about the importance of the

IEP during the K–12 school years, and let them know how important it is for them to place an increasingly major role on arranging for the services and supports they need to be successful."

I pointed out that not every student is ready to assume this responsibility, and cannot think beyond high school, either to a college experience or to career goals.

"That's why it's important to begin this transition planning process early. You have to involve the child at whatever the level of interest might be, and be sensitive to their ability to understand their needs and participate in this strategic planning. Going over every little detail in the IEP is not necessary and, for some students, might be boring or even seen as intrusive. On the other hand, you should not make any assumptions about the student's interest in these details. In fact, some students are relieved to see 'proof' of their struggles as reflected on their IEP. Whatever the situation, plan for a meaningful handoff of information over time and give the student many opportunities to communicate what they know about themselves as learners and what support they need to be successful. This will help your child to fully understand both the challenges and the opportunities that lie ahead."

The National Center for Learning Disabilities recognized a parent's need for information during this crucial time and created a brief called *Transition Under IDEA 2004: Statutory Requirements and Strategic Planning for Transition to College*. This brief, found on the NCLD website at www.ld.org, includes a checklist that focuses on transition issues and is meant to supplement the wide range of materials available to students in planning for college. Each of the items on the list can be incorporated as IEP goals as students progress through high school.

All students with LD can benefit from understanding their IEP, no matter what their eventual goals. If the IEP indicates weak math skills, these weak skills will carry over into life after high school and will be an area that will cause difficulty whether the student goes on to college or directly into a job. For instance, your son or daughter doesn't leave LD behind when they go out bowling. They have to keep score. They have to make change. They have a hundred things they do every day that can be affected by their skills or lack of the same. The IEP captures the information about those skills and puts it down on paper. It helps students understand who they are and how best to handle the challenges ahead.

And parents, transition issues present challenges for you as well. Rules, regulations, changes, legal language, obscure words, acronyms you have never heard of, and long strings of numbers referring to bills and laws all conspire to leave you feeling more lost and confused than ever. But take heart. Teachers and administrators, and especially LD and vocational counselors, are there to help you.

Don't expect or even try to do it all alone.

Remember that you are also in a state of transition during this time, and your child is not the only one facing an uncertain future. You are too. It is never easy to watch a child who is completely dependent upon you transition into an adult, still dependent in some ways, but also trying mightily to gain independence. Even so, your job now is to help in any way you can and to make sure you do not become an obstacle to independence. It is all too easy for parents to foster "learned helplessness" in their children. Though well intentioned, our incessant hovering may create an unhealthy dependence—the exact opposite of what we want to achieve. This time of transition for your child is a good time to consider your own transitions as well, and how you can best shift your intense day-to-day focus into the broader view of helping your young adult child as he or she takes the first steps along the path to independence.

11

The Fearful Student: Finding Your Child's Interests

Whenwe think of a student preparing for college, we often imagine someone in tenth or eleventh grade who is gung-ho about the process, eager and willing to sit down and plan for a bright future. There are students like this, of course, but if we already know there are parents with unrealistic expectations about their child's college plans, it stands to reason that there are students with equally unrealistic notions of education after high school. Someone who reaches far too high is an obvious example. No one should discount goals and determination, and I hesitate to advise anyone to lower their expectations, but logic dictates that someone in a special school who can barely pass the simplest math test is probably not the best candidate for a degree in nuclear physics.

A counselor at a special school told me of a student with severe LD who came into his office to ask how he could get the catalog for Yale University. "The truth is," he told me, "if you need a lot of help on how to get the catalog, Yale may not be the right school."

More common than overreaching (at least as far as the LD student is concerned) is the opposite problem of a student reaching too low or not at all. It is easy to imagine a young man or woman in that same special school who has found a place where they finally feel comfortable with themselves and with others, maybe for the first time in their lives. And now graduation day appears on the horizon, and with it comes a possible end to that comfort. They may have no desire to leave home, either. In their daydreams they may see themselves spending the rest of their days in high school, living at home, with no scary changes coming their way and nothing to upset the balance.

We all understand this. The future *is* scary, and change *is* scary, and some of us deal with both of these by ignoring them or pretending they don't exist.

Dr. Arlyn Roffman, a professor of special education at Lesley University, was asked about this situation in an online chat. A mother asked what she could do for her son, who could not face the idea of leaving school or being out on his own. The young man had severe learning disabilities. He was found to be of average intelligence, with good reading skills but dramatic deficits in math. His mother had no idea how to help him try to discover what he wanted from life.

Arlyn's first words of advice were to respond to the young man's fear by getting him to talk to his parents, a teacher, or a counselor at school, who could reassure him that he would not be cast out on his own and set adrift before he was ready. This might strike some as an unnecessary step to take. "He doesn't need reassurance," a mother might think about her son. "He already *knows* we would never just throw him out!"

Does he? Teenagers are not renowned for clear, logical thinking. On one level, yes, the young man surely realizes his mother would not set him adrift, but it is possible for this same young man to have a concurrent thought, a lingering anxiety not far below the surface, that tells him his life of security and routine is coming to an end. Easing these fears would help to "unstick" him enough to start expressing some interests and dreams for his future.

Arlyn then suggested a formal evaluation, including an Interest Inventory and a hands-on vocational assessment, which evaluates both skills and aptitudes. Each state has a Department of Vocational Rehabilitation that can help with this evaluation. As for the Interest Inventory, she suggested the Strong-Campbell Interest Inventory. This is a tool used by school vocational counselors to help students consider possible career paths by discovering what types of things interest them.

THE KEY OF LIFE:
FINDING YOUR CHILD'S INTERESTS

Sitting down in a formal way in an attempt to figure out what interests us might seem to be a bit overdone—how can individuals be so unaware of their own interests that they must resort to filling out a form in the hope of finding an answer? I had trouble understanding it, since my son's unshakeable passion for filmmaking and Allegra's love of skating were both formed at an early age. There was never any question of what interested them.

I almost passed over this subject, but when talking to a young man who has had a particularly difficult struggle with ADHD, I happened to mention that I thought most young people had a pretty good idea of what they wanted to do by the time they left high school.

"Are you *kidding?*" he asked, quite taken aback. "I had *no* idea what interested me or what I wanted to be. Finding out what interests you is one of the most difficult things of all for someone with LD, especially if you have had a long history of failure. The problem is that knowing what interests you is also the key of life!"

As we talked further, I realized that even students with strong interests may be fearful of discussing them or putting them forward as possibilities. Why? "You don't think you'll be taken seriously," this young man told me. "You might be so beaten down and have such low self-esteem that the idea of having an interest that might lead to success seems to be impossible."

Many young people face this situation. They honestly don't know what interests them, or more to the point, how to articulate those interests or see them as leading to a career of some kind. They simply cannot see the opportunities. Using a tool like an Interest Inventory not only helps these students discover their interests but also suggests a pathway to success using the interests they already know they have.

INTEREST INVENTORY

Interest Inventories such as the Strong-Campbell Interest Inventory, also known as the Self-Directed Search or SDS, allow students to focus on their interests as they relate to career possibilities. Of course, just because someone is interested in something doesn't mean he or she has the ability to work in that chosen field. An interest in nature, for instance, does not guarantee success in advanced biology classes. Even so, by organizing interests into broad themes and occupations, a student may hit upon possibilities never before considered. An interest in nature could lead to a job in the National Park system or at a local zoo.

Before suggesting your son or daughter take an Interest Inventory, it might help for you as a parent to think about what interests your child. Do you know? I had it easy, as skating became Allegra's consuming passion, but how many of us are unaware of the secret delights that might be hiding in our child's heart?

Most Interest Inventories start by focusing on six general types of interests. Some may apply more than others to LD adults, but I have listed them all below with a brief explanation of what distinguishes each type from the others.

• **Realistic**

> Qualities: practical, hands-on, physical coordination.
>
> Interests include machines, engines, computer networks, athletics, or working outdoors.
>
> Possible occupations include operating equipment, using tools, repair work, providing security, or construction work.

• **Conventional**

> Qualities: attention to detail, accuracy, ability to work with numbers.
>
> Interests include organization, information systems, data management.
>
> Possible occupations include organizing and keeping records and files, bookkeeping, setting up procedures and systems, working in a mail room or other support service within a company.

• **Investigative**

> Qualities: independent, curious, mathematical or research ability.
>
> Interests include science, math, research.
>
> Determination and ability to think in ways others do not are also traits of the LD adult, and these can be invaluable in careers where "thinking outside the box" is often vital to success.

- **Enterprising**

  Qualities: risk-taking, competitive, verbal ability.

  Interests include business, entrepreneurship, leadership.

  Possible occupations include sales, management, marketing. At first glance, these also might not appear the best fit for someone with LD or ADHD, but once again, an ability to think in new and different ways can be the key to success. (In the "Interviews" section, we'll meet several prime examples of this.)

- **Artistic**

  Qualities: independence, imagination, creativity, musical and artistic expression.

  Interests include self-expression, communication, and culture.

  Possible occupations include visual or performing arts, graphic artist. This is an area filled with people with LD. The visual arts in particular are a magnet for those lacking ability in reading and math.

- **Social**

  Qualities: people skills, verbal ability, service to others.

  Interests include community service and volunteerism.

  Possible occupations include caring for elderly or for children, teaching assistant, working at a health spa, hotel services, or as a greeter at a restaurant.

This gives a general idea of what an Interest Inventory entails. (The actual inventory is far more specific and detailed. Contact your state's Department of Vocational Rehabilitation for more information.) It can be a valuable tool for students with LD who have no idea which path to take, and can help alleviate some of the fear of the immediate, scary future.

12

LD, ADHD, and the SAT

And speaking of scary...

We who are no longer in high school easily forget how much anxiety we felt as the day approached when we were to take the dreaded SAT test. At the same time, I don't think there is a high-school student alive who fully appreciates the level of anxiety experienced by their parents over this very same test. Parents know how important it is and how it can influence our children's entire future...or at least we *think* we know that. But do we? It goes without saying that worry and apprehension are heightened for students with LD and their parents, but it is all too easy to overdo the nail-biting, the sleepless nights, and the endless meetings with teachers and school administrators over accommodations. I do not mean to minimize the importance of the SAT but rather to minimize a parent's anxiety over it.

The letters SAT used to stand for Scholastic Aptitude Test, but now they stand alone and are used to describe two types of tests, the SAT Reasoning Test and the SAT Subject Test. (The American College Testing, or ACT, test is an alternative and is accepted by all colleges and universities.)

The SAT Reasoning Test is the standard SAT test. It measures the critical thinking skills needed for success in college and includes sections on critical reading, math, and writing.

SAT Subject Tests are designed to measure knowledge and skills in particular subject areas, such as English, history, mathematics, science, and language. Many colleges use the Subject Tests for admission, for course placement, and to advise students about course selection. Some colleges specify the Subject Tests they require for admission or placement; others allow applicants to choose which tests to take.

The majority of students will take the SAT Reasoning Test, but before making a final decision on the type of test to take, it's best to figure out which college the student hopes to attend. Its catalog will list its test requirements. It may turn out that the college of choice does not require SAT Subject Tests. It may even turn out that the college of choice doesn't require any SAT test at all.

THE SAT AND STUDENTS WITH LD AND ADHD

Thousands of students with LD and ADHD take the SAT test every year, most with accommodations. These accommodations are determined by the College Board, the company that administers the SAT. Students at The Churchill School in New York City, for instance, have to have a full psychological education evaluation done outside of school, and then they get time and a half, double time, one on one, readers, or scribes when taking the SAT, depending on their profile.

This process is not without controversy. As Kristy Baxter, the head of Churchill, says, "Because so many students in the mainstream are asking for accommodations—everyone wants extra time—the College Board has become very restrictive in terms of the criteria they use. That's understandable, but it's hurting our kids. Some of our kids are being turned down for accommodations, even though they are in a school for students with LD. This happens because some of the testing they use is limited. For instance, if you haven't had a specific type of reading test to show you're at a certain reading level, then you can't get certain accommodations. But we have documented files on our kids that show that they have a documented learning disability and need these services. So our kids are getting hurt and others are getting turned down, and it seems to be done in arbitrary ways. Kids that we think are going to get time and a half end up with double time, and kids who need double time get time and a half."

Gaston Caperton, former governor of West Virginia and currently president of the College Board, is also on the board of directors of the National Center for Learning Disabilities. He has dyslexia and understands the tribulations of those struggling with LD. I met him in his office at the College Board. The early part of our conversation focused on his personal experience with LD (included in the "Interviews" section). I then turned to the subject of so much concern to Kristy and many parents, namely, the SAT.

His advice is sound and comforting. It won't completely remove all anxiety, but I hope it will help parents see the larger picture.

The SAT lingers in our minds long after we take the test. Governor Caperton, during his second interview for the job of president of the College Board, admits that he had a sudden worrying thought that they might ask to look at his SAT scores!

"I had very average SAT scores," he says. "That experience and that thought popping into my mind after all these years show that I still carry the experience of having LD with me. When you end up in a competitive situation, you tend to think about and worry about your weakest qualities, and that's what happened to me. After all those years, that little voice inside still worried that they might look at my SAT scores and see that I didn't do so well in reading. I was in business for twenty-five years, governor of West Virginia, taught at Harvard and Columbia, and I *still* worried about my SAT scores."

I brought up some of the changes he's made to the SAT, specifically a greater emphasis on writing, which could present some difficulties for those with LD.

"The mission of the College Board," he explained, "is to prepare kids for college success and opportunity, and to focus on two things: Equity and Excellence. Every person in this country has to know how to write. A person's ability to write is critical to any job they have, and the reason we put so much writing on the SAT was to encourage people to write. In a continuing competitive society, which is much more internationally competitive than it has ever been, we have to make the education system in this country better all the time. That is the Excellence part. The Equity part says that we have to give every child an equal opportunity. We have people who live in good neighborhoods and have good schools, and we have kids who are poor who have terrible schools. We try to address that so we work very hard on both Excellence and Equity, and writing is extremely important no matter where you are. If you can't write, you can't collect your ideas and you can't express them to others. Writing is critical, even if it's only writing to yourself or for yourself."

"And for the student with LD?" I asked.

"Yes, let's talk about the SAT as it relates to the student with LD. We have about fifty thousand students a year with LD out of about 3 million. We understand that it is harder for students with LD to take tests than it is for other students. Before I came along nobody cared about that at all. Parents and students are all anxious about the test. Taking a test to go to college is a rite of passage and it is not much fun. Nobody likes it. Everybody is terrified. But let's say you are a parent of a child with learning disabilities. The anxiety for those parents and that child goes way up, so we try to accommodate those students as fairly as we can. We give it a lot of attention, but we've got to do it in a way that is both fair to the individual with LD and consistent across the board. Some parents have kids who have gone to very special schools and have had special attention paid to them; and often we can't give them the exact accommodations that their school would give them. They're probably getting a national norm . . . what we think is fair. And they *don't* think that's fair and I can understand that. But we are restricted in some ways as to what we can and can't do."

He then explained the process to me. The student fills out an application. The school supports the student and helps them with that, and the College Board tries to give the student the same accommodations he or she gets from the school. "The problems come about when people try to do things at the last minute," he said. "They get nervous because they haven't heard back from us. They need to remember that if someone has special needs it takes us longer to process their application. The biggest piece of advice I would give to parents about this is that the sooner they can get it done, the better. It's very difficult when they call up a day or two before the test and complain they haven't heard from anybody. We need time to process these requests. Parents and teachers don't realize it, but we spend a lot of time and money on this. Due to my own past and my own difficulties with LD, we are very sensitive to what needs to be done. We have a whole department that does nothing but look over those applications."

I asked him what a parent could do to lessen the stress of the SAT apart from getting in the documentation early.

"First of all, they should not expect there to be more pressure on them than on parents who don't have a child with LD—or, at least, not more pressure from us. I tell all the people who work at the College Board that parents of a child with LD are going to be harder to deal with than others because they're already under more pressure. We need to realize and accept that because it's true—they *are* under more pressure. But truly, the best way to ease the pressure is to get everything done early. That way you don't find yourself five days before the test without knowing what the accommodations are. But apart from that, there is no additional pressure. Taking the SAT test for a child with LD or ADHD is no different than for any other child. You should do as much as you can to make sure the accommodations are in place. You should also prepare the child. Don't let the SAT be the first time the child takes a long test. Do two or three practice tests."

Parents should consider having students take the PSAT, or Preliminary SAT/National Merit Scholarship Qualifying Test. It's a standardized test that serves as practice for the SAT. There are many benefits to taking the PSAT. Students become familiar with the types of questions and the exact directions they will see on the SAT, and will have an opportunity to discover areas of weakness and strength before they take the actual SAT.

By preparing students through practice tests and getting accommodation requests in early, parents can bring their children to the same level of stress that everyone else faces. And regardless of whether or not they get the exact accommodations they might in school, it's extremely helpful for them to know the type of accommodations they *will* have, and to know it well in advance.

Students should not be worrying about accommodations the day before the test: they should be worrying about the test, the same as everyone else (after all, eliminating *all* worry about the SAT is beyond the abilities of humans).

Governor Caperton had some additional words of advice. "Students and parents should also be aware that schools look at things beyond the SAT scores," he said. "I am one of the judges on your scholarship, the Anne Ford Scholarship at the National Center for Learning Disabilities. I look over all those applications and even though the kids might not have high academic marks, they do remarkable things in school. They get into very good colleges. That doesn't mean they aren't going to have to work awfully hard when they go off to those schools, but colleges and universities have sensitivities to those things that they never had even ten years ago. The SAT is an important part of college admissions, probably second in importance after overall grades. But the extracurricular things count for a lot.

"A good admissions process, which most schools have, is done in a comprehensive way. They look at SAT scores, they look at grades, they look at extracurricular activities and how the student writes an essay. They try to know as much as possible about a student, and they take everything into consideration. If a student has LD or ADHD and they've done all these extra things, they really do take that into consideration. As a non-LD-related example, think of English as a Second Language. Schools don't expect a student who has been in the United States for a year and a half to write an essay as well as those who have been here all their lives. People are sensitive. They are trying to find good kids to bring into their school. There are also plenty of schools with open admissions. Fifty percent of all students in higher education go to community colleges, and they all have open admissions. So people put themselves under a little more pressure about this than they need to."

Governor Caperton's simple advice to parents can make a world of difference for students with LD and ADHD who are facing the SAT. As mentioned, there is no way to completely eliminate the worry and stress, but following his suggestions can go a long way toward alleviating them. Here are his suggestions again:

1. Submit paperwork and requests for accommodations *early*.
2. Students should take two or three practice tests such as the PSAT. Areas of weakness will be discovered and extra help can be found to focus on those areas.
3. Don't sweat it. Even if the student doesn't do very well on the SAT, that does not mean college is no longer an option.

Now let's take a look at the process of finding the best and most appropriate college according to a student's interests and abilities.

13

How to Find the Right College

The first step in choosing the right school for the student with LD or ADHD is to find information about those schools that offer courses in your child's chosen field. Some parents, especially those whose children have not yet entered high school, may wonder if there are colleges that accommodate students with LD or ADHD. Indeed there are! Most colleges and universities accept students with LD and ADHD and provide services. Some colleges, such as Landmark College in Vermont and Mitchell College in Connecticut, are entirely devoted to educating the LD student—in other words, *every* student there has a learning disability.

The College Board has an online service called the College Matchmaker that allows students to submit their preferences and interests, such as school size or type of campus. I made a quick search by checking a box to indicate that I wanted to find a college that provides services for those with learning disabilities. Two seconds later a list of 2,710 colleges appeared. *2,710!* Some were universities, some community colleges, some technical schools, and each one provides some type of service for the LD student.

Many of these colleges also have programs specifically designed for students with LD. These programs may have separate admissions procedures and support systems. The Threshold Program where Allegra went after high school is a good example. It is a program within Lesley University.

After making a list of possible colleges that fit your child's interests and career choices, you need to find out about the specific learning disability services provided at each one. These vary from college to college.

Unlike high schools, there is no requirement for colleges to follow a standard set of procedures and rules throughout the country, and so reading about the services provided at one college doesn't mean they'll be provided in the same way at all the others.

THINKING OUTSIDE THE BOX

The first thing to do, especially for those parents who cannot imagine their child going on to any type of college, is to expand our notion of postsecondary education. Yes, "college" is an option, but there are many more.

Here is a list of possibilities.

College/Degree Programs

Four-Year Colleges. Four-year colleges and undergraduate university programs (including four-year technical schools) vary in size, admissions criteria, academic standards, course offerings, location, and cost. The curriculum leads to a Bachelor of Arts (B.A.) or Bachelor of Science (B.S.) degree. Most of these schools will offer LD support services and programs.

Two-Year Colleges. Two-year colleges provide a chance to prepare for further education, to learn an occupational skill, or to change careers. Students earn an Associate of Arts (A.A.) degree, and credits earned at the two-year college can usually be transferred to a four-year college or university.

Community Colleges. These schools offer liberal-arts subjects in addition to training in specific occupations such as hotel management or automotive mechanics. Most have remedial or developmental courses that can help upgrade basic academic skills, if needed.

Junior Colleges. Most private junior colleges are small residential schools that prepare students for transfer to a four-year liberal-arts college. Some offer occupational training. Entrance exams are usually required, however work experience and extracurricular activities are also considered in the admissions process. Students earn an Associate of Arts degree.

Vocational/Trade Schools. Similar to community and junior colleges, these schools offer career-oriented programs. Some courses of study lead to an Associate of Applied Science (A.A.S.) degree following an intense program in one very specific skill area. These schools also offer non-degree certificate programs.

Nursing Schools. There are two kinds of nursing schools.

- A school affiliated with a hospital, where students receive R.N. degrees after training.

- A school affiliated with a four-year college, where students receive both a B.S. degree and an R.N. degree, and are prepared to enter the field of nursing administration.

Military Schools. There are two kinds of military schools. Both offer degree programs in engineering and technology, with a concentration on various aspects of military science.

- Federal Military Academies prepare officers for the Army, Navy, and Air Force. Institutions such as West Point, Annapolis, and the Air Force Academy require recommendations and appointment by members of Congress.

- Private and state-supported Military Institutes and the Coast Guard Academy operate on a college-application basis.

Business Schools. At some colleges it is possible to specialize in business administration or to take a two-year secretarial course along with liberal-arts courses.

Certificate Programs

In addition to the trade or vocational schools, students may want to consider schools with non-degree certificate programs. Some, like the engineering colleges, may seem out of reach for most LD students, while others such as art schools may be ideal.

Engineering/Technical Colleges. These are independent professional schools that provide four- or five-year training programs in engineering and the physical sciences. They are often known as Institutes of Technology or Polytechnic Institutes.

Film/Art Schools. These schools prepare students for careers in film and art.

Cooking Schools/Culinary Arts. These schools offer programs ranging from six months to three years and provide students with hands-on training in a variety of cooking techniques. Students leave these programs with a certificate in the culinary arts.

Health Service Programs. More than 3,500 vocational school programs, including practical nurse training, EMT preparation, and dental assistant training, are currently available for students interested in a career in health care.

Life Skills Programs. Some students with LD need more intensive services than a community college, university, or technical school can offer. Life Skills programs are postsecondary educational programs that help young people learn the skills needed for independent living. The programs are provided in a residential setting and often offer training in such important life skills as time management, vocational training, banking/budgeting, and perhaps most important of all, social skills.

Some of these programs can be found as part of a college system, like the Threshold Program at Lesley University, or they may be run at an independent living center.

ADMISSION STANDARDS AND DISCLOSURE

After identifying the type of school and choosing several candidates, take a look at the admission standards for each one. Typical admission standards for a four-year college measure abilities in English, math, science, foreign language, social studies, fine or practical arts, and health and physical education. They also take into account a student's high-school grade-point average, rank in senior class, and, of course, the SAT.

If a student is at or above the average SAT score and grade-point average, he or she will probably be accepted, but what happens if a student is below average? There are still ways to strengthen an application. Extracurricular activities, work experiences, hobbies, teacher recommendations all add to a student's profile. In addition, the impact of LD should be considered, and for that we come to the issue of disclosure.

No college will ask if a student has a disability. A college may have the best disability services in the state, but it will not actively seek out candidates to fill them. That is up to the student.

This is a huge issue for some young people. Regardless of their high-school experience, some simply do not want to enter college with the "label" of LD. This is certainly understandable, but there are undeniable benefits to disclosing a learning disability, especially for those students who are below the minimum standard for admission to the college of choice. By itself, the very fact that a student has learned to compensate for LD says a great deal about his or her perseverance, ability to handle challenges, and determination. Colleges will take these things into account, especially if the student makes a request by enclosing a letter with the application. The letter should include a statement that the student has a learning disability, which admission requirements the LD affects, additional information such as extracurricular activities or work experience the student would like the college to consider, and documentation of the disability by a professional.

Some colleges will specify the type of LD documentation they require, which may mean making updates or changes to the documentation the student already has. *The Postsecondary LD Report* lists the following six elements as part of the documentation acceptable to most colleges.

1. A diagnostic statement by an appropriate professional identifying the disability, date of most current evaluation, and date of the original diagnosis.
2. Description of the diagnostic tests, methods, and/or criteria used.
3. Description of the current functional impact of the disability, including specific test results and examiner's narrative interpretation.

4. Treatments, medications, or assistive devices/services currently prescribed or in use.
5. Description of expected progression or stability of the impact of the disability over time, particularly over the next five years.
6. Credentials of the diagnosing professionals.

If your son or daughter is reluctant to disclose LD or ADHD, don't shrug and say, "Okay, fine with me." While you may understand this reluctance, helping your child understand the benefits of disclosure truly is in his or her best interest. Students who are upfront about their LD or ADHD can tap into a wide range of resources and services they might not expect to find.

ABOUT COMMUNITY COLLEGES

Location, financial aid, academic programs, entrance exams: some or all of these factors come into play when searching for the right school, and for a majority of students with LD, the two-year community college has the most appeal. Why might your son or daughter be attracted to a school like this?

For one thing, community colleges have open enrollment. This means students can attend even if they did not achieve a high score on their SAT, or if they have a GED instead of a high-school diploma. Many entrance exams at community colleges do not require a student to take the SAT (and students can take these entrance exams with accommodations). In addition, tuition costs for community colleges are well below those of four-year colleges, and there are often more opportunities for financial aid.

There are two additional reasons I believe community colleges can greatly benefit the LD student, even those planning to go on to a four-year college: location and ease of transfer.

Location

In my interview with Kristy Baxter, head of The Churchill School, we talked about the difficulties many students have when it comes to leaving home. "Many of our kids are fragile learners," she said. "Certain kids have less resiliency than others. It's part of their temperament.

Other kids are very resilient. They come into the world and they have to struggle in school, but they have a temperament that gives them the resilience to push through it. Students who are fragile learners don't have this resilience. They don't have the ability to push through. It's as though the struggle overwhelms them."

"Is it something hard-wired into them," I asked, "or is it a matter of parenting, maybe a parent who was too protective?"

"I think it's how they're wired. Some students can snap back and stay in there, and others can't. And when you add attentional problems to that fragility, it can cause a lot of difficulties. Many of our kids are very talented in the arts, and many go on to art schools. We have one student who was accepted at the Art Institute of Chicago. They accepted him because the quality of his work was so good, but his teachers and advisers didn't want him to go there, because we felt the pressure would be too much for him. He wasn't a student who would respond well to a high level of pressure and competition, so instead, he went to the Maine College of Art, which is perfect. He's in a good art school that's manageable for him.

When we look for a college for our kids, it's really a matter of understanding the whole makeup of that child. Some of our kids have academic ability, but they don't have the emotional wherewithal. One of the trends we have found is that our kids do not do as well the farther they go from home. They don't have to actually live at home, but we've found that students have more difficulties when they go to schools that are far from home."

Kristy's experience does not necessarily dictate that students with LD or ADHD must go to a college in their hometown in order to succeed. The school could be in the same state or a neighboring state, but still within range of home, even if it's only a psychological illusion. When Allegra was considering a program after leaving high school, we found two possibilities: one in Chicago and one a little closer, in Massachusetts. Practically speaking, both were about equal in terms of travel, maybe an hour's difference by plane. But somehow that additional distance to Chicago unnerved us both. It was too far from home, too difficult to imagine hopping in the car and driving there ... and so she settled on Massachusetts without regrets.

Obviously, if leaving home is too great a challenge for your college-bound student to bear, a community college within driving distance is an attractive option.

Ease of Transfer

The other benefit a community college offers the LD student is ease of transfer. Suppose a student really wants to attend a four-year college but simply cannot handle the basic courses required by that particular college—math, for instance, or science. All is not lost. The student can attend a community college for two years and take courses that satisfy the basic requirements of the four-year college. The courses at the community college generally parallel the freshmen and sophomore offerings at the four-year college, but the student with LD will have the benefit of accomplishing them in an environment that may be more supportive, with smaller class sizes, and closer to home.

Those students already accepted into a four-year college should not lose sight of the community-college option, especially if trouble appears once they arrive at school. Let's say a student is required to take a course in math in order to satisfy the requirements of their major in Art. If this same student barely scraped by the math section of the SAT and is hopelessly lost when it comes to advanced mathematical formulas, it is perfectly acceptable to take an easier math course at a local community college and transfer the credits to the four-year institution.

14
Financial Aid

Whenit comes to issues concerning college-age adults with LD, the majority of calls to the National Center for Learning Disabilities are those requesting information about financial aid. Most callers hope to find out about specific scholarships or resources directed toward students with LD, but alas, there are few of those to be found. NCLD instituted a scholarship in my name after I stepped down as chairman. The Anne Ford Scholarship receives hundreds of applications every year, all from qualified students, and it is always an ordeal to choose the final recipient.

In general, there simply aren't enough LD-related scholarships to keep up with the ever-increasing demand, and while grants and scholarships are important, they are overshadowed by the largest source of financial support and the one that all students should look to first: the federal government.

FAFSA: THE FREE APPLICATION FOR FEDERAL STUDENT AID

FAFSA is the only application a student needs to complete to be considered for federal financial aid. This aid can come in several forms.

- Grants, such as federal Pell Grants, which do not have to be repaid.
- Loans, which do have to be repaid, with interest.
- Work-study programs, which allow students to earn money while enrolled in school to help pay for education expenses.

Federal financial aid is awarded on the basis of the student's financial needs. The U.S. Department of Education uses the information on the FAFSA to calculate an Expected Family Contribution, or EFC. The school of choice will then subtract the EFC from the total cost of attendance, and the resulting number is considered the student's financial need. (Even though the EFC is called the Expected Family Contribution, it is not the amount that the family is expected to pay for the student's education, nor is the amount of financial aid the student will receive equal to the total cost of attendance minus the EFC. The EFC is used as a general guideline to indicate the amount of financial aid the student is *eligible* to receive.)

Even if you don't think your child will be eligible for any financial aid, it is still a good idea to fill out the FAFSA form. Many states, schools, and private funding sources use the FAFSA data to award aid from their programs. Many also require it as part of their application process. The form can be completed on paper or online at www.fafsa.ed.gov.

More than 80 percent of all applications are submitted electronically. It's faster, easier, and the schools listed on the application receive the student's processed information more quickly than by regular mail.

The first thing to do when applying for a FAFSA is to apply online for a Personal Identification Number (PIN) that will be used to sign the application. This is used for identification purposes when signing the online application, the same as the PIN number used at an ATM machine. This isn't required when filling out and sending the paper application, but it is the fastest way to sign an application and it's the only way to access and sign a Renewal FAFSA in years to come. With the PIN number you can access up-to-date information on your loan process, submit corrections, or add a school code to your application. You can apply for the PIN at www.pin.ed.gov.

If you do not have access to a computer, you can still get all the information you need by calling the Federal Student Aid Information Center (FSAIC) at 1-800-433-3243. The FSAIC provides the following services:

- Helps you complete or make corrections to FAFSA on the web.
- Helps you complete the paper FAFSA.
- Answers questions about the PIN.
- Checks the processing status of the FAFSA.

- Changes your paper address and e-mail address.
- Changes the schools you listed on your application.
- Explains the Student Aid Report (SAR) and how to make corrections, and also mails a duplicate SAR.
- Checks on whether a school participates in federal student-aid programs.
- Explains who is eligible for federal student aid.
- Explains how federal student aid is awarded and paid, and the verification process.
- Sends requested publications.

FINANCIAL NEED

In general, financial need is defined as the difference between the student's educational expenses and the amount of money the family is expected to contribute. Educational expenses include things such as tuition, fees, books and supplies, computers, room and board, transportation, and (for students with LD) could include the cost of services for personal use or study, such as readers or note takers.

Once these expenses have been identified, the student and parents should provide the college's financial aid administrator with documentation of these expenses. Some colleges may only require a statement written by the student. Others may require an official document from a professional. Make sure to check the guidelines of each financial aid office.

OTHER SOURCES OF FUNDING

1. State Vocational Rehabilitation Agencies

In addition to the FAFSA, state agencies for higher education can be a source of financial aid for the student with LD. The contact information for these state agencies can be found online at www.ed.gov.

Students with LD may also be eligible for assistance from their state office for Vocational Rehabilitation (VR) Services. The mission of these agencies is to provide counseling and training for individuals with disabilities to become employable. For some, this means college-level study, in which case the VR agency may provide help with tuition expenses, room and board, books and supplies, reader services, and technological aids and devices.

These services must be authorized in advance in an Individualized Plan for Employment, which, in an apparent effort to confuse as many parents as possible, is known as the IPE. Please note that this is *not* the IEP, or Individualized Education Plan, used in high school.

State financial aid associations and Vocational Rehabilitation administrators work together to provide financial aid for students with disabilities, but the process is not easy. Students and their parents should contact both the VR agency in their state and the financial aid office of the college they plan to attend to be sure to meet both of their deadlines. The college will determine the student's eligibility for financial assistance and develop a financial award package. At the same time, the VR will try to award funds to take care of the student's disability-related needs. Those things not covered by the VR can be added to the student's expenses, which may then increase the student's financial aid.

2. Supplemental Security Income (SSI)

Supplemental Security Income (SSI) is a federal program that provides assistance to individuals with disabilities who have little or no income or resources. Work-study programs or other employment can affect SSI benefits, but if the Social Security Administration approves a Plan for Achieving Self-Support, the student can set aside income that is being used toward a specific vocational goal such as tuition and continue to receive SSI payments. These plans can be developed by Vocational Rehabilitation counselors, public or private social agencies, parents, or the student. Contact your local Social Security Administration office for more details.

3. Federal "TRIO" Programs (Talent Search, Educational Opportunity Centers, and Special Services for Disadvantaged Students)

These centers are federally funded programs. Some are connected with a college and some have been set up as part of a private organization. They were established to provide counseling and other services to disadvantaged students and student with disabilities, and can be very helpful to students trying to negotiate financial assistance with their college of choice. Some provide financial assistance as well. Check with the college to see if there is a Special Services Program and the type of services offered.

4. States

Most states offer some form of financial aid. High-school guidance counselors and college financial-aid administrators will have lists of state agencies that offer grants and loans.

5. Colleges

Some colleges and universities provide direct financial aid such as merit- and need-based scholarships, loans, or work-study programs. Students should check with the financial aid office when applying to the school.

6. Private Sources

Many private scholarships are based more on merit or performance than on financial need (and here is where the ability to compensate for LD comes into its own as a measure of a student's performance). Once again the best place to start the search is on the Internet. I have listed the most helpful websites in the Resource Guide. Students can register for free with online databases that match such things as their heritage, high-school performance, talents, interests, and achievements with listings of available grants and scholarships. Unfortunately, there are very few scholarships available specifically for students with learning disabilities.

The HEATH Resource Center at George Washington University has provided the following checklist for parents and students searching for financial aid.

Pre-College Financial Aid Checklist

During the Junior Year of High School:

- Explore college profiles and programs. If possible, visit the colleges that most interest you.
- Investigate financial-aid opportunities with your high-school counselor.

- Write to the college(s) of your choice for applications and financial-aid information.
- Begin the application process with Vocational Rehabilitation and/or Social Security.
- If you are involved in special education services at your high school, be sure that your IEP Transitions Services Plan includes your academic and vocational goals.
- Collect information and document expenses for completing the financial-aid forms.

By the Senior Year of High School:

- Obtain the FAFSA online or from your high-school counselor. Using the most accurate income-tax information possible, complete the form.
- Mail the financial-aid form as soon as possible after January 1, since forms postmarked before then do not count. (Be sure to check the application deadline for each college to which you plan to apply.)
- Complete and return to the college(s) all application materials and any financial-aid documents requested by the college by the date indicated by the institution (usually February/March).
- Keep track of the date on which you sent in each form. You should receive a Student Aid Report (SAR) within four weeks. If you have not received any response within four weeks, call the student-aid center at the number listed on the FAFSA.
- When the SAR arrives, contact the financial-aid offices of the colleges on your list to see if they need a copy of it.
- Keep in touch with the college financial-aid offices during the course of the application process to verify that they have received your application data and that they are processing your aid package.
- If you are a VR client, be sure that your counselor is in touch with the financial-aid offices at the colleges on your list.

- Be on time and accurate in filling out the application forms. If possible, have a third party read them and check for accuracy. Keep at least one photocopy of each completed form for your own record in case problems arise.

Now let's move to a discussion of the young adults who did not receive a high school diploma.

15

The GED: A Second Chance

Exciting possibilities await young people newly out of high school, and that certainly includes those whose LD or ADHD does not allow them to attend a traditional two- or four-year college. You wouldn't think such a thing possible after reading statistics such as this:

- 39 percent of students with LD drop out of high school.
- 46 percent of students with LD who graduate do not receive a standard diploma.
- 66 percent of students with LD are considered unqualified to enter a four-year college.

What happens to the 39 out of every 100 who never graduated from high school? It would seem that, for them, all doors to educational opportunity have slammed shut, but that is not the case. Indeed, one of the greatest challenges for these adults is to believe that any opportunities exist for them at all.

I don't know if you have ever had any late-night discussions with a good friend who revealed the deep dark secret that he or she never graduated from high school. I have. It was a shock, because this friend is so accomplished. I knew he had gone to college and had an outstanding professional career. Even so, the fact remained that he had not graduated from high school. He dropped out and eventually took the General Education Development test, or GED, which then led to all the doors opening onto his success.

Some hold the GED as a guarded secret. Others make it a proud and open statement of accomplishment and determination. Either way, the GED promises a way upward to those whose high-school careers came to an untimely end. Ninety-five percent of U.S. colleges and universities recognize the GED. As far as these institutions are concerned, a student who passes the GED is at the same level as someone who graduated from a traditional high school. Some colleges may require additional tests such as the SAT to qualify, or they may require the candidate to undergo further counseling and testing. Each college has different requirements, which the student should look into when deciding whether to apply.

THE GED AND FORM L-15

Candidates for the GED who have learning disabilities or ADHD are entitled to accommodations similar to those they had in school, or if diagnosed since leaving school, whichever accommodations are deemed appropriate. In either case, candidates can't simply walk into the testing center, say, "I think I have LD," and expect to get the help they need. They have to fill out Form L-15, which is available at the GED testing center in their particular state. It's important to note that not all states use this form. As usual with bureaucracies, some states use similar forms but with a different name, or with a slightly different format, so when you first contact the GED testing center, *make sure you get the right form,* or it will be returned to you. (For our purposes, I will use Form L-15 to explain the process. Even if a different form is used, it will be substantially the same.)

Here are the steps to take in order to get accommodations on the GED.

1. **Request Form L-15** (or the appropriate form). You can get this at your local GED testing center, which can be found in your phone book, online, or through your state Department of Education. If you need help figuring out which is the correct form, the staff at the center will assist you. The form is free, and you must fill out the original— not a copy.

2. **Do not schedule a testing date.** Do this only after Form L-15 has been completed, submitted, and accepted by the GED administrator. Documenting a learning disability is not always easy or quick.

3. **Find and provide the required information.** Some candidates may already have documentation from their high-school years, such as their IEP. Even so, a licensed professional qualified to assess and diagnose LD or ADHD must

fill out one section of the form. If the professional is unavailable, an advocate may fill out the form using information from the professional diagnostician's report. The report must include a clear diagnosis from the professional and provide information on current limitations that might affect the candidate's ability to take the test under normal conditions. For instance, a student with ADHD who is easily distracted may find it hard to take the test in a room full of other people. An appropriate accommodation in this case might be to allow the candidate to take the test in a private room.

4. **Return Form L-15 to the local GED office.** The form will be forwarded to the GED administrator and then to the GEDTS (the testing service that runs the GED), which will review it and make the final approval. Nearly 90 percent of requests for accommodations due to LD or ADHD are approved. When a request is not approved, it's usually because the form was not completed properly or necessary information is missing. When that happens, Form L-15 is returned and the whole process of requesting accommodations begins again. For that reason, it's best for the candidate to ask a parent, an advocate, or the diagnosing professional to help fill out the form.

Once the GED is passed, either with or without accommodations, the candidate is free to look into and take advantage of the many educational opportunities that await.

ADULT BASIC EDUCATION (ABE)

Another outlet for adults who lack a high-school diploma is Adult Basic Education, or ABE. These programs provide instruction in the basic skills of reading, writing, math, and critical thinking in order to prepare adults for opportunities in employment, higher education, or vocational training. Some programs help students prepare to take the GED or provide life skills workshops with topics such as resume writing, budgeting, parenting, and interpersonal communication. Some also provide individual tutoring and special classes for adults with LD.

The courses are usually given through county boards of education at learning centers or high schools, through continuing education departments at colleges, or through private programs and jobs.

You can find ABE and literacy programs in your area by calling the National Literacy Hotline at 1-800-228-8813.

16

The College Student with LD or ADHD

For many parents, seeing their child in the rear-view mirror as they drive away from the college campus is the first time they feel truly separated. I remember speaking to the headmistress of a school for LD students who told me she used to be a little impatient with the emotions of parents upon leaving their child at the school for the first time. "But then I sent my daughter off to college," she said, "and I can never forget the intense, bone-crushing grief I felt. I was quite shocked by it, and ever since then I've been much more sympathetic."

The adult child's grief over separating from a parent can be equally intense, though I suspect there are far fewer who would describe it as "bone-crushing." There is usually an element of excitement involved, even for those whose first day at college is spent lying on the dorm-room bed, clutching a pillow, and crying. Even so, we should not minimize this grief, especially for those who have been so dependent on parents and teachers to help them get by.

The best way to help young adults work through separation problems is to make sure they are as prepared for college life as it is possible to be, and for this, a parent can be invaluable.

SELF-ADVOCACY

Self-advocacy is number one on the list of things new college students with LD and ADHD must learn to do, especially since the helpful parents and teachers they relied on for so long are no longer there. Sure, a telephone call brings them closer and even allows them to solve an occasional problem, but for the most part, LD students are now "out in the big world" and must learn to fend for themselves. This move from dependence on others to an ability to stand up for oneself is as much a transition issue as is taking practice tests for the SAT.

I love the word "advocate," so feisty, positive, and action-oriented. I picked up a thesaurus to look for other words that mean the same thing as advocate and found these: supporter, promoter, and believer. If that's what an advocate is and does, then obviously self-advocates support themselves, promote themselves, and most important, believe in themselves.

Back in the early 1990s, the National Center for Learning Disabilities invited a young woman named Shelley Stanzel to join the board of directors. Shelley was fresh out of Dartmouth College, where she was the only named complainant in a case brought against the school on behalf of students with disabilities. Her troubles began in her sophomore year in a Spanish language class. Shelley grew up in Texas surrounded by farmhands who spoke Spanish, but even as the rest of her family picked the language up rather easily, she could never get beyond a few basic words. She went to Dartmouth specifically because of their Rassias method of language instruction. She thought the heavy emphasis on auditory drills might help her master Spanish, but in fact, it set her on a course to failure. No matter how hard and how long she studied, she made no progress at all, and for the first time in her academic career was faced with an F.

A professor suggested she get tested for LD, and as you may already have guessed, the test showed that she had an auditory processing disorder. As usual with a late diagnosis of LD, Shelley met the news with shock and relief—shock because she had never suspected the presence of LD and relief because the diagnosis finally explained her lifelong difficulties with the Spanish language. She enrolled in a Spanish immersion course in Spain during the winter term and to her surprise discovered she could learn quite easily when taught by a different method. Back at Dartmouth she began to lobby for changes in the way languages were taught. The school administrators resisted. Some were openly hostile. Left with no alternative, Shelley gathered other students with LD and organized a class-action lawsuit along with the U.S. Department of Education that led to extensive reforms in the way Dartmouth (and other colleges) meet the needs of students with LD.

Now, due in large part to the self-advocacy of students like Shelley, colleges across the nation provide accommodations to those with LD, ADHD, and other disabilities as a matter of general policy. Even so, they only reach out so far to the student with LD. They won't track these students down. They won't, and can't, directly ask if a student has a disability. Students with LD who choose to hide their disability (and there are many!) have two options: the first is to suffer through classes where a minor accommodation could make all the difference in the world; the second is to accept their own diagnosis and take the positive steps necessary for success in college.

So how do they do this? And what is a parent's role?

I'll answer the second question first, because it's the same answer I would give during each step of a student's efforts to become a self-advocate. Parents must support, encourage, and help their young adult children to see the positive side of what can be a frightening prospect.

"I don't want anyone to know!" your daughter might say. Do not simply discount this fear, but acknowledge it and help her understand that disclosure doesn't necessarily mean being labeled in a negative way. I think a lot of young adults are very mindful of, and possibly traumatized by, their experiences as a "special ed kid," singled out from all their friends to go to a separate classroom. Who can't understand the shame of a young man in parochial school who has to cross the schoolyard in full view of his fellow classmates to attend special classes in a trailer that, owing to separation of church and state laws, is parked outside the school grounds? And who can't relate to the shudder a young woman feels when she is constantly termed "special," since for her the word instantly brings to mind images of the Special Olympics? These experiences leave young people with LD and ADHD feeling anything *but* special, so how can we expect them to cheerfully bound up the steps to the college dean's office and announce, yet again, that they are not like everyone else?

Some students have no problem with disclosure, and this works to their advantage, but for those with LD who are reluctant to disclose, the best thing a parent can do is to lay out the benefits. There are also parents who for one reason or another don't want their children to disclose their LD. "I don't want him to be labeled" is usually the phrase I hear. I wonder what such parents think is going to happen when their son goes from an environment of support and accommodation to one where nothing is provided at all, due to his lack of disclosure. Do they think he'll magically be able to do the work that, hitherto, he has only been able to manage with some sort of help? This is as unrealistic as the old daydream that the LD would someday simply go away.

Disclosure is the foundation of self-advocacy. Without it, there is no point in learning to advocate at all. What on earth would you advocate for?

PRACTICE SELF-ADVOCACY

Parents can also help their adult children learn the best ways to ask for help. Don't expect them to know how to do it, especially those with proven deficits in social skills. Practice role-playing. Take the part of a professor or college administrator and invite your son or daughter to come into your "office." Ask them to explain why they need accommodations and what type of accommodations would most help them.

This is a chance to prepare them for some of the realities they will face in college. Remember, not every professor or administrator will be open and enthusiastic about the idea of accommodations. Indeed, some are as hostile to the idea as those long-ago administrators at Dartmouth who refused to listen to Shelley Stanzel. Their reasons are well known as we hear the same statements from the general public or from some politicians. "It's giving them an unfair advantage," some say, or "Some without LD are using the system to get accommodations they don't really need." We may see this as narrow-minded on their part, but the fact is they are right. There *are* students who cheat and there *are* parents who seek unfair advantages for their children, but they are small in number. The more important and truthful fact is that for students diagnosed with LD or ADHD, accommodations do not give them an unfair advantage, but bring them up to an equal starting point with their peers.

For every college official hostile to the idea of accommodations, there are many more who are supportive or, at worst, simply don't care one way or the other. Regardless of the reaction encountered, the primary responsibility for getting the needed accommodations remains with the LD students, and it is in their best interest to learn to speak up for themselves in a mature, nonconfrontational way.

First, they must learn how to describe their disability and explain their needs. Without some input from LD students, it's very hard to guess the type of accommodations they need. By the time they reach college (unless they have a recent diagnosis), students should have a pretty good idea of what does and does not work for them. Ask your child to start by explaining his or her disability to you. Don't allow any "I don't know" or "Well, ummm...I guess it's kind of like a reading thing."

You can help your son or daughter along by telling them all that you know about their LD. Parents invariably know more than their adult child about the disability. They have studied it for years; they know every detail and every potential pitfall. Often parents keep this information away from their child, not out of an overdeveloped sense of secrecy but because it was simpler that way. They didn't share the information when the child was in first grade, and the pattern continued through grammar school and high school. It's time to break your silence and share your knowledge. Your child needs to know and to be able to tell others.

COLLEGE SUPPORT SERVICES

Once your child knows how to explain his or her own disability and the accommodations that work best, you can then look into the support services available at the colleges of choice. Most colleges, trade schools, and adult-education classes will have some sort of office of disability support services. As soon as possible, students should visit and register with this office and make themselves and their needs known.

Documentation is key. All the work with the IEP, all the diagnostic tests, all the written details about strengths, weaknesses, and individual learning styles now come to the aid of students with LD. It's all there in black and white, and can be used by students to buttress efforts to define who they are and how the office of disability support services can help.

Students should also understand that the counselors in the disability office have *not* taken on the role once filled by the parent. They will not become a student's primary advocate. Students still have to go to the professor and request accommodations.

Parents can prepare students for this as well, especially for those times when the student is confronted with a professor who is openly hostile to the concept of accommodations. Go back to your "office" in your living room and conduct an imaginary interview in which you play the part of the hostile professor meeting your college-bound child. Be tough. Act like someone who doesn't believe in LD or accommodations. Say things like, "I think it's just an excuse to get out of doing the work," or "If I let you have these accommodations, you'll have an advantage over everyone else and that's not fair."

Watch how your child responds. Does your child handle the situation in a mature fashion, or does your child lash out with a hostile response. Pay attention to social skills, too! When you confront the student as the hostile professor, does your child raise his voice? Does she become flustered and storm out of the room in tears? Bring your child back into the room and show how to respond in the proper way, with appropriate eye contact and a tone of voice that is not too loud or aggressive. Of course, there may be a lot of laughter, since your child knows you believe wholeheartedly in accommodations. Even so, you will still get a general idea of how your child will handle the real situation and can adjust your advice accordingly.

COLLEGE LIFE

If grades and accommodations weigh heavily on a parent's mind, we now come to the issues that are of paramount importance to the student: dorm life, roommates, socializing, and friends.

All of these involve social skills to one degree or another, and once again, the students are on their own. The parent who is the "best friend" is no longer there, nor is the large group of understanding friends back home. I don't know how many times I've heard of two strangers meeting for the first time as college roommates and taking an immediate dislike to each other, only to develop a friendship that lasts years after leaving college. At the same time, we've all heard roommate disaster stories. In my experience, most parents should be prepared for the second scenario.

A college roommate will be the first non-family person most young adults with LD will live with. Any quirks, oddities, or annoyances tolerated by family members may not be so acceptable to a stranger in what is undoubtedly going to be tight living quarters. The young man with ADHD who cannot stay organized might call for a level of patience not often seen in young men without ADHD. Problems with social skills of all kinds come into play in roommate situations, the same way they do in friendships and all other interpersonal relationships. The most parents can do is to continually reinforce the needed skills *before* they ship their child off to college.

It seems likely that sooner or later (probably sooner) most parents will get a call in the middle of the night from a teary young adult wanting to come home, or leave school, or make some other drastic change. Most of the time this can be put down to fear and anxiety due to all the changes, and in that case, a parent should be reassuring and understanding but not so reassuring and understanding as to give in. Three days after moving off to college is not the time to agree to let your child come home. Do everything you can to encourage your child to stay and work on whatever problem has come up.

At the same time, parents and students should be aware that leaving a particular school is not the end of the world. Sometimes it simply doesn't work out. If, after giving it his best shot, your child is still miserable and is unable to keep up with the work, there is no shame in allowing him to leave the school. Do not look upon his leaving as a failure, and even more, do not let *him* look upon it that way. He can always return or go to a different college. The important thing here is to make sure the college experience hasn't so traumatized him that he point-blank refuses to consider an alternative.

Most college students with LD or ADHD do not fail because of low intelligence. They fail because they can't structure their lives properly, or they haven't learned to ask for the help they need. For some, troubles with classwork and social lives could be alleviated by reaching out to other students with LD. The office of disability support services will be able to help them locate others who are in the same boat, and that can make a world of difference when trying to navigate an unknown sea.

17

The Helicopter Parent

When Alessandro went away to college for the first time, I carried a small suitcase up to his new dorm room. Inside it were framed pictures of me, Allegra, and other family members. I spread them out on his bureau and then made his bed. His new roommate's father had a camera and took pictures of all this because, as he said, "I've never seen anything like it!"

In my defense, I will say that I was only expressing my sense of wistful sadness and, far more important, that I *did* eventually go home.

Some parents of young adults with LD or ADHD cannot quite bring themselves to leave. They may not stay in the dorm room and make the bed, but they do hover in the background. They are on the telephone all the time. They nag the disability office. They sometimes call professors to "explain" their child's disability. They entangle themselves in roommate disputes. They may even try to enlist someone as a spy, maybe a campus official or dorm supervisor who can tell them everything that's going on with their child.

These parents are known as "helicopter parents," so called for their tendency to hover over their children and get involved in all aspects of college life. I found the term in an article in *The Wall Street Journal* by Sue Shellenbarger, who talked about parents of non-LD students who interfere and meddle in situations ranging from campus-safety concerns to parking passes to curriculum matters. Most of the parents interviewed justified their involvement by pointing out the high cost of tuition and the necessity of ensuring their child gets the education they're paying for. Understandable, I suppose, and when we add a disability into the mix, we can be certain that parental hovering can rise to a level of a Black Hawk helicopter gunship.

Every parent reading this can justify their reasons for meddling, and those of us listening can usually nod our heads in agreement. There *are* times when students with LD or ADHD have gone to the disability counselors, professors, roommates, and friends, all to no avail. The problem could be over accommodations or housing issues or any number of things. They are floundering and have no one else to turn to, so parents, put on your white hats and ride to the rescue!

Trouble comes when you make a cavalry charge over *every* issue. If you call up your son's roommate and bawl him out because he's supposed to understand that your son Jack has trouble making friends and therefore it is up to him to include Jack in his own plans . . . well, that's when things have gotten out of hand.

We can divide the college experience into two categories, hard and soft. In the hard category I include things like financial matters, class choices, accommodations, and dealings with the disability office. These make up the bones of your child's education, and I think it is perfectly fine for a parent to stay involved and take direct action when necessary. Direct action, by the way, does not mean storming into an office of any kind or yelling into a phone. Think of it as an extension of your child's self-advocacy, especially at those times when your child's own efforts are not enough.

The soft category is all those things that make up the social side of campus life: the friends, the roommates, the dorm parties. Parents, try as hard as you can not to get involved in these affairs unless directly asked. Even then use common sense to decide if your involvement is necessary or even advisable. Sometimes a squabble between your child and a friend is best left alone, thereby allowing the friendship to flourish, based on a deeper understanding of each other's point of view, or to drift apart as some friendships unfortunately do.

Do not pressure the roommate or anyone else to give you information about your child. You may think you have a right to know what time your son Jack got back to the dorm room last night, but if you ask Jack, he might very well think it's none of your business. He certainly won't be pleased to learn that his roommate has been sharing the information with you.

Try to calm down and give the helicopter a rest. Sift through the various aspects of your child's situation and make a list of what does and does not require your direct involvement. Understand that this first foray into the world outside your own home is your child's first major step toward independence. That's the ultimate goal, and success comes from learning lessons on one's own, from fighting one's own battles, and most of all, from realizing that Mom and Dad are not always going to be there to step in and solve all the problems.

PART IV

On the Job: Employing the Adult with LD and ADHD

18

Defining Success

Employment can be the greatest challenge in the life of an adult with LD or ADHD. Those newly out of school have joined "the real world" with employers who may have had no exposure to LD and coworkers who expect them to carry their own weight. They no longer have the protection of special education teachers and guidance counselors who knew every detail of their particular disability and could often predict behavior before it happened or help them learn from their mistakes while keeping their self-esteem high and intact. These helpful souls have been replaced by the competitive young man in the next cubicle, eager to make his way ahead and not at all reluctant to do so at the expense of his colleague with ADHD, or the manager who might understand accommodations in an intellectual, abstract way, but who is far more concerned that the employee with LD is lowering the productivity in his work group.

Finding the right type of work in the first place can be a challenge. Many young people with disabilities are unable to find stimulating, satisfying jobs. Some have difficulty finding any job at all.

The Bureau of Labor Statistics is not very encouraging.

- An estimated 10 percent of working-age adults with LD are unemployed.
- Adults with LD earn an estimated 36 percent less per hour than their peers without LD.

Why is this the case? Because they can't read very well? For some, yes. Deficits in basic reading, writing, and arithmetic can lead to workplace problems, but as usual with LD and ADHD, much of the trouble is caused by less tangible factors. Poor attention span, an inability to follow oral instructions, difficulty with organization or time management, and most of all, that old culprit, weak social skills, lead to the most serious problems on the job.

Let's take time management as an example. We can all imagine (and probably know) employees who are chronically late for work or for meetings. No matter what they do, no matter how many times they are reprimanded, they can never quite get themselves together on time. It's more difficult to imagine and understand the employee who is chronically early. This is someone like Nancy, who cannot get anywhere on time because she simply cannot figure out the process. She needs to leave her house, drive through town, find a parking place, get settled at her desk, and print out a few pages for a ten-o'clock meeting. The meeting has been held at ten o'clock every Tuesday for the last six years, and yet, every Tuesday, Nancy finds that she has misjudged her timing and has arrived at half past eight. She then decides to go back to her desk and work on something else, loses track of the time, and ends up dashing into the conference room fifteen minutes after the meeting has started.

This may sound like an exaggeration, but I assure you, this is the sort of thing that happens every day to individuals with LD or ADHD. As someone well versed in the field of learning disabilities, I have tried many times to understand how the LD brain works, but I remain baffled by the thinking process that causes someone to go so completely off-track day after day. Imagine how baffling it must be to an employer who has never even heard of LD or ADHD before.

I once met a young woman who was distraught about her difficulties with time management . . . actually "distraught" is too gentle a word for the anguish I saw that day. She had already lost several jobs because she could not arrive at the office on time, no matter how hard she tried. "I get up four hours before I'm supposed to," she said. "Four hours! But even so, I *still* arrive forty-five minutes late. I'm about to lose this new job, and I don't know what to do about it." I asked her if she had ever been tested for ADHD. She hadn't, and I could tell that my suggestion opened a door never before considered and that the possibility of receiving an answer to the reason for her troubles gave her an immediate sense of hope.

Casey Dixon, a Life Coach whom we will meet later in this section, claims that time-management problems lead most of her clients to seek

professional help, but nothing beats problems with social skills for causing the most day-to-day misery on the job. We can tell ourselves that an
inability to interact well with others does not necessarily affect a person's work, and this would be true if by "work" we mean sitting in an isolated office crunching numbers all day. But work is so much more than
the actual task at hand. It is a subtle interplay of egos and hierarchies, of
encouragement and criticism, all of which must be navigated in ways
some with LD or ADHD find challenging or even impossible. As they
did in school, these individuals may have trouble meeting new people or
working with others in a cooperative, give-and-take atmosphere. They
may be unable to understand the nuances of humor or how best to handle criticism. This, in turn, can lead to isolation, frustration, and
ridicule—the very things they hoped to leave behind when they left
school. We have all heard the expression "children can be cruel," but
the sad truth is that adults can be cruel, too, and schoolyard taunts all
too often reappear as jokes told at the water cooler.

Adults with LD and ADHD can compensate for the challenges presented by the workplace. Those with time-management problems can
improve their lives in immeasurable ways by using a datebook or computerized calendar like the one that comes with Microsoft Outlook, or
even by setting their watch ahead by fifteen minutes—it literally can be
that simple.

Employers who hire those with LD can certainly help with such
problems, but the worker with LD *must* step forward to both acknowledge their disability and know what to ask for. Again, things are not the
same as they were in high school. If a worker remains silent about a
learning disability, no one will proactively seek out accommodations on
that worker's behalf—indeed, it is illegal to even *ask* if someone has LD,
much less take action based on such an assumption. Workers with LD
must be partners in this and do everything they can to help the employer help them. No teacher or parent will step in to provide all the
answers.

Success in the workplace is an important goal for all adults with LD,
but what is success? The word itself is so deeply ingrained in American
culture that we all too often and too easily judge others as being some-

how unsuccessful because they have not reached the heights only a few can hope to achieve. When it comes to their own abilities and aspirations, those with LD or ADHD are often the harshest judges of all, and they make themselves so miserable over their perceived lack of success that they avoid doing the things that could actually improve their lives.

Dr. Marshall Raskind of the Frostig Center answered the question in this way. "Success is really not easy to define," he wrote in an article for Schwab Learning. "It means different things to different people and it may mean different things at different times in a person's life. That said, I think we can find certain commonalities among people in terms of the factors that might be considered important to being a successful individual, such things as having friends, positive family relationships, being loved, self-approval, job satisfaction, having physical and mental health, financial comfort, spiritual contentment, and an overall sense of meaning to one's life."

He then lists the following attributes of such people:

- Self-awareness
- Proactivity
- Perseverance
- Goal setting
- The presence and use of effective support systems
- Emotional coping strategies

Dr. Raskind wrote the article in hopes of sensitizing parents to these attributes and the possibility of instilling them in their children before they reach adulthood. In looking at each attribute in turn, we can find ways for parents to do the same for their children who have already become adults.

Self-Awareness

Is your adult child aware of his strengths and weaknesses? Is he aware of his special talents and abilities? Does he really understand his learning disability, and does he accept it? Can he "compartmentalize" his learning disability by thinking of it as a single facet of who he is rather than as the defining aspect of his identity?

The most successful adults with LD or ADHD are those who understand the impact of LD on their lives. They know and accept their strengths and limitations, and factor both into their quest for work. They know, for example, that their poor reading and writing skills make them poor candidates for a job as a journalist, but they could be ideal candidates for a job requiring the excellent verbal skills they know they possess. This may seem obvious to most of us, but you would be surprised how often a lack of self-awareness lies behind a failure to find a job.

Proactivity

Does your adult child make decisions and act on them? Does she take responsibility for those decisions? Is she assertive and self-confident?

This is a difficult attribute to acquire for both children and adults with LD or ADHD. They have been so conditioned in school to the belief that any answer they give will be the wrong one, or that they will invariably misunderstand even the simplest interaction with their peers, that they lose confidence in their ability to judge any situation or answer any question correctly. They never even entertain the possibility that they could be right. Parents can help by making it clear to their adult children that their opinions are welcome and valid, and by never belittling those opinions or answers, even when they are wrong. Individuals who always think they are wrong can also fall into a pattern of blaming others. It is much easier to pawn off the responsibility on another person (or another thing, such as the clock that is broken or the car that wouldn't start) than to own up to making a mistake. Another way parents can help is to explain that taking responsibility for something said or done usually helps solve the problem far more effectively than blame or evasion does.

Perseverance

Does your adult child understand the benefits of persevering? Does he know how to deal with obstacles and setbacks?

Unlike proactivity, perseverance is a common trait in those with LD or ADHD. Many adults with LD have had to struggle all their lives with things the rest of us take for granted. They've had to work twice as hard to get the same result, and they have developed this stubborn, sometimes plodding resolve into a real asset. They will work on something long after their coworkers have given up on it. Difficulties arise when they can't seem to recognize that it's time to reevaluate their strategies or, in some cases, the goal itself. There's no sense in beating your head against the wall over and over for a goal that will remain elusive—as did, for example, the young adult who kept trying to become a journalist even though he couldn't read or write beyond a second-grade level. There comes a time when enough is enough, and a parent can help ease the adult child into that realization.

Goal Setting

Does your adult child know how to prioritize? Are her goals realistic? Does she understand the various steps necessary to reach those goals?

Parents can help with this by focusing on the "big picture." Some adults with LD or ADHD have attainable career goals, but they have no concept of the possible obstacles they may encounter, nor do they understand how to get beyond those obstacles.

Effective Support Systems

Does your adult child know when he needs help or how to get that help? Does he have strategies to cope with various situations (including the use of technology)?

Dr. Raskind suggests that parents ensure their adult children understand the benefits of using support systems, recognize the various signs that indicate they are in need of help, learn how to accept help, and develop trust in others. He also suggests helping them develop an awareness of the disability laws that protect them.

Emotional Coping Strategies

Along with knowing when to get help, adults with LD also need to know where and how to get help. Is your adult child aware of the situations that produce stress and the various strategies for alleviating that stress?

Learning disabilities and ADHD can produce a great deal of frustration and stress in a person's life, which in turn can lead to anxiety, a loss of self-confidence, depression, or substance abuse.

Successful individuals with LD or ADHD are able to reduce and cope with this stress. They do this in three ways. First, they are aware of the situation that triggers the stress (reading a business report aloud in front of people, for example). Second, they have an awareness of the stress itself and how it manifests itself (heart palpitations, hyperventilating). Third, they have access to various coping strategies, some of which are internal (deep breathing exercises to calm down). These coping strategies range from reliance on accommodations in the workplace, to planning ahead for difficult situations, to something as simple as sharing feelings about the situation with a coworker or family member.

You, as a parent, can become a part of these coping strategies by making sure your adult child knows you are available to listen whenever they want to talk about their problems at work. They need to know you will listen and that you can do so without being judgmental. The question for you then becomes: Can you do this? Don't lure your adult child into difficult admissions of feeling inadequate and then pounce with accusations or remarks that will only reinforce that feeling. Be honest with yourself. If you can't help or if your adult child is too wary of your help, put aside your hurt feelings and help your adult child find someone they feel comfortable with, someone they can talk to and openly share their deepest concerns.

Creativity

I would add creativity to Dr. Raskind's attributes of success for adults with LD or ADHD. Innovation and creativity are the great strengths of people with LD. The arts and sciences are filled with people who could barely read when they were in school, and look how much richer our world is because of them. Creativity is not confined to the arts. These adults have had to work around so many problems in their academic careers and figure out ways to compensate for their disability that they often become the most adept at finding creative ways to fix a problem in the workplace. They approach things from an oblique angle, discovering the unexpected and finding new ways to do old things. It is not uncommon for coworkers to rely on them as the "idea people."

When looking at the various components and attributes that lead to success, we find ample evidence that adults with LD and ADHD can and do succeed in the workplace. It is important for the employer to realize that. It's especially important for the LD adult to realize that, too, but let's not leave out the person not usually considered in an employment situation, and that is you—the parent.

Rick Lavoie, one of the top leaders in the field of learning disabilities, tells a story that illustrates the dilemma so many parents face. A restaurant in Boston took on a young man as a new employee to help out in the kitchen. He had severe LD, but his enthusiasm and willingness to try new things impressed his new employer. After a month on the job, the employer called the young man's mother and asked her to stop by the restaurant. He told her that he had tried his best to provide a job for her son, but it wasn't working out and they had no choice but to fire him. The mother was devastated. "But why?" she asked. "He's always on time, he loves his job, he's willing to do everything you ask." His response was: "All that's true, and our problem is not with him—our problem is with *you*!"

This mother was calling every day, all day long. She showed up at the restaurant. "Is he wearing his boots? Has he eaten? Is everything going all right?" She made such a nuisance of herself that the employer was forced to let her son go—the one thing she most hoped to avoid.

So much of our child's success comes down to our own ability to let go.

If they are ready to go out into the world and look for a job, let them go. You must let them go *even if you do not think they are ready*.

If they want to try a job you think is not suited to their skills, let them try. You should step in only if and when it becomes apparent that they are unable to give up on what is obviously a wholly misguided plan. Let them give things a try. They may lose a job or two, but your role—your *job*, if you will—is to be there to tell them it's not the end of the world and help them get back in the saddle to try something new.

19

Business 101

THE FIRST JOB IS FINDING A JOB

"What do you want to be when you grow up?"

That's one of the hardest questions for any young adult to answer, especially those whose school careers consisted mainly of varying degrees of failure or of struggling just to keep up with everyone else. For them, a lack of self-esteem leads them to question the possibility of finding *any* job, much less one based on their passions and interests. If young adults with LD are floundering about, without any sense of direction and seemingly unable to articulate what they want to do with their lives, there are ways to open their eyes to various possibilities. In the College section, I suggested using an Interest Inventory to help them pinpoint their own interests when trying to decide on a focus for their studies. Obviously, this can also be helpful when considering the type of job that will make best use of their interests and strengths.

Finding the right job isn't always easy. If the need for income isn't immediate, young adults with LD can benefit tremendously from internships and volunteer positions. These are an excellent way for them to try out a job to see if it suits their abilities or discover if it is something they might like to pursue further. Hospitals, social service agencies, day-care centers, and schools make use of volunteers, and many companies offer internship programs. These positions, whether voluntary or part of an apprentice or intern program, can lead to part-time or full-time positions within the same organization or company. At the very least, they provide solid experience that can be included on a resume and built upon when searching for a similar position.

Parents can help in the job search through suggestions and encouragement. They can also help by redefining unemployment from a negative state into one of action and hope. You do this by instilling the idea that the first job for young adults is finding a job. By shifting their viewpoint, you help them get used to the idea that they are *not* unemployed—they are working to find a job. This could be planning out a daily schedule that includes a specified amount of time looking at the help-wanted section in the newspaper or online, or going to a mall to look for openings in the various stores or restaurants. It also includes preparation for getting a job such as writing a resume, going on interviews, and following up after each interview.

When looking at Dr. Raskind's list of attributes for success, we spoke of how important it is that young adults understand the realities of the type of job they hope to get. This goes for the parent, too.

We all have concepts of what we would like to see our adult children with LD do for work. For instance, you may want your son to dress up in a jacket and tie, or maybe you envision your daughter in a corporate setting, with a job that interests her and has room for growth. Beautiful images, but do they fit the reality of the child's abilities? As with the parent of the severely LD student who still dreams of a Harvard graduation, we can easily find parents who expect their children to land careers far beyond their range of talent. At the same time, I once again urge parents not to short-change their children's prospects. Some with LD and ADHD, especially the milder forms, find spectacular success in the workplace far beyond what anyone imagined back when they were mediocre students. Every single one of the CEOs interviewed later in this book was a mediocre student in school, yet they all went on to successful careers—not by overcoming their LD but by finding ways to use it to their best advantage.

Most parents of young adults with severe LD are realistic about their adult child's abilities, yet even they can take a wrong turn when it comes to helping that child find a job. A good example of this came up in an interview I conducted with Jim Rein, founder of the Vocational Independence Program (VIP) at the New York Institute of Technology. "Let's say a mother hopes to find her son a position in a little mom-and-pop store or a post office in a small town," he said. "It sounds like an ideal work environment, but for some disabled adults, it's the exact opposite of what they need. In a small store or office with few employees, they have to be able to do everything. In a larger operation they can specialize. They can be in charge of stocking inventory in a large store, or delivering interoffice mail in a corporation."

One of the keys to success on the job for many young adults with severe LD is repetition. Sometimes the very things that cause people without LD to recoil in horror—repetition, routine, or a monotonous work environment—are the very things that appeal to those with LD. Many individuals with LD, both children and adults, have an aversion to change. Nobody likes change, but in my experience, nobody truly hates it as much as those with LD (some with ADHD are quite the opposite and actually thrive on change). I mention this only as a factor when parents are helping their young adult children with LD consider a career. How do they handle change? Are they much happier in a routine? Don't criticize a job choice as being monotonous and dull when, in fact, it may be the job that best suits their disposition.

"They often thrive in a job where they only have to do one thing," Jim said. "Let's say they want to work in a restaurant. Maybe they would be far more successful as a prep-chef cutting the carrots in a large restaurant rather than being in charge of the kitchen and preparing elaborate four-course dinners in a smaller one. Many parents think that the small, homier setting will work out, but in a larger company, the kid stands a better chance of having one specific job and dealing with a specific group of people."

Parents also make a mistake when they don't understand the full range of a job. They may think their son would make a terrific carpenter. He's good with his hands and loves to build things, but what about reading blueprints and understanding measurements?

"Sometimes what seems to be a perfect job has hidden challenges," Jim said. "Essentially, there are two basic types of jobs. The first is one where all you have to do is be good at what you do. A chef is an example of this. If I go into a restaurant and order prime rib rare, that's what I want. I really don't care what the chef knows about Shakespeare or if he can write a research paper. I want the prime rib to be the way I want it, that's all. The second is a type of job where, no matter how good you are, if you don't have the certification or the degree, you can't do it. For example, if you want to be a cosmetologist, you can take all the courses and get straight As and be great at what you do, but if you don't pass the certification test, you're basically sweeping up hair in the shop."

If your son or daughter has high hopes for the second type of job, be sure that all the challenges are examined and thought through, especially when it comes to testing for a license or official certificate.

THE RESUME AND COVER LETTER

Even if an employer does not specifically ask for a resume, it is always a good idea to offer one when applying for a job. A resume is a first impression on paper. If your son or daughter shows you one covered with coffee stains and full of typing errors, you might want to suggest coming up with a revised, cleaner copy before heading off to the interview.

The same goes for inaccuracies in the resume. To say that individuals shouldn't lie or exaggerate their work experience on a resume would seem almost too obvious for comment, but it's amazing how many applicants do it. I saw one resume where a young man listed several positions in retail sales, mostly in clothing stores. Right in the middle of his resume he included a six-month position as a "Chemical Engineer," in which he specialized in mixing various chemical formulas. It would take a strong person indeed not to pause and wonder, and eventually ask about it. When I did, he admitted that he had been a bartender.

Lesson: If you worked as a bartender, write "Bartender" on your resume. Do not try to fool someone into thinking you have an advanced degree in chemistry.

Stay away from exaggeration! Nothing stands out quite as starkly, and nothing makes an employer less likely to hire someone. At the same time, don't be so truthful that you hurt your chances. It is not necessary, nor advisable, to state that your reason for leaving your previous job was because "my boss didn't like me."

These are the things to include on a resume:

- All personal information such as name, address, telephone number, and e-mail address.
- Career Goal. For example, "To obtain a job in sales in a major retail store."

- Work Experience. For each job, include the name and location of the employer, the dates of employment, job title, and a brief description of job responsibilities.
- Education.
- Skills and Achievements.
- Volunteer Experience.

This information should be organized under headings and should be typed out neatly and clearly. If using a word processor, be sure to use Spellcheck before printing the resume. Even then, someone other than the job applicant should proofread it. An employer shouldn't have to read as a career goal: "To obtane a job in sals."

A cover letter should always be sent along with a resume, especially when responding to a help-wanted ad. This can include information not included in the resume, such as skills and strengths most suited to that particular job.

THE INTERVIEW

Here's a scenario many parents can relate to:

Your son applies for a job in a mailroom for a small shipping firm in your town. He's called in for an interview. An hour later he calls you in a rage, telling you the person who interviewed him was rude and dismissive, and he didn't get the job. You offer to take him to lunch to make him feel better. You arrive at the restaurant and you wait...and wait...and forty-five minutes later your son comes in without an apology or explanation, wearing an old sweatshirt, ripped jeans, and filthy sneakers and obviously without having washed or combed his hair since the day before.

"Were you late for the interview, too?" you ask.

"Yeah, but only ten minutes or so. No big deal."

"And is that what you wore to the interview?"

"Yeah. Why?"

"Don't you think you should wear a nice shirt to an interview like that?"

"Why? It's a shipping company. Nobody dresses up. It's no big deal."

Guess what—it *is* a big deal.

Granted, it isn't necessary to wear a three-piece suit and tie for a job interview at a fast-food restaurant, but an attempt to appear put together, even in a casual way, is very important. This may appear self-evident, but that's because *you* are reading this. Is it so evident to your son or daughter? Young adults with LD all too often downplay or ignore the importance of appearance and grooming, and are surprised by the negative reactions of others.

Someone in charge of hiring for even the most casual job is going to pay attention to the subtleties of a candidate's appearance and behavior. In a conversation with a friend, you might not mind that your friend is snapping gum every ten seconds; but if this is someone you don't know and whom you might have to work with, chances are you will be acutely aware of the gum. "Next," you say, dismissing the irritating gum-snapper in favor of the person who makes an effort to appear serious about the job.

Adults with LD are already burdened by problems and limitations caused by their disability—why add to them, especially when trying to make a good first impression?

These are the basic rules for an interview.

- Be on time. That's the primary rule, the one that must not be broken. Showing up a half-hour late is not going to get someone the job. It may not even lead to the interview.
- Dress appropriately. Even if the job is casual, an effort should be made to wear casual clothes that are clean and neat—no holes, no tears, no sneakers with broken laces.
- Bring a pen. Undoubtedly some sort of application will have to be filled out. (This is a good time to point out the difficulties many adults with LD have in holding a pen correctly. If your son or daughter holds a pen like a dagger, you might try to see if that can be changed.)
- No gum. No hard candy. No smoking.
- Smile. This is a good time for parents to gently remind their son or daughter that people respond favorably to a smile and positive outlook. This suggestion was not lifted from an outdated etiquette book. The men and women who head the largest companies look to a positive attitude as the major indi-

cator of success in the workplace. This applies to *all* levels of work, from the loading dock all the way up to the executive suite.

Most interviewers will not rely solely on applications and personal appearance but will ask questions. Is your son or daughter prepared to answer them? We can all too easily imagine a young adult with LD being asked, point-blank, "What are your strengths?" and answering with a mumbled, "Umm...I don't know." It's not uncommon: lots of people have trouble thinking quickly in a high-pressure situation like a job interview. Parents should smooth the way by conducting a test run where you play the interviewer and ask a variety of questions, coaching your son or daughter on the answers to give. By doing this, the questions will not come as a surprise.

Here are some questions typically asked at a job interview.

1. Why are you interested in this job?
2. What do you know about our company?
3. What special talents or skills can you bring to this job?
4. What are your career goals?
5. What are your two greatest strengths?
6. What is your greatest weakness?
7. Tell me about yourself.
8. In your last job, which tasks did you enjoy most? Least? Why?
9. Why did you leave your last job?
10. Are you a "team player"? Can you give some examples?
11. How well do you work under pressure?
12. What is your salary requirement? What benefits (i.e., medical, dental, vacation time) do you expect?
13. Why should I hire you?

The job candidate should also write a follow-up letter to thank the interviewer for their time, and to express a continued interest in the position. It is usually expected and *always* appreciated.

DISCLOSING A LEARNING DISABILITY

Whether to disclose a learning disability in a job interview is one of the most difficult of all issues to address with any degree of confidence. You can find experts on both sides of the issue. I come down on the side of *not* disclosing right away, especially if the learning disability is not severe. Others insist that the adult with LD should always be upfront and honest right from the beginning and let the chips fall where they may. Well, fine, except that sometimes the chips fall in all the wrong places. The words "upfront" and "honest" are the sticking point here, as if to imply that withholding information about a person's LD is somehow devious and untruthful, when that is not the case at all.

Let me give an example. Let's say a young man has severe ADHD. He has high energy, a quick mind, and great enthusiasm, and he is applying for a job as a waiter in a very busy restaurant. In that case, having ADHD can actually work to his advantage. Many adults with ADHD prefer and are far more successful in a busy, fast-paced work environment than in a quiet, subdued office. Why would this young man put his employers on notice that he has a disability?

"But they should understand," I hear some of you say.

Of course they should! Everyone in the world should understand, but they don't.

Most experts I have talked to, and *especially* most adults with LD I have talked to, advise against disclosing in the interview. There is no certainty that the LD will affect the person's job performance in either a positive or negative way. Many people find and hold a job for years, even a lifetime, without ever telling their supervisors or coworkers they have LD (think of all the people diagnosed late in life, after long careers, with everyone, themselves included, in the dark about their disability).

What happens if the LD or ADHD directly interferes with their job performance? I once spoke about LD and Employment at the headquarters of a bank in New York City. A few minutes after I started, I noticed a woman seated in the back row begin to cry. I couldn't take my eyes off her the entire time ... rocking back and forth, with one hand over her mouth, soundlessly crying from the time I started speaking until I finished. When I left the stage, I approached her and asked what was wrong, certain she would tell me about her child's difficulties at school.

Instead she whispered, "I'm in way over my head. I have LD and I'm afraid I'm going to be fired." She couldn't keep up with her coworkers, her supervisor wasn't happy with her performance, everything was going wrong, and she didn't dare tell anyone about her disability. Bear in mind that my entire speech and the introductions leading up to it were centered around finding help in the workplace. The very company the woman worked for sponsored the event and was obviously reaching out to help workers in her predicament, but she didn't hear that. She couldn't. In her mind, she had to suffer in silence for fear of losing her job.

This is so unnecessary. No one should spend their days like that, terrified of falling behind, fearing for their job, unable to tell the truth when their coworkers accuse them of slowing things down or their supervisor gives them low marks on their performance review. I tried to tell her this, and though she seemed to take to heart my suggestion to disclose her disability to the human resources department, I never heard the end of her story. I hope it all worked out.

DISCLOSURE AND THE LAW

The Americans with Disabilities Act (ADA) requires that reasonable accommodations be made by employers who have fifteen or more employees. Its purpose is to allow qualified individuals with a disability equal access under the law to college or employment. Please note that a "qualified individual with a disability" is defined as someone who, *with or without a reasonable accommodation*, can do the work or perform the essential function of the employment position. In other words, the person with LD or ADHD must be able to perform the work required in order to be covered by the civil-rights protections of the ADA. If the person cannot perform the essential functions of the job, even with reasonable accommodations, there is no discrimination in either failing to hire or in firing the person.

The law also forbids employers from asking about any disability during a job interview, and if and when the disability is disclosed, they cannot divulge this information to coworkers.

Because the employer cannot ask, the person with LD must self-identify as someone with a disability and must provide documentation to verify that disability. This means the employee cannot walk into his manager's office on a whim and say, "I have ADHD and I demand special accommodations," unless he is prepared to back up that claim with written documentation.

Disclosing a learning disability must not be done in a spirit of anger or during a crying jag. It's not the sort of thing to hurl back at a supervisor in response to criticism or to justify poor performance on the job. LD may be the root cause of the poor performance, but it's important to disassociate the disability from anything resembling an "excuse." For instance, let's say a frustrated supervisor accuses a coworker of being lazy. In the supervisor's mind, at that moment, that is the entire source of the problem—laziness. If the employee comes right back with an immediate defense against the charge by disclosing LD, the disclosure will probably be viewed as an excuse. The best action to take in such a situation is to accept the criticism and wait for things to cool down a bit before bringing up the real reason. Disclosing LD or ADHD needs to be done in a mature, calm way that emphasizes the positive aspects of the disability and includes suggestions for ways to improve any problems caused by it.

HOW TO DISCLOSE

Dale S. Brown, in an article for the National Institute for Literacy, listed the following steps when planning to disclose a learning disability or ADHD. It is telling that she wrote these suggestions under the heading: "The best accommodations are those that are won without resorting to complaints and lawsuits."

1. Disclose the disability and request accommodations verbally to the supervisor or human resources department.
2. Have medical documentation available. Employers can demand proof of a disability before providing accommodations.
3. Clearly describe the disability and the accommodations needed. Because employers can legally turn down accommodation requests if they can prove they cause an "undue hardship," employees should propose the least costly and time-consuming accommodations.

4. Follow up with a written request, recapping the description of the disability, accommodations, and how they will help meet the employer's goals.

Glenn Young, an expert on LD adults, gave similar suggestions for those planning to self-identify as an individual with a disability, but in addition, he listed two others.

- Take the risk to self-identify.
- Face a wide range of uncertainties.

Risk and uncertainty are not as clear-cut as the other suggestions, nor are they inevitable, but they should always be included when weighing the benefits and drawbacks of disclosure.

Perhaps we can settle on a point of disclosure that lies midway between the initial job interview and the point where poor job performance threatens the loss of the job. In the example of the waiter whose ADHD has no impact on his work, there seems little reason to disclose. But at the first sign of trouble, before anyone else is aware of it, he should give serious consideration to disclosure, and he should do it well before the troubles get out of hand.

A recent article in *The Wall Street Journal*, written by Sue Shellenbarger and titled "For Adults with Learning Disabilities the Hardest Part of a Job Is Keeping It," confirms this. "Caught in limbo between a fear of being stigmatized," she wrote, "and the risk that their disorders will hurt their job performance unless they receive accommodations, many [adults with LD or ADHD] try to hide their impairments at work. The strategy often backfires, getting them fired anyway because of performance problems linked to their impairments. If they disclose their disorders at that point, employers generally look at that as an excuse. David Fram, the director of the National Employment Law Institute, said that 'more employers might accommodate workers if they asked for accommodations before they started having problems on the job.'"

THE DEFINITION OF "REASONABLE"

Let's talk about that word "reasonable" in the phrase "reasonable accommodations." In the perfect world dreamed of by parents and other advocates for the disabled, every employer and coworker already understands the needs of those with disabilities and happily makes every effort possible to accommodate them, often at the company's expense. I sometimes feel that advocates hand out advice based more on these idealistic hopes than on reality. An example of this can be found in a suggestion made by an advocacy organization for those who have trouble getting to work owing to issues with time management. Rather than exploring possibilities like a wake-up service or figuring out a more efficient commute, they say: "If being on time or working a full eight-hour day is a problem for you, a modified work schedule will allow you to come to work later in the day. Or you may be able to work shorter periods by working part-time or by job-sharing with someone else who wants to work part-time."

The second half sounds reasonable, but what about the first? "A modified work schedule will allow you to come to work later in the day." This may be the perfect solution for you, but when viewed from the standpoint of a coworker, the notion of requesting permission to come in late to work could cause friction and alienate you from your coworkers. We should always try to connect the word "equitable" to "reasonable" when thinking about accommodations. Certainly, if coming in an hour late results in an hour's less pay, then it sounds both reasonable and equitable, but if it means coming in an hour late but with the same pay, some coworkers simply will not care that it is an accommodation due to a disability. They will perceive it as unfair treatment, and no matter how well or often it is explained, they will continue to view it as unfair.

Why does this matter? We already know the difficulties presented by a lack of social skills. These difficulties can separate the adult with LD from his peers and set him apart as someone "different." Accommodations perceived as being unfair can do the same thing. Resentments build among coworkers, they band together against the person with the accommodations, and before long an adversarial relationship develops that may require even more accommodations. Bear in mind that management, by law, is not allowed to tell the coworkers the reason for the accommodations. If the worker doesn't step forward and talk about LD and the reason for the adjusted work schedule, the coworkers will have no clue and assume it's a form of preferential treatment.

In such cases it does no good for parents and advocates for the disabled to huff and puff and expound on what the disabled person's coworkers *should* feel in this situation. It's what they *do* feel that matters, and if the accommodations aren't reasonable or presented in a reasonable manner, there could be trouble ahead.

In addition, we should not fool ourselves about the realities of discrimination. Laws can protect against overt discrimination, but what about the more subtle forms? Career advancement can be undermined in subtle ways that are difficult to detect—especially by someone whose learning disability causes difficulty in understanding social cues and behavior.

I based the negative scenario outlined above on a situation involving secrecy by the disabled employee, an unclear understanding of what "reasonable" means, and coworkers who are not sympathetic. The good news is that this is not the only scenario found in the workplace. More companies than ever throughout the country now actively recruit people with disabilities.

The ADA requires employers who have fifteen or more employees to provide reasonable accommodations, and obviously, it is in their best interest to help all their employees be as productive as possible. Most reasonable accommodations cost nothing at all or very little. If an employer believes that a proposed accommodation is a hardship to the company, they can propose a different one. It's all a matter of compromise. For instance, I heard of one woman who had a difficult time writing her weekly reports but was highly skilled in verbal communication. She proposed the use of assistive technology, in her case a computer program that turns speech into written text. Her employer was hesitant to provide it, in spite of the obvious benefits. Did she file a grievance claim and take him to court? No. She bought the program herself, for less than a hundred dollars. Her reports now come in on time, written in the same smooth manner as her verbal reports. She doesn't have to agonize over them for hours, nor does she have to hear the weekly criticism that used to come her way.

Of course, it would have been better if the employer had provided the accommodation, but it's reasonable to assume that he's seen the improvement in her productivity and will be more receptive the next time someone approaches with a suggested accommodation. The chances are also good that he'll be more amenable to any promotion or salary increase based on her improved performance, which will more than make up for her initial outlay of a hundred dollars.

HOW TO DETERMINE THE NEEDED ACCOMMODATIONS

Many young adults don't fully understand their own disability and have a difficult time suggesting accommodations that might work for them. For many, the words "lazy" or "not trying hard enough" are hardly new, and they may glumly accept such accusations without ever mounting a proper defense.

Here is something that could help: the Office of Disability Employment Policy within the U.S. Department of Labor offers a free service called the Job Accommodation Network, or JAN (the website and address can be found in the Resource Guide). JAN bills itself as "Your comprehensive source for job accommodations," and it does this by providing individualized accommodations solutions for both workers and employers, along with advice and information about the Americans with Disabilities Act.

The JAN website is full of useful information on the topics I have covered, including job interviews, resume writing, and disclosure—all tailored for those with disabilities. JAN also has a Searchable Online Accommodation Resource called SOAR, which is particularly helpful for those looking for suggestions for accommodations to help them improve their work performance.

As an example, I went to the section called "Learning Disabilities" and chose, at random, "Individual with Deficits in Reading."

The suggested accommodations are:

- Voice Output software that highlights and reads (via a speech synthesizer) text on a computer screen.
- Locator dots for identifying numbers or letters on the keyboard (these are adhesive-backed raised dots in various colors and sizes that can be felt by the fingertip).
- Books on tape.
- Tape-recorded directives, messages, and materials.

- Line guide for computer screen.
- Use of a Readingpen, a handheld device that scans words and gives auditory feedback.
- Use of materials that are not handwritten.
- Use of large-print text or double-spaced text.

These are only a few of the suggestions. The Job Accommodation Network can spur workers with LD to consider new ideas and possibilities. It can also help explain both learning disabilities and accommodations to employers.

20

"Show Me Spark!":
Corporate America and the
Adult with LD

W hen assessing the employment options of our adult child with LD, especially a child with severe disabilities, we often think small, maybe a business with two or three employees run by someone who understands our child's personality and needs. We don't consider the large corporation, even though, as Jim Rein pointed out, "adults with LD do much better in a company where they only have to do one thing rather than the smaller one where they have to do everything." We tend to think that our son or daughter will be little more than a number in the larger company, a cog in a gigantic machine that couldn't care less about the needs of an employee with LD. That might have been the case once upon a time, but the corporate environment changed with the passage of the Americans with Disabilities Act in 1990. Now most large corporations are not only supportive of employees with disabilities, but actively recruit them to join their work force.

I am occasionally asked to speak to employee groups at various corporations, usually about raising a child with LD. The first time I did this was at the invitation of Joan McGovern, head of AccessAbility, the disabilities program at JPMorgan Chase. Joan and I met again recently to discuss some of the issues facing young adults entering the corporate workplace. We started with one of the most difficult employment issues of all—finding a job in the first place. "A lot of people with disabilities think that finding a job in the corporate world can be tough," Joan said. "But it only appears that way. In reality, there are a lot of services out there to help students and experienced workers with disabilities find employment. For example, in New York City we have the Mayor's Office for People with Disabilities. They reach out to a number of colleges in the area as part of National Disability Mentoring Day and bring disabled students in for job shadowing or mentoring."

Job shadowing involves spending anywhere from an hour to a half day to a full day with a manager, following them around to different meetings and watching whatever else they do for that day to get a sense of the workplace. Mentoring is a similar program that pairs a young adult with an employee for a longer period of time. In both instances, especially when conducted as part of some type of Disability Awareness campaign, the need for disclosure is not an issue.

But what of the young adults who choose not to disclose or are in denial about their LD, or who do not even know they have LD or ADHD at the time they are hired? They obviously wouldn't come into the company as part of a disabilities-related program. What happens to them when they discover they need additional help to keep up on the job?

Once again, Dr. Raskind's first attribute of success—self-awareness—is critical.

I once heard a young man interrupt his mother after she mentioned he had LD. "I *used to* have LD," he said. "It's gone now." Embarrassment, shame, or even a genuine belief that the disability has been cured or lessened can lead to such denial. In some ways it's understandable: school forces children into close quarters with subjects and circumstances that shine a glaring light on a learning disability, and after leaving school, it is easy for some young adults to believe they have left their learning disabilities behind, too.

Denial such as this can create serious problems in the workplace. Even if the employers are convinced beyond a shadow of a doubt that someone has LD or ADHD, the Americans with Disabilities Act prevents them from acting on those suspicions. They cannot ask someone if he or she has a disability. The only thing an employer can do is ask if the employee needs anything to make the job easier. If the disabled employee says no, that's as far as it can go.

"It can be very hard to sit back and watch them struggle," Joan McGovern said. "Apart from asking if there's anything you can do to help, you can also mention any sensitivity sessions or awareness sessions within the company, both internally and externally, or any support groups you're familiar with, or you can say that someone in your family is experiencing this particular disability. In other words, you can offer support by dancing all around the subject, but if they don't want to accept the help, there is nothing you can do. The employee with disabilities is the only one who can begin the conversation about disabilities at the workplace."

The employee who is unwilling to disclose is *legally* assumed to have no disability at all, even if the disability is apparent to everyone else.

"IT ALL COMES DOWN TO PERFORMANCE"

Disclosing a disability does not automatically guarantee ironclad protection against losing a job, nor does it prevent disability-related problems from arising. Disclosure smooths the way for accommodations or a job change within the same company.

"Every company goes through periods of downsizing when they have to lay people off," Joan said. "That's when the human resources executives take a look at the big picture and see where everyone fits on the spectrum in their particular department. Who do we reduce? Who do we advance? Who do we let go? There have been times when they tell me an employee with disabilities falls into the area of those they have to let go. It all comes down to performance. Is the employee meeting their job objectives? Are they keeping up? If they need assistance, that's when the manager steps in and asks if there is anything the company can do to help. If the employee doesn't say anything, then the manager can come back with, 'Well, I have to tell you that your performance is not satisfactory. I'm trying to help you get where you need to be, but you have to work with me.'"

This is the time for the employee to ask for reasonable accommodations. The manager will provide the accommodations (or work out a reasonable alternative) and see if the performance improves. If the problems persist, the manager might ask if the employee needs additional help. At a company like JPMorgan Chase, if the problem remains after all the accommodations and suggestions have been tried, the employee then goes to career services and gets transferred to another position within the company. The company also has a number of partnering organizations that it deals with, such as Abilities Inc. and The American Association of People with Disabilities. After the employee exhausts all internal possibilities, he or she can contact one of these partners to continue the job search. "That way we give them a warm hand-off," Joan explained, "and at least some level of hope that the partnering organizations will be able to find them another job."

SOCIAL SKILLS ON THE JOB

Workplace problems resulting from deficits with social skills are not always easy to categorize as disability-related. In some ways, that is true of LD and ADHD as a whole, due to the lack of visible signs of the disability. A blind employee or one in a wheelchair is not going to rouse the same sort of resistance or even hostility as the employee with ADHD or LD—once called "the hidden handicap" by the LD community. No one will accuse the blind man of laziness if he can't read the computer screen, nor will anyone tell the young woman in the wheelchair that she could walk "if she only tried."

Some nondisabled people have trouble categorizing problems with reading and writing as a disability, but this pales in comparison to the trouble they have accepting poor social skills as a disability. I asked Joan McGovern what would happen in a company like JPMorgan Chase if the disability-related problems were caused solely by social skills. "Let's say the employee is constantly interrupting and asking inappropriate questions," I said. "What happens when, three months after he gets the job, everyone around that person cannot stand him, and he becomes isolated by his coworkers?"

"That would be something the manager would pick up right away," Joan said, "either on their own or from the person's coworkers. Much of this depends on the culture of the company. Within our firm, our employees are empowered to speak out on an issue and be upfront about their inability to work with this coworker. From there we'll do whatever we can to help the situation. If employees can't do the work they were specifically hired to do and there are no accommodations that work, we try to get them something else in the firm, but sometimes at the end of the day, you just have to let them go. Of course, that's the very last resort."

I asked if a company can legally suggest that an employee go to see a doctor or therapist. I used the example of a young woman with ADHD who would have been fired from her job had she not discovered a certain medication that allowed her to concentrate.

"It depends on the size of the corporation," Joan said. "We have a unit called Employee Assistance Program, and that's where they address the mental condition of the issues. We have psychologists and psychiatrists on staff. But once again, the employee has to initiate it. Someone from Employee Assistance Program cannot approach the employee and say, 'I understand you're being very disruptive and we think you need to go on drugs.' That is absolutely not allowed."

Parents can play a role in all this, especially when we have the combination of a terrible work environment and a young man or woman who simply refuses to acknowledge or accept his or her own disability. That is when parents can step forward and say to their child: "You have to talk to someone. You have to tell them about your disability."

Joan agreed. "Absolutely. A parent could do it. In fact, a parent *should* do it, if they see that type of situation. A friend can do it, too. And maybe most relevant, a coworker can do it. And once the employee *does* say something, the company has to help. It's all done under the strictest confidentiality, too. It's important that employees feel that confidentiality is in place."

"How often do these types of situations arise?" I asked.

"Hundreds of times a day."

OPPORTUNITIES IN CORPORATE AMERICA

Joan also had words of advice for the young adult who is looking at the corporate world as a possible place of employment.

"When you speak to a company, don't assume you know what positions they have available," she said. "Agencies that help the disabled should also not assume this: they should visit the company and find out what's available instead of just advising the clients to look on the website for the jobs listed. The Internet is a wonderful resource, but if you look at a company's website, you might think you don't have the skills or abilities they need. For instance, people might think JPMorgan Chase only hires bank tellers. We don't! We have jobs in the mailroom, in the cafeteria, in building maintenance and security. But individuals and the agencies that place them have to make an effort to find out what else we have available. We could have fifteen hundred jobs available in a given week, and once you find an area you're interested in, you can get the details about the specific jobs available.

I also tell people to send in a resume and to be sure to fill out a section we call Profile Information. That's where you put information such as job shadowing or mentoring. You have to market yourself or have someone help you market yourself. Write down all the things you have done. It's all experience. It's all knowledge. It's all something particular that you have picked up that your peers haven't. And the main thing with all of this is your confidence going into the interview."

"In other words," I said, "if you get there on time, you probably get the job."

"Right! I talked to a group of disabled people who were entering the job market for the first time, and I told them that if they come to me for an interview and set their resume down in front of me and say, 'Before we get started, I would like to tell you one thing I'm excited about— you'll see on my resume that August through September, this was an initiative that I did, which resulted in, etc. etc.'; then already I'm sitting back and thinking, 'Tell me more!' I begin to think more about where I can place this person rather than whether I want to hire them at all."

I pointed out to her that business leaders often give similar advice. Jim Rein of the New York Institute of Technology told me of a seminar he hosted for his Vocational Independence Program. When the head of human resources at a major corporation came to speak to his LD students about the realities of the workplace, Jim raised his hand from the back of the room and asked, "What is the most important quality you look for when hiring someone?"

"Reliability," she said without hesitation. "If someone just shows up, we will train them for the job."

David Neeleman, founder and CEO of JetBlue, had similar advice. "Anyone who comes to work on time and has a good attitude is already ahead of 75 percent of the work force."

Joan McGovern agrees. "Show me spark," she says to potential employees. "If you can do that, your chances of getting a job are good, especially in a huge corporation. There are so many opportunities. If you don't work out in one department, you can go to another, or you go to another company and then come back in. I tell disabled students not to look at the job market in the traditional way of internships, full-time or part-time employment. They also need to look at programs like mentoring and job shadowing that help people get used to being out in the workplace. And it doesn't matter where you start. You can work in the cafeteria or work in maintenance and work your way into different jobs if you'd like.

"Remember, time reinforces things for those out of work. If you start out saying you have never been able to do a certain thing, then you end up saying that you can't do it. Eventually that becomes 'I can't do anything,' and over time that attitude gets deeper. I always tell people in this situation, 'You need to go out and give it a try. It doesn't matter where, or at what level. You need to show enthusiasm. You need to show me spark, and I know you can do it. Everybody can!'"

21
Motivation

THE DOWNWARD SPIRAL

I often use the phrase "the downward spiral" when talking about the young adult who has given up on the job search. Think of a young man fresh out of school, starting off with high hopes, searching through the Help Wanted ads for a position that suits his talents and interests. Maybe he can't find the exact job he wants, but that's okay. He finds something similar, but after only a month on the job, he is fired. No one gives him a reason, but in his heart he suspects his dismissal came because of his LD. He goes back to the ads, now avoiding any job similar to the one he just lost. Another company hires him, but again, before the probation period is up, he is let go.

Now the Help Wanted section seems more of a threat than a source of optimism and possibility. Each job listing requires skills the young man thought he had only a few months before, but since the loss of the two jobs, each now seems beyond his abilities. Doubts increase, and soon he questions *all* his skills and abilities, even those that never caused a problem in the past.

Time reinforces things . . .

Soon his focus no longer looks outward toward finding a job but retreats inward toward ways of getting by without working. Maybe his parents will let him live at home for a while longer, or maybe they'll give him enough money to get by until "something turns up." With his confidence spiraling downward, he no longer buys the newpaper, no longer bothers to look at the help-wanted section. He may start to view the whole concept of employment as something for "other people"—but not him. He may claim to be a rebel, an artist, or a slacker—whichever term best fits his self-image—though inwardly the term "loser" echoes louder than the others.

He spends his days sleeping and is up most nights playing computer games or watching television, and he always has an excuse when his parents ask him when he's planning to find a job.

I know parents with adult children in this situation. One young woman quit her job after a "bad experience" (which she has never shared with anyone, including her mother) and has never worked since. A young man has lived in his parents' converted basement for nearly five years without paying rent, barely scraping by on an allowance from his father. The parents in both cases shrug their shoulders and say, "What can we do?"

They already know the answer—surely they have no shortage of well-meaning friends and relatives who tell them to throw the kid out of the house or cut off his allowance, anything to force him out to get a job; yet they are unable to do it. Much of this comes down to difficulties with letting go, but let's face it—sometimes it's just easier to let an adult child hang around the house rather than endure the frustrations of forcing him to get a job. These parents know they're not helping the situation, but they need a break from all the forcing and encouraging and advocating that have taken up so much of their time for so many years. They throw their hands in the air and say, "We're done."

How nice it would be for someone else to take over for a while, someone to listen to the excuses and complaints, and to instill enough motivation and encouragement to stop the adult child's downward spiral before it reaches rock bottom. If you feel this way, don't despair and don't beat yourself up if you sometimes grow weary of giving the never-ending encouragement. There are people who can help. They can give you a break and allow you to recharge for the inevitable time when you will once again be asked to step into the role you know so well.

LIFE COACHING

A friend of mine who is not learning disabled told me she had hired a Life Coach to help her get through a difficult transition period at her job. Out of curiosity I looked up Life Coach on the Internet and discovered that some coaches specialize in helping adults with LD and ADHD. This surprised me, especially after working so long in the LD field. I wondered why Life Coaching had never appeared on my radar screen before.

When looking at the list of Life Coaches who specialize in LD and ADHD adults, I randomly chose Casey Dixon, a coach based in Pennsylvania, and I contacted her out of the blue to talk about her work. My first question was the most obvious and basic of all: "What is Life Coaching?"

Casey defined it as a partnership between a client and a coach that helps the client move toward goals and take actions that will enable them to become the person they want to be in a more focused and rapid way than they would be able to do on their own.

About 60 percent of her clients first come to her because of employment problems. Some clients, similar to the young man I used in the example, are not employable at the moment because they are dealing with too many life-skills issues and are not ready to move forward.

When bringing them to a point where they are employable, Casey first focuses on self-awareness to help them learn about their own strengths and their own difficulties and challenges (she uses Dr. Raskind's work as inspiration). "A lot of my clients have already been through the psychological wringer," she says. "They already know a lot about their own disability and how it affects them. Others don't know anything. But whether their LD or ADHD is severe or mild, they need to understand that it is a part of who they are and that it is not going to go away; but also that they can learn to live with it, manage it, and find the strength within to cope and move forward."

When coaching someone who is unable to find work or keep a job owing to problems with social skills, a Life Coach will try to get to the root of *why* things break down socially at work. Is it because of impulsivity and a lack of inhibitions? Is it the emotional instability that often goes along with ADHD? Is it because the person has a nonverbal LD and doesn't understand social cues?

"Coaching is different from teaching because I'm trying to get the adult client to provide the answers for themselves. When teaching a child I would say, 'This is how you do it, let's practice it, let's repeat it.' It is a very structured sequence. When coaching adults with LD, I come at them knowing they are a whole person, and I try to provide the support and structure they need to figure out their issues and problems on their own. I'll ask them to break things down into pieces. Let's say there is a project due and the person is freaking out and can't handle it. I'll ask what is involved in doing the project and have them break it down into its component parts. I'll ask which part they feel they aren't capable of handling, and then ask which part they feel they *are* capable of handling. We focus the coaching session on trying to solve a problem by making a change in their habits, behaviors, or beliefs. I do that by asking them to talk to me about the problem, ask where is it going to fall apart, how they know that, and what they can do to make sure it doesn't happen. The key is moving them from inquiry and understanding toward action."

Life Coaching for LD or ADHD is not the same as psychotherapy. Life Coaches approach life problems or employment issues with the goal of giving concrete advice rather than focusing on feelings. If someone with ADHD has trouble at work because he or she keeps blurting things out during meetings, a psychiatrist might try to get to the root causes. A Life Coach will try to get at root causes too, but without spending a lot of time on questions like "Why do think you feel this way?" A coach will drill down into very specific situations and settings to come up with individualized methods to fix the problem. For instance, when working with clients who blurt things out in meetings, a coach will try to help them figure out how to use their own particular skills to solve the problem. "I might ask if they can recognize things in their body that tell them when they're about to blurt something out," Casey said, "or if there is something they can do to keep it from happening, such as writing their thought down on a notepad so they won't lose it. Many people with ADHD blurt things out because they are afraid they will forget something important."

Sometimes the problems associated with employment can be so large that they are not even perceived as problems at all—in other words, they consume so much of a person's life that, in time, they *become* that person's life. Casey gave me the example of a woman who works on the loading dock at a company, loading heavy crates all day long. "She was stuck in that job because she couldn't read very well. Her situation presented a very typical scenario. By the time many people with LD become adults and join the work force, they have been beaten up by the education system or their parents or society at large, and they are so desperate to do something well and to please someone that they become overly dependent upon what other people think of them. This woman on the loading dock was working much harder than any of her peers because loading crates was how she gave herself a little bit of self-esteem and self-worth. As her Life Coach, I helped her reorient herself to her life goals. We first had to determine what those goals were. Is it to be a better crate loader? Or is it to learn how to read so she can move away from that? It took her a while to articulate those goals, but when she did, we were able to focus her energy toward doing the things necessary to avoid loading crates for the rest of her life."

Low self-esteem and a need to please others are not confined to the loading dock. Some executives with LD get into trouble because they are so eager to please and so dependent on other people's opinions that they are simply unable to say no. Casey has a client who owns a multi-million-dollar business that he built himself, but who is so overtaxed and overworked that he is afraid his business is going to suffer. When they looked into how he spends his time and energy, he told her that he'd spent over an hour reinstalling emergency exit lights that morning. "I asked if that was the best use of his time. I don't ask *why* he did it— we already know the answer is that he's dependent on other people's opinions. The more important question is what he could have done differently and what is he going to do the next time somebody says they need a lightbulb changed or the stapler refilled. It's a matter of moving toward more productive action rather than focusing on the 'why' of something."

"WHAT YOU PAY ATTENTION TO GROWS"

Time-management problems are the number one reason people seek out coaching, but Casey finds that most of the problems associated with time management are actually a result of people having trouble managing their energy rather than their time. She has clients who don't know how to schedule their day and wish they could develop a routine. A Life Coach can help with that, but surface changes to a daily routine will usually not last if they don't address the issue of where the clients put their attention and focus and energy. "A lot of people with LD and ADHD give a lot of attention and time to things that drain all the energy out of them," Casey explained. "I have a client who needs to be better at doing paperwork, but every time she looks at the pile of papers she goes into a negative thought cycle. She starts to think, 'Why am I so bad at this? I can't believe that pile of papers is still there,' and she goes into her own belief system of 'I'm an idiot and I can't, I can't, I can't.' She gives the pile of papers too much power and allows it to drain all her energy. I try to get my clients to pay attention to the things that *give* them energy, so that by the time they have to do that paperwork, they have some options. They can create structures and systems that allow them to take care of the paperwork in an effective way, or they can delegate the job, or outsource it, or get support for it."

Negative belief patterns can become so intractable—our young man who has given up the job search and spends his time on the sofa watching TV is a case in point. He has settled upon a negative belief pattern that tells him he doesn't have the skills to get or keep a job. "Changing the negative self-talk is so difficult," Casey says. "It's probably the most difficult issue of all. I've had clients who make dramatic improvements in their lives, and yet the minute something goes wrong, they start cycling back into those negative beliefs. We work a lot on awareness about how you talk about yourself and to yourself, and how to stop the negative patterns. There is an expression used in the Life Coaching field—"What you pay attention to grows." If the unemployed person spends a lot of time paying attention to all the negative feelings behind their inability or refusal to find a job, they will keep driving down that same road until it's a major highway. Instead, we can focus on how they will benefit if they get a job and on the strengths they have. Focus on positive things. Ask what they can do this week to move in that direction. Just one thing. That one thing can sometimes start things off, especially for those who are really stuck."

Accountability is another important aspect of coaching. When clients agree to take action and move forward with a coach, they are more likely to actually follow through because they have to report back to the coach in their next session. Casey calls it "accountability without shame," as the coach does not use shame or say how disappointed they are if the client is unable to take action. Instead, the coach will help the client discover what kept them from being able to do what they said they wanted to do, and then help them solve this newly discovered obstacle. For example, let's say a young man said he wants to manage his time so he is able to go to the gym three times per week. If he only gets there once, the coach won't approach this in a negative way but will point out that going once is a healthy start and help him figure out an improved schedule to meet his goal of going three times. The key here is that the young man realizes he has someone *who is not a parent* who cares about his progress and checks in with him on a regular basis so that his goals do not get put on the back burner.

HOW TO FIND A LIFE COACH

There are several organizations that can help you find the best Life Coach for your needs. The largest is the International Coach Federation (ICF) (www.coachfederation.org). The ICF is an international organization that is setting professional standards for the coaching field. Another group, the ADHD Coaches Organization (ACO), lists 126 Life Coaches on its website, all specializing in coaching clients with ADHD (www.adhdcoaches.org)

Each Life Coach will have his or her own pricing range and method, though in general, the price ranges from $250 to $500 a month, depending on the location. Sometimes this fee is paid as a retainer, which allows a certain number of sessions per month (for example, three hour-long sessions a month with check-ins as needed). Some coaches have daily sessions for five to ten minutes. Some have appointments for an hourly fee that can be scheduled as needed.

Life Coaching is a wonderful hands-on approach to helping the unemployed young adult with LD, but chances are fairly good that the parent will be paying for it. For those without the means (or willingness) to pay, there are alternatives. Returning once again to our unemployed young man, we can safely assume that insecurities about his own skills and abilities have contributed to his reluctance to find a job. Let's not discount the fact that he might be right! He may not have the skills or the right type of skills for the job he wants. In that case, Vocational Rehabilitation could be the answer.

VOCATIONAL REHABILITATION

In my interview with Joan McGovern of JPMorgan Chase, I asked if she had any advice for someone who lived outside a major city and didn't have access to programs such as those affiliated with the Mayor's Office for People with Disabilities in New York City. "What happens if we have a little store in rural Minnesota with five employees," I asked, "and the guy working in the back stock room just can't do his job? Nobody there knows that he has LD and ADHD, and he ends up getting fired. If you were this man's friend, how would you help him?"

Joan suggested a Vocational Rehabilitation Center. "Every state has one," she said, "and every county has one. They'll talk to him and they'll analyze him, usually for free since it is a tax-funded organization. He can visit them in person, or call them, or go online to get information. If the young man is tested and they discover he has LD or ADHD, they'll provide lists of agencies and organizations they work with that can either hire him, train him, or if he's already working, help him acquire the additional skills needed to land a different and better job."

I went online and checked out the Minnesota Vocational Rehabilitation website to see what the young man or his parents might find. The first question they answered is the first one most of us would ask: "Who can get Vocational Rehabilitation (VR) Services?"

Answer: "You may be able to get Vocational Rehabilitation Services if you have a disability that makes it hard for you to get a job." That pretty well sums up the situation of our young unemployed Minnesotan.

Using reports from doctors that document the disability, VR counselors will interview candidates to see how well they do in seven areas:

- Getting from one place to another
- Talking and listening to others
- Taking care of yourself
- Making plans or carrying out plans
- Getting along with other people
- Having the skills to work
- Needing changes at work to do a job

People who have serious limitations in these areas will get services first.

The Minnesota VR then describes the relationship between the disabled adult and the counselor: "VR counselors know about disabilities and what it takes to enter the world of work. You and your counselor will talk about what you are good at, what you like, and what you need. This is your first step in choosing a good job or career. Then you and your counselor will set up an Employment Plan to meet your work goal. Your VR counselor can help you develop all or part of your plan. If you want to, you may develop your plan on your own. You decide how much help you want. Your counselor is responsible for deciding if your goal will lead to a job, the services needed to reach your goal, and if your plan is complete."

In addition, the VR office determines if additional training is needed and helps the candidate find it. It gives advice on finding the right job and on the interview process. There is no charge for the counseling or job placement services, though if the candidate already has an income above a certain level, there is a sliding pay scale based on income and family size.

Remember, these specifics are from the Minnesota Vocational Rehabilitation Office. Contact your own state office for details specific to your area. VR offices are usually listed in the state government pages of your phone book under "Economic Security," "Employment and Economic Development," or "Work Force Center."

For parents, it's important to follow these leads or encourage your adult child to follow them. It's especially important that you don't fall into the same inertia and negative thought patterns that so paralyze your adult child. "He can't do it, he'll never be able to keep his job, there is no help for him." These thoughts can prevent you from taking action, or even trying to summon the energy to make the attempt.

Joan McGovern consistently urges the positive approach. "You may think there is nothing out there for you, especially if you live in rural areas. But it's not true. There are organizations and people throughout this country who are willing and eager to help those with disabilities. Life Coaches, Vocational Rehabilitation, the Job Accommodation Network. There are so many organizations listed on the Internet, and if you don't have access to the Internet, you surely have access to a library. The same information can be found there."

VOLUNTEER WORK

As a final word on employment, I would like to once again mention the benefits of volunteer work—unpaid, yes, but also fulfilling.

Whenever I have been asked what parents can do to help an adult child who has given up hope of finding work, I tell them two things:

1. Get him up off the sofa.

2. Look into all the various programs available to help him find work, and if he still can't find a job, encourage him to do volunteer work.

If nothing else, volunteering for even one day a week accomplishes the first task. Nothing makes a situation appear more hopeless than sitting around all day with nothing to do but think of how hopeless our situation appears to be.

Volunteering can halt the downward spiral of lethargy and negative thinking. It has the added benefit of getting someone used to a schedule and being around other people, and there is always the potential for learning new skills. Volunteerism is truly what makes America great. Out of a population of 300 million, the Bureau of Labor Statistics estimates that each week 64.5 million of us take time out from our busy work schedules and family lives to help others. In doing this, we are able to put our own troubles and concerns in perspective. Helping others can build self-esteem, too, and by doing that, the LD adult who volunteers for a worthy cause stands a much better chance of finding and keeping a job.

PART V

Managing on Their Own: Life Concerns for the Adult with LD and ADHD

22

Staying Healthy

W hen our adult children move out on their own, whether to college or into their own apartments, their health remains a concern, though for most of us it is a distant concern along the lines of "I hope he's taking his vitamins" or "I hope she's making regular visits to the dentist." When they lived at home, we made all the appointments for them. Now we must hope they are doing this on their own. Good health, our own and our children's, is something most of us take for granted until it is threatened. Good health ambles along its own sunny way, unnoticed, but when health takes a turn for the worse, everything else falls away and it becomes the center of our lives.

Some parents of adults with LD face this on a daily basis. They may have a child who is chronically depressed, or in the throes of alcohol or drug abuse, or who has physical problems unassociated with LD. For these parents, health issues move front and center, and the old familiar difficulties and challenges presented by LD or ADHD now pale in comparison. These parents long for the days when their child's academic problems loomed in their minds as their greatest concern.

Not all health problems affecting adults with LD or ADHD are life altering or insurmountable. They have the same health problems as everyone else, and according to many experts, in no greater numbers than the population at large (though, as you'll see, I take issue with some of these claims).

In this chapter, I will discuss health issues ranging from mild to severe. We cannot consider learning disabilities themselves as a matter of "health" in the same way we think of a disease or injury, but to discuss general health problems in a book of this kind without mentioning the effects of LD defeats its purpose. LD is *always* related somehow.

Let's imagine we have a twenty-five-year-old man with ADHD, in perfect physical health, never had a problem of any kind, never hospitalized, rarely had a cold. What possible reason could we have to be concerned for his health? Admittedly, little; but what about his inability to make (or keep) regular appointments of any kind? Has he seen a dentist? When was his last physical? And what if he does happen to come down with something that requires a regimen of antibiotics taken for a specified length of time and at specific times during the day? Anyone with a son or daughter with ADHD is probably nodding right now and saying, "Uh-huh."

Most of us will not go to the lengths of calling a twenty-five-year-old man twice a day to ask if he's taken his penicillin, but we can at least acknowledge our concern and admit to ourselves that LD has affected yet another aspect of our child's life. Those whose adult child has severe LD and is living away from home in a group facility or school may want to consider creating a Medical Overseer. This is a fancy name for someone who keeps track of your disabled child's medical needs, such as doctor and dentist appointments, medications, and pharmacy needs. This person could be a family member or someone hired for the job.

PHYSICAL HEALTH

Eating Disorders and Obesity

When we talk about obesity in America, we can't isolate any specific population as most at risk—we're *all* at risk! Those with LD can have a problem with weight gain, and so can those who teach about LD in a university. Many parents who read this may think, "Hmm, don't know if I can bring this one up, since I have the same problem myself!" That may be true, but don't lose sight of the fact that adults with LD may not be equipped to tackle the problem of obesity, no matter how much they may wish to try. Let's say you have a young woman who is desperate to lose thirty pounds. She has the discipline, she has the will, she has everything except an ability to read and understand food labels or diet books or guides to nutrition. She could certainly use a little help, even from someone with weight problems of their own.

Weight gain or obesity among those with LD seems to be one of those issues that doesn't quite make the radar screen of many experts. I can't find a whole lot of information linking the two, nor can I find anyone who says there is a definite link between having LD and having troubles with weight. What I *can* find are countless parents who have told me this is a major concern. I'll give you one example. I was talking to another mother about an unrelated LD issue. She has a son who lives in a group home in Texas. I happened to mention that I was working on this topic and couldn't find much information about obesity in the LD population, and she practically jumped through the phone. "Oh, it's a terrible problem," she said. "The home where my son lives is very well regarded, one of the best facilities in the country, yet nearly everyone who lives there is overweight. When I talked to the administrators, they said that it wasn't a serious problem. I don't know if they were in denial about it or didn't take it seriously, but it truly was a serious problem. Finally some of us parents visited the home as a group to make our position crystal clear. We wanted something done about this. At the very least we wanted the staff and administrators to understand our concerns. This wasn't only about weight, but their overall health. Weight problems can lead to diabetes, heart disease, and all kinds of other health problems, and we wanted to try to avoid those things as much as possible. And I'll be honest with you. I worry more about the health of my LD child than my children without LD. Those without LD have husbands and wives and families of their own to take care of them down the road. My LD son only has me. If he becomes incapacitated due to weight-related health problems, who will take care of him, especially when I'm no longer able to do it? It's really a big concern."

Let's look at a few reasons why adults with LD or ADHD might have difficulty maintaining their proper weight.

The magazine *ADDvance* conducted a survey of adult women with ADHD about their eating habits. The results did not indicate a high rate of eating disorders such as anorexia or bulimia, though it did indicate that many had a great deal of trouble with compulsive overeating, or binge eating. Many of the respondents said they used food, especially carbohydrates such as bread, starchy foods, or sweets, as a way to calm down or to self-medicate. Surely we can all relate to this. We've had a stressful day, maybe we didn't have a chance to eat a proper meal, and now we're home, ready to unwind. Do we cook a healthy meal of a salad, followed by a broiled chicken breast and vegetables? Of course not! We reach for the macaroni and cheese, especially the kind that doesn't require too much work. Throw it in the microwave and ding! It's done. And then we can curl up on the sofa and unwind, and let the cares of the day slip away.

But what if every day is stressful, and not only because of outside influences like a project deadline or a demanding work schedule, but because you bring the source of stress with you wherever you go in the form of LD or ADHD? What if simple acts taken for granted by most others become a daily source of anxiety? In these cases, the occasional self-medicating dose of comfort food may become a daily fixture, and with it come the added pounds and expanding waistline.

Another challenge for those with LD or ADHD is planning ahead. The truth is that eating in a healthy way is not easy. I can already hear the wails of dissent, telling me that anyone can do it and that it is the easiest thing in the world to prepare a healthy dinner. These people, no doubt, are the very ones who have no trouble at all standing in front of a stove for the, oh, four or five hours it takes to boil brown rice. It doesn't matter how many books are published filled with "easy five-minute recipes for healthy living." The five minutes they focus on usually involve the simplest part of the process. What about shopping ahead of time? What about planning the time correctly so those precious five minutes become available when needed?

Fast-food restaurants have ideal customers in adults with LD or ADHD. They provide a ready-made product, whenever it's needed, requiring no advance planning. They certainly appeal to a majority of Americans without LD. I imagine the attraction is even higher for those unable to plan out their day with evenly spaced, healthy meals.

I met a woman named Mary at a conference in Phoenix whose daughter, Elaine, is overweight. Like the mother of the overweight son in the group home, Mary is quite concerned. Elaine is one of four children, the second oldest and by far the heaviest. I have never met Elaine so I didn't know the situation, but even if I had known, I would never have brought it up. Mary brought it up first by voicing the thought so many of us have. "I know LD has a lot to do with my daughter's weight problems," she said. "In fact, I think it has *everything* to do with it."

We discussed the difficulties so many adults with LD and ADHD have with planning ahead and how easy it is to buy junk food, but then she brought up something I hadn't thought of. "Elaine seems to have no sense of balance," she said. "She doesn't appear to have a self-image like that of many other young women. I know there are lots of girls in their twenties who are overweight—some of them so overweight they are classified as morbidly obese. But at least they *know* they're overweight. Elaine seems to be unaware of her situation. Or if she's aware, she simply doesn't care. I can't quite figure out which it is. She doesn't have a sense of boundaries. No matter how many times we talk about the difference between eating doughnuts or eating salad, it never seems to stick. She gets it—I know she does, at least for a little while—but then when it comes time to eat, all that knowledge flies out the window. There is also an unthinking quality to her overeating. She seems to be completely oblivious. I've seen her take enormous helpings at dinner without batting an eye, and the fact that her plate is the only one piled high with food doesn't seem to register or cause the least bit of concern."

What can a parent do in this situation?

In Elaine's case, I find myself going over possibilities one by one and rejecting them all. Short of hovering over her at every meal—certainly an impractical feat, since she lives hundreds of miles away—it's difficult to come up with a way for a parent to break through that wall created by a lack of self-awareness.

Allegra has had a couple of times in her life when she put on too much weight. Her case is unusual in that she spent so much time skating that she never had to worry about her weight; but during those times when she hasn't been as active on the ice, she has experienced what so many other Americans have. The skirt that suddenly doesn't fit any more. The jeans that can't be buttoned. Unlike Elaine, Allegra does have a healthy self-image. She might not know all the details of nutrition and a healthy diet, but she certainly understands that jeans that can no longer be buttoned did not suddenly shrink on their own. Still, the first time it happened I was concerned when I saw no sign that she was trying to change.

I decided to talk to her about it. This is always a risky thing. No one wants to hear about how much weight they have gained, and I didn't know how Allegra would take it. We went out to dinner one night, and I tried to keep the conversation light. I didn't want to go into this radiating a sense of negativity or seeming that I might be issuing some dire pronouncement. In the middle of our talk, I said, "I've noticed that you've gained a little weight." Before she could respond, I followed up with, "and I just wanted you to know that I can help you with it."

Luckily, my observation did not come as a surprise, nor was it particularly resented, and Allegra was more than happy to let me help her. We started off by going to the store and looking at food labels. I didn't even try to go into the various vitamins or the differences between saturated and unsaturated fats.

I focused on two numbers: total calories and total fat content. I picked up two cans of a similar type of food and said, "Let's say you have these two choices. Instead of picking up the first one you see or the one with the prettier label, look at the chart at the back of each one. See? This one has 170 calories and this one has 150. It's not a huge difference, but it adds up."

After she went home we faxed menus back and forth to each other. Nothing formal or typed out, just handwritten lists of what she planned to have for dinner. If a fax machine hadn't been available, we could have done this by phone or e-mail. The trick is to make it fun and a challenge—an *easy* challenge, I should say. There's no point in turning the act of eating into a thing of drudgery, nor will it help to insist that your child follow a diet based on rice cakes and lettuce. Moderation is the key.

Coupled with moderation is knowledge. Food and eating are the simplest things in the world—too simple, of course, for that is what gets us into trouble in the first place. But in reality, nutrition is anything but simple. We all take in information during specific moments in our lives, some based on fact, some based on falsehood, some based on old wives' tales, and some based on facts that have since been proven to be wrong. For instance, I always thought steak was good for you, low in fat and high in protein. Well, yes, it is, but not *all* steak. Even better examples are the phrases "low-fat" or "fat-free" that scream from packages all through the grocery store. All right, fine, they're fat-free, but are they loaded with sugar? If so, where is the packaging that shouts out that sugar gets converted to fat? Truth in advertising isn't really truth: it is shades of truth, which divert your attention from one pitfall so you can be led straight into another one. Even my recommendation to look at calories has a hidden danger, and that is serving size. *Calories per serving* is straightforward, and many of us stop there. "That's not too bad, 170 calories," we think, and then we see that the small can in our hand actually contains 3.5 servings, which means we now have to multiply 170 by 3.5. I don't know about you, but I can't do that kind of math in the middle of a crowded supermarket. Who makes up these serving sizes anyway? 3.5 servings in a single can? Who are they feeding? Elves?

My point in all this is to show the complexity of something we all have to do every day, and further, to wonder how on earth individuals with LD are supposed to know all this if they've never been told. Don't take it for granted that your adult child knows that vegetables have fewer calories than bread, or that canned foods might be more convenient but are often loaded with fat.

If you, the parent, don't know these things, it's a good idea to start learning. Buy a book. Talk to a nutritionist. Arm yourself with knowledge so you can pass it on to your child.

MENTAL AND EMOTIONAL HEALTH

Some people mistakenly lump LD or ADHD together with mental illnesses such as depression or schizophrenia. Certainly a person with LD can have a mental illness, but the two conditions are separate and should be thought of that way.

LD is a lifelong condition that starts before adulthood as a result of genetic or developmental factors, or from brain damage at birth. Most forms of mental illness first present themselves in adulthood (though some do appear in childhood) and usually are not thought of as a "lifelong condition"—unlike LD, it is possible to recover from a mental illness.

When I think about what adults with LD go through every day and have faced most of their lives, I can only wonder that more of them do not suffer from some form of depression at some point. Arlyn Roffman, in her book *Meeting the Challenge of Learning Disabilities in Adulthood,* wrote: "It is difficult to grow up with LD and experience repeated failure and relentless taunting from peers without developing secondary psychological issues, often referred to as emotional overlay. Emotional overlay does not always develop into diagnosable mental health problems but the symptoms can be quite debilitating nonetheless."

This can be especially true for those who were not diagnosed with LD in childhood. For years they endured the frustrations, humiliations, and repeated failures in school, all without an official explanation. Along with teachers insisting they didn't try hard enough and classmates calling them stupid, a great deal of damage is caused by self-criticism and the drumbeat of "I'm not good enough" that plays over and over in their minds. They grow up, they go to college or enter the work force, and the drumbeat doesn't stop. It beats on and on to affect jobs, relationships, family life—everything. Adults who were diagnosed early may get off a little easier, but not much. Even with the official explanation, "I'm not good enough" can follow them from childhood into adulthood with the same insistent beat.

Is it any wonder that depression, mood swings, irritability, or anxiety come into play? I can find estimates in medical journals ranging from 70 percent of adults with ADHD or LD suffering depression at some time in their lives all the way down to 15 percent. I won't try to pin down specific numbers of individuals, especially since most of us are concerned with only one, anyway—our own individual child. For those of us whose adult children do not suffer depression or anxiety, it is enough to know they could have a problem down the road. Those whose adult children are already touched by one or more of these conditions may wonder how they can help, or if they can help at all.

Depression

Who in the United States doesn't know someone who suffers from depression? They may never have admitted it to us or told us they are taking an antidepressant, but the condition is so common that even without knowing for certain that a friend or relative suffers from it, we can make a guess based on our own observations. Lethargy, sadness, lack of interest in things they used to enjoy: these are symptoms we recognize. They may be symptoms of depression; they may be symptoms of something else. Regardless, when we see them in a loved one, we know without question that "something is wrong."

Depression takes two forms. The first is biological or chemical and is not linked to any specific outside cause like the loss of a job or the death of a loved one. If someone with LD or ADHD suffers from this form of depression, it's a safe bet that they would have suffered from it whether or not they had a disability. The second form of depression is reactive and is caused by outside factors. This form of depression could have a direct link, not to LD itself but to the myriad problems arising from LD such as low self-esteem, difficulties with social situations, or a lack of friends or romantic partners.

In some ways the first, biological type of depression is easier to deal with, at least for the parent (though for those who are suffering, I'm sure it is a nightmare). Antidepressants can give enormous relief by correcting the chemical imbalances that caused the depression in the first place. The second, reactive type is more daunting because even if we know the cause, we may not have the first idea what to do about it.

Reactive depression can also be a little difficult for some parents to detect. If their child has a sudden change in personality caused by a chemical imbalance, parents are sure to notice, but if the outside forces that cause reactive depression have been around for so long, and the reactive depression has become a chronic condition, parents may simply assume that it is just their child's natural personality and fail to view it as something treatable.

There are also varying levels of severity within the two forms of depression. These range from major depression, which can interfere with a person's ability to work, study, sleep, or enjoy activities they once enjoyed, to a less severe type of depression known as dysthymia. While dysthymia does not disable a person, it does interfere with their ability to function normally or enjoy a happy life. The National Institute of Mental Health also includes bipolar disorder in their lists of types of depression, but that is so connected with the biological forms of depression that I am not including it here.

Signs of Depression

What should parents look for if they suspect their adult child is depressed? First of all, they should understand that the presence of a learning disability does not create symptoms of depression any different from those seen in people without LD (though, as with LD itself, not everyone has the same symptoms, and the severity of the symptoms varies from person to person). These are some of the things to look for:

- Persistent sad, anxious, or "empty" mood
- Feelings of hopelessness or pessimism
- Feelings of guilt, worthlessness, helplessness
- Loss of interest or pleasure in hobbies and activities that were once enjoyed
- Decreased energy, fatigue, or feelings of being "slowed down"
- Difficulty concentrating, remembering, making decisions
- Insomnia, early-morning awakening, or oversleeping
- Loss of appetite and weight loss or overeating and weight gain
- Thoughts of death or suicide. Suicide attempts
- Restlessness, irritability
- Persistent physical symptoms that do not respond to treatment, such as headaches, digestive disorders, and chronic pain

Some of these symptoms may not be obvious to parents. How, for instance, would we know if our adult children have had thoughts of death or suicide without asking them (which also assumes they would tell us)? In addition, there truly are people whose personalities or other medical conditions cause traits similar to the symptoms of depression. I most definitely include adults with LD or ADHD among them. Some of these symptoms may even be caused by the disability itself: how easy it would be for parents of an adult with ADHD to read that "difficulty concentrating, remembering, making decisions" is a symptom of depression and therefore conclude that their son or daughter *must* be depressed.

The only sure way to find out is through a professional diagnosis. The doctor or psychiatrist may suggest antidepressants and/or therapy, depending on the results. This all sounds nice and clear-cut, but an additional difficulty awaits the parents of an adult child they suspect suffers from depression, anxiety, or any other mental health problem, and that is a reluctance on the part of the adult child to accept the possibility of yet another "mental problem" or to seek treatment at all.

Using my daughter as an example, there was a time when I thought she might be going through a mild bout with depression. She never said she was depressed, and even though she didn't appear to be overly sad, she didn't appear overly happy either. The word "blah" comes to mind. But more than that, she definitely lost interest in activities she once enjoyed. She seemed to become lethargic suddenly, preferring to spend time alone on the sofa watching television rather than visiting with her friends. I asked her if she was depressed, and with little or no thought she said, "Only when I think about my father." (This was understandable—I get depressed when I think about her father, too.) Even so, I didn't buy it. She hadn't been on good terms with her father for many years, so her answer seemed to be off the mark, with little bearing on the symptoms I noticed. Why, after over thirty years, would her father's absence suddenly cause lethargy and a lack of interest in formerly enjoyable things?

I saw this as a surface answer, one that she came up with as an automatic response to my question, "Are you ever depressed?" Her answer could easily have been, "Only when I think of global warming," and it would have had as much meaning as the one she gave. My guess is that even if she did have depression, she would have been unable to articulate any clear-cut reason for it. That's true of many who suffer from this condition, especially when it is caused by biological factors. They can think of no obvious reason for it, so they'll try to come up with something that sounds legitimate.

Allegra eventually worked through all this, and we never did find out if she had suffered from depression. Like many parents in a similar situation, I had my suspicions, but I sat back and waited, telling myself that I would deal with the situation if it got out of control. I certainly hope I would have followed through on that promise to myself, but would I? I don't know. Eventually, I suppose I would have. I might have been too afraid not to. We've all heard horror stories of suicide attempts or even actual suicide; and though I cannot imagine Allegra ever entertaining such thoughts, we can never truly know what lies deep within the thoughts of another.

My point is not to scare parents but to urge them to consider possibilities apart from LD or ADHD when they notice changes in their adult children's behavior. It is not enough to rely on the adult children to figure out what is wrong. They may not have enough self-awareness to realize they are suffering from depression and not just going through another LD-related problem.

Anxiety

Closely related to depression, and also common among those with LD or ADHD, is anxiety. Again, this is so understandable once you take into consideration all they must face on a daily basis. Frustration, failure, humiliation: such things have shadowed them since grade school and can turn every new experience from one of possible adventure or opportunity into yet another chance for them to fall short of expectations. They may approach life and daily interactions with feelings of dread and pessimism, always expecting the worst.

Most parents of an LD child or adult can relate to anxiety in their own lives. I told someone recently that I had never been an anxious person until I had Allegra. Having an LD child creates all sorts of worries, but rarely are they truly debilitating. This is not always the case for adults with LD: for them the anxiety goes far beyond mere worry. It goes hand in hand with nearly every activity and in a much greater way than for most of us. We all relate to feeling anxious if we have to speak in public, but imagine that same fear and anxiety filling your day over things that usually don't cause a hint of worry in others. Small things during a typical day can take on great import and raise worrisome questions: "Will I get lost on my way? Will I be able to read the memo? What if I make a mistake?"

Such fearful questions set up expectations of failure, and before long LD adults find life a whole lot easier and calmer if they simply retreat from doing anything except the things they absolutely must do. They don't try for a better job. Social situations of any kind cause intolerable anxiety, so forget going on a date or asking someone out. They don't take risks. They don't do anything that might set them up to fail.

Allegra suffers from a level of anxiety, though I'm certain she doesn't view life with anything approaching dread or pessimism. For her it comes in the form of taking the easy route, free of unknowns and free of risk. When she was in the structured environment of school or skating full time, the discipline and the atmosphere of expectation and achievement kept her on a forward track. For all of us, the more we do something, the easier and less frightening it becomes; but once the outside pressures of a structured environment ease up, then we too have a tendency to ease up. We take fewer chances. We don't put ourselves out in front as often as we once did. If anxiety makes the withdrawal from the arena even more prolonged than usual, then it can be doubly difficult to get back in the game.

This is what a young man with LD, a computer professional, wrote about the issue in an online chat room: "I have a learning disability and anxiety. I am very confused sometimes as to where one begins and where the other begins. I have low self-esteem. I feel like I may be able to beat the anxiety, but the LD will never go away so I will always struggle. I have a great deal of trouble remembering things. Being in computers, there is so much to remember and I constantly have to study, but when I don't understand something or cannot remember how it connects with other things I start to feel stupid and my mind starts to go and I feel like a failure. I start to wonder if me not understanding is my LD or is it my anxiety, and I have it set up in my mind that I will not understand the material. I put a lot of pressure on myself to learn and feel stupid if I don't because coworkers get it easier than me. I feel like I have to get this stuff because I have to get a better paying job to support my family. I feel overwhelmed with all the material I have to learn. I don't need to be rich. I just want to support my family."

He then went on to give a few tips to others who might have both LD and anxiety.

Some things that help me through the day

- Beat the fear, beat the disorder.
- It is all in your mind.
- You have been through worse and gotten through it.
- When it really hits the fan, people with anxiety are usually the people to lead because they have imagined it many times already.
- When you have a setback, that must mean you are going in the right direction.

I love these thoughts, and I love the idea of someone using them to get through tough times during the day. I especially admire the wisdom of the last two. What a great way to turn anxiety and a tendency to dwell on troubles into positive attributes, for who better to take charge in a situation than someone who has already imagined every possible worst-case scenario and what could be done to solve each one?

Viewing a setback as an indication that you are going in the right direction also has value and is a good lesson for everyone with LD. The only people who do not face obstacles or setbacks are those who never try to do anything at all. Don't think of obstacles as a constantly negative part of life but proof that you are taking action. Obstacles affect only those who are moving forward.

ALCOHOL AND DRUG ABUSE

This is another area that common sense tells us has great potential to create problems for those with LD or ADHD. "That's not true," say many in the professional community. "Studies have shown that there is no direct link between the two." On the other hand, some professionals are coming around to the opposing view and say there is indeed a link between the two, especially between ADHD and substance abuse.

I have heard enough firsthand accounts from parents to believe we can go further than the link between ADHD and substance abuse and say there is a link between LD and substance abuse, too. On an intellectual level I will accept the fact (if proven) that the prevalence of substance abuse in the LD population is no greater than in the general population, but most parents who have an LD adult who is spiraling out of control due to drugs and alcohol *know* there is a link. They feel it in their heart, they feel it in their gut, and all the theories and studies in the world cannot change this.

The attorney Robert Shapiro started a foundation named after his son Brent, who died of a drug overdose and who also had ADHD. Included in a statement of the Brent Shapiro Foundation's mission are these words: "We intend to search for biological markers of alcohol and drug dependence and study the apparent increased risk between common childhood problems such as ADHD, other learning disabilities and the susceptibility to this disease."

That is the statement of a parent who *knows*.

The National Center on Addiction and Substance Abuse at Columbia University, or CASA, also knows. Back in 1999, CASA's President, Joseph Califano, and I cosponsored a conference on the issue, for even then we knew there was a growing problem of substance abuse among those with LD and ADHD.

With the help of the National Center for Learning Disabilities, CASA released a study in September 2000 called *Substance Abuse and Learning Disabilities: Peas in a Pod or Apples and Oranges?* This study grew out of the earlier conference, and as you can see, the title reflects the ongoing debate. Our press release at the time positioned the study as a "Challenge for the Scientific Community." The controversy, for the most part, doesn't seem to be over whether those with LD are more susceptible to addiction or substance abuse, but whether LD actually *causes* it. I don't know the answer, and so I will leave those concerns for others to work out. It may be that the only study parents really need to consider is the one they undertake themselves. Here is Robert Shapiro again, during an appearance on *Larry King Live* in June 2006. "And parents," he said, "if you think there's a problem, you're right. There probably is."

Connecting the Dots

For those who do require more tangible proof, can we at least acknowledge that the subject requires our attention? As usual with learning disabilities, most studies focus on children; but we, as parents of adults with LD, can certainly learn from these studies. Here are some facts from the CASA White Paper and from NCLD. These facts alone do not directly connect all the dots, but they certainly lay them out in a way that allows us to connect them for ourselves. Here is one set of facts:

> **Fact 1:** *Children with LD are at greater risk of school failure. 39 percent of them drop out of high school.*

We can easily connect this with a second fact.

> **Fact 2:** *Academic failure and peer rejection are common risk factors associated with substance abuse. So is the low self-esteem that accompanies social problems and academic failure.*

The risk factors for adolescent substance abuse—low self-esteem, academic failure, loneliness, depression, and the desire for social accept-ance—are similar to the social and behavioral effects of learning disabilities. Once again, this does not mean that LD itself *causes* drug or alcohol abuse, but it certainly generates the conditions that lead adolescents down that path.

Joseph Califano, in the same *Larry King* interview with Robert Shapiro, said of those with LD and ADHD, "These kids are at much higher risk of substance abuse than other kids. It's important for parents to know that. It's important to identify the learning disabilities and the problems early, so you can help these kids."

Here is another set of easily connected facts, this time involving ADHD:

> **Fact 1:** *Those with LD are twice as likely as the general population to suffer from ADD or ADHD.*
>
> **Fact 2:** *ADD and ADHD are associated with early onset of substance abuse and a greater difficulty recovering from addiction. Half of those suffering ADHD self-medicate with drugs and alcohol.*

The connections go on and on. We also know that individuals in substance-abuse treatment have a higher incidence of LD than the general population (one study revealed that 40 percent of people in treatment for substance abuse have LD). CASA even goes a step further and reverses the *LD = Addiction* equation by stating that *Addiction = LD*. Its report states that "children exposed to alcohol and illicit drugs in the womb are at higher risk for various developmental disorders, including LD."

The LD Teenager and Substance Abuse

The teenage years are a troubling time for many with LD and ADHD, when low self-esteem and academic failure are at their most pronounced, and the desire for acceptance by one's peers is at its highest. The quest for acceptance can lead to the use, abuse, and sometimes the sale of drugs and alcohol. We all have an image of the "cool kids" in school. Maybe this image reflects our own time in school when motorcycles, leather jackets, fast cars, cigarettes—all the things that sent shivers down our parents' backs—were the very things that most attracted us. Many if not most of those who go through such phases eventually straighten themselves out. But what if you have a limited ability to understand your own feelings and emotions, or your social skills in any situation apart from those involving the use of drugs and alcohol are woefully inadequate? It may not be enough to simply hope LD teenagers will straighten themselves out.

Before we can look for a solution to a problem, we have to discover if there is a problem in the first place. One unfortunate attribute of those addicted to drugs or alcohol is an insistence that they are not addicted at all. They'll go to all kinds of lengths to prove this is the case. They'll blame others or their circumstances. They'll continue to drink or use drugs in spite of the obvious problems caused by the behavior. They'll even resort to lying about their alcohol or drug use. (This does not apply only to teenagers. Anyone with a drug or alcohol abuse problem behaves the same way. The denial and lies grow more frequent and elaborate as the problem intensifies.)

There are signs to look for if you suspect your teenager may have problems with substance abuse. The Centers for Disease Control has put together a list of things to look for, but remember that even if some of these warning signs are present in your teenager, that does not automatically mean he or she is drinking or abusing drugs. In addition, the parent of a teenager with LD or ADHD will find some overlap between the effects of LD or ADHD and the signs of substance abuse. For example, "Bad Performance in School" is often listed as a sign of possible teenage drug and alcohol abuse. Parents of teens with LD already know that poor academics is going to be a factor in their child's life, so they need to adjust their observations and look for unexpected things around the margins of what they already expect. Instead of looking for "Bad Performance," they may want to look for a sudden change in school performance, regardless of how good or bad that performance might normally be. Parents must use their judgment and do so honestly, without slipping into denial. Don't attribute something completely to LD or ADHD if you suspect there might be more involved.

Warning Signs: Physical and Emotional

- "A New Crowd." Is your child suddenly hanging out with a whole new group of people, or maybe one or two new friends? What do you know about these new friends? Are they older?

Do you suspect they use drugs or alcohol? If they do, ask yourself why they have suddenly befriended your son or daughter,
especially if your son or daughter has had trouble maintaining
normal friendships in the past.

- Smell of alcohol or marijuana on breath or body.
- Unexplained mood swings and behavior. The teen with LD
  and ADHD may have more mood swings than the general
  population (or go the other way and seem never to have a
  mood swing at all). Extreme changes are the thing to watch
  for in this case.
- Argumentative, paranoid or confused, destructive, anxious,
  verbally abusive. Violent outbursts.
- Overreacts to criticism, acts rebellious.
- Sharing few if any of their personal problems.
- Doesn't seem as happy as they used to be. Lack of motivation.
- Overly tired or hyperactive. The parent of the teen with
  ADHD will need to take particular care not to assume hyper-
  activity is a definite sign of alcohol or drug abuse.
- Drastic unexplained weight loss or gain.
- Unhappy and depressed, withdrawn, apathetic.
- Cheating, stealing, lying.
- Always needs money or has excessive amounts of money.
- Neglected appearance or hygiene.

Warning Signs at Home

- Loss of interest in family activities.
- Disrespect for family rules, withdrawal from responsibilities.
- Valuables or money missing, or valuables suddenly appearing
  in the child's possession.
- Not coming home on time, not telling you where they are
  going.
- Constant excuses for behavior.
- Spending a lot of time in their rooms.
- Lies about activities.
- Evidence—Bottles missing from liquor cabinet or medicine
  cabinet. Finding drug paraphernalia around the house: ciga-

rette rolling papers, pipes, roach clips, small glass vials, plastic baggies, remnants of drugs (seeds, etc.).

Warning Signs in School

The following warning signs are included for the young adult still in school, but again, the parent must weigh the impact of LD when trying to determine if they are a sign of substance abuse.

- Sudden unexpected change in school performance.
- Truancy.
- Loss of interest in learning.
- Not doing homework.
- Poor attitude toward sports or other extracurricular activities.
- Reduced memory and attention span.
- Not informing you of teacher meetings, open houses, etc.

The LD Adult and Substance Abuse

The warning signs of teenage alcohol and substance abuse flow right into the signs of adult alcohol and substance abuse, with some obvious differences. School truancy will no longer be an issue. The behavior is there, but now it's called absenteeism from the job or cutting class in college. Living alone or with roommates, your adult child is no longer under your watchful eye. You may not see anything firsthand and will have to rely more on intuition or remarks heard from others. Maybe it's a phone call from your son, during which he slurs his words or says strange things. A friend of your daughter's might approach you and say, "You know, I'm really worried about her drinking."

You will know when the time comes to pay more attention to your intuition and those little clues you catch from time to time. As Robert Shapiro said, "If you think there's a problem, you're right. There probably is."

One of the challenges we all face is a general acceptance of the problem. Few people condone substance abuse by young teens, but once a person passes the legal drinking age, society not only tolerates, but encourages alcohol use. We still have laws against drug use, though they haven't prevented the availability and open use of drugs, especially in our cities. I know of one case where the parents of a young man with severe LD quite openly accept his use of marijuana. They don't promote it, but they certainly haven't tried to curtail it. Why? They explained it to me this way: "He had no friends in college. None. But when he used and sold marijuana, at least he met others who did the same."

I didn't know how to respond to that. I found it difficult to imagine that they couldn't see the end result. It's so understandable for parents to want their children to have friends. We see their loneliness and ache for them. We can imagine parents going to any lengths to ensure their children have a social life of some kind, but it's possible to go too far. Can we in good conscience risk the possibility of serious addiction, with all its attendant problems involving physical health and legal difficulties, simply to satisfy ourselves that our son or daughter has friends? Even if the answer to that is yes, we surely know that a friendship based solely on the sale and use of illegal drugs stands little chance of evolving into a deep and lasting relationship. Think these things through before you act on them or let them slide by without comment.

Most of us will not go to such extremes, but disapproval of your adult child's alcohol or substance abuse doesn't always guarantee an end to it. Let me tell you about Lynn and her daughter, Alison. Alison and Allegra were close in age, and together Lynn and I watched our daughters grow up facing the challenges of LD. We were also able to confide in each other about the problems that inevitably came our way. It was a safe, comfortable relationship for both of us. As our daughters grew older, they grew apart—not owing to any falling out but more because of circumstances. It was similar to the friendship I described earlier between Allegra and her fellow ice-skater, Hilary. Like Hilary's, Alison's life took a different path, in a different city, far from where Allegra lived. Lynn and I remained close, however, and I was able to be there for her when Alison underwent what must have been the worst crisis of their lives.

When Alison was about twenty-three, she met a young man and fell in love. Lynn was so happy when her daughter announced her engagement. I too was happy, as I knew my friend very much hoped to see her daughter get married. Very soon after the wedding, Alison's behavior began to change. She had both LD and ADHD, so Lynn was already attuned to problems in her daughter's life. But this was different. There were unexplained mood swings. She would call sometimes, crying hysterically, yet couldn't seem to explain what was wrong. She began to miss appointments—not unusual in someone with LD and ADHD, but still...there was something different this time, something almost willful in her disregard, as if she was now purposely avoiding family get-togethers rather than simply forgetting about them, as had happened so often in the past.

It turned out that Alison's new husband was a heavy drug user and convinced her to do the same. She also started using alcohol for the first time.

Over the years Lynn and I had had conversations about the possibility of such a thing happening. We did not actively fear it, but we did have some concerns that our daughters might not be able to resist the temptations that might come their way. Many young people have troubles now and then, but for those with LD, the lure of drugs and alcohol can be particularly strong—not because they have a heightened physical susceptibility to substance abuse but because their desire for acceptance and friendship makes them more susceptible at an emotional level. This is what happened with Alison. Soon after meeting her future husband she fell right into his patterns. In her case (at least in the beginning) it was due more to her desire to fit in and please him rather than a desire to use drugs.

About a year or so after the wedding, the marriage broke up. Alison's drug use tapered off, but her alcohol consumption skyrocketed. Lynn was terrified. This was something completely beyond her experience and brought all sorts of real and imagined dangers. Eventually the family conducted an intervention. They gathered friends and family members together to confront Alison. They did it in a loving but firm way, and persuaded her to go to a rehabilitation center. After rehab, Alison became a member of Alcoholics Anonymous and has been sober for nearly eight years.

The Solution

For me, the words "Alcoholics Anonymous" used to conjure up an image of a group of old men wearing dirty raincoats, sitting in a church basement and mumbling about their terrible lives. I had trouble understanding the actual disease of alcoholism, too! Like many who do not have it, I simply could not understand why someone couldn't have a drink or two and call it a night. Why did they crave more or drink to such an extent that they couldn't function?

I thought it was a matter of willpower. Through Alison, I've learned that it's an actual physical addiction, more like an allergy than anything else. Sober alcoholics have a saying: "A hundred drinks are not enough, and one drink is too many." What they mean is that the first drink sets up a craving, and once they start to satisfy that craving, they simply cannot stop. The trick is to find a way to avoid having that first drink.

I've talked to many knowledgeable people about this and they all come down to the same conclusion: Alcoholics Anonymous is the only long-term solution that seems to work. With this in mind, I sat down and talked to Alison about her experiences. The first thing she did was to correct me on a few erroneous ideas I had about AA.

1. *It's a group made up mostly of old men in raincoats in a basement somewhere, mumbling about their rotten lives.* Not true. Oh, I suppose there must be one or two lurking about, and yes, it's true that many AA meetings are held in church basements; but for the most part, the people who go to AA are leading productive, satisfying lives and come from all walks of life and income levels.

2. *It costs money or there is an initiation fee.* There is no fee and there are no dues. A basket is passed at each meeting and most contribute a dollar. That's all.

3. *It's a religious cult.* They do speak of a "Higher Power," but each individual defines what that is in a personal way. It can be God, it can be the group itself, it can even be a chair or a dog. The point is for the alcoholic to realize that he himself isn't the higher power.

In discussing the positive side of AA (I haven't heard a negative side yet), Alison opened my eyes to the possibilities available to the LD person now addicted to alcohol or drugs. "One of the first and strongest suggestions for anyone coming into AA is to get a sponsor," she said. "A sponsor is someone with a little time under their belt, at least a year."

"Is the sponsor a professional?" I asked, thinking of addiction counselors.

"Not at all! A sponsor is another recovering alcoholic who helps the newcomer to AA stop drinking. Another big part of AA is what we call Fellowship. After every meeting, many of us go to a diner for coffee. Before I had kids I used to do this almost every night! And I have to admit, for someone with LD who had trouble making friends, that was a real godsend. No one ever asked if I had LD. No one cared if I made a mistake reading the menu. The friendships I formed in those days are so strong, much stronger than any friendships I had while I was drinking. They're still my friends today."

I pointed out that the social side of AA is what so many young people with LD or ADHD desire in their lives—friends, companionship, something to do at night, someplace to go.

"That's right!" she said, enthusiastically. "And in my case it led to my second marriage. He's also in the program, and we've been together for six years now, with two children. Things are a whole lot different than in those days when my mother spent every night worried sick about me."

That last remark resonated with me. I can't imagine anything more worrying to a parent than to know your child is out there somewhere, living in the hell of addiction. The sense of helplessness could overwhelm even the strongest of us.

So parents...if your adult child is having trouble with substance abuse of any kind, do not despair. Yes, it's an ordeal—perhaps the most frightening you will ever face; but there is help out there, and it may be closer than you think. Neighbors, friends, coworkers—chances are someone around you knows something about this problem. Contact them. Talk to them. Ask for advice. You may actually find this terrible dark cloud in your child's life bears that silver lining we always hope for but have learned not to expect.

23

Medication and ADHD

Controversy surrounds the use of Ritalin for students with ADHD. I am not going to take sides in this battle except to say that both sides have their points: medication has been a tremendous help for some, and it has caused problems for others. I know a man in his mid-thirties who has experienced both. Everyone in his entire family, both his parents and all his siblings, has diagnosed ADHD. "We never knew why none of us could finish anything," he told me. "We'd start a project or job and stay with it for a while and then lose interest. Finally my brother was tested and found to have ADHD. I got tested, too, and I also had it, and so did everyone else in the family. I take Ritalin, which really helps. The trouble is that it only lasts a certain length of time. After a few months it stops working, and I have to go off it for a couple of months. When I start taking it again, it starts to work again ... and then it wears off. It's a predictable cycle. The problem is, it wreaks havoc with my life. When I'm taking it, my life is pulled together. I get things done. I'm organized. I don't have problems at work. Then I go off it and everything falls apart. By the time I can go back on the medication, I've created such a mess that I have to spend most of my time trying to fix it all again. It's very frustrating!"

Most ADHD medications like Ritalin, Concerta, Focalin, and Adderall are stimulants and are usually the first choice of treatment for adults with ADHD. They affect the regulation of two neurotransmitters, norepinephrine and dopamine. A second choice of treatment is anti-depressants, because they, like the stimulants, affect norepinephrine and dopamine. A new medication called Strattera is not a stimulant and is often prescribed for those who have had problems taking the older ADHD medications.

I first heard of Strattera when I interviewed David Neeleman, CEO of JetBlue Airways. He told me that a young man of his acquaintance named Shawn had started taking it and considers it a wonder drug. I later met Shawn and asked if he would talk to me about his experiences with the medication. At twenty-seven, he has already had a remarkable life, and rather than focus solely on his use of Strattera, I'd like to share more of our conversation. It's an illustration of the challenges faced by some young adults with LD and ADHD. In Shawn's case, it also shows how determination and a positive self-image can help when facing those challenges.

"I grew up in Michigan and had ADHD my entire life," Shawn told me. "I knew it at an early age because my mother got me diagnosed when I was about six years old. But she just couldn't handle it. I was always hyper, I couldn't focus in school. I was put on various medications, but they never worked. My mother actually abandoned me because of it. She had a boyfriend who is now a doctor, and he is the one who really hated the fact that I had ADHD. He would make me sit against a wall for hours, because he would get so angry because I wouldn't sit still.

"When I was ten years old, my mother abandoned me. And I look back . . . you know, I forgive them for everything. I just know they probably have problems of their own, and I can see how hard it must have been for them to have a kid who can't sit still, who's always running all over the place. So when I was ten, I was put into group homes and foster care, and then I dropped out of high school in tenth grade. I couldn't focus. I couldn't sit still. Dealing with people was so hard because I would blurt things out, and I was constantly a laughingstock. I was always ashamed of myself, and this constant shame progressed with me into adulthood. The fact that I was abandoned because of this disorder ruined my entire life."

"Did you question your own intelligence?" I asked, "or did you think of yourself as intelligent, but with problems caused by ADHD?"

"The second. Intelligent, but with problems caused by ADHD. I think my brain counteracted the ADHD in some ways. I believe that happens for most people with ADHD at some level. For me, I had to learn things more quickly than others. I didn't have the ability to sit and pay attention in class or in social situations, and so my brain compensated. I went to college when I was twenty years old, but by then I was already a broken man. And I know it sounds like I'm blaming something. That's a problem with ADHD. You have it, but you can't say everything that goes wrong in your life is because of ADHD. If you do, then people say it's a crutch and that you're blaming your problems on something else."

"That may be true," I said, "but you could also look back and say that your mother abandoned you because of ADHD. It's more than a crutch. It's something real, and in your case, it led to a devastating situation early in your life."

"I guess that's true. Even now as a grown man I still struggle with ADHD, but I've also learned how to compensate for it in many different ways. I dropped out of high school, took the GED, and went to college at twenty years old. I finished in four years with a degree in E-commerce, international business, and Japanese. In college, I struggled a lot, but I also noticed that I was starting to learn things quicker. When I couldn't write a long paper, I would write a short one instead, but a very, very creative and intuitive one. That's what got me through."

"Did you take Ritalin?"

"When I was younger, yes. I took it for a year, but I couldn't deal with it. It overstimulated me. Even worse, it gave me a side effect that resembled Tourette's syndrome. I was in high school. It was awful. My peers shunned me because the drug gave me vocal tics and I made noises. But even with that—and I'm sure a lot of LD people can relate to this—at times you get shunned so much, and you're ashamed of yourself so often, that you reach a point where you don't care anymore. And strange as it sounds, you can find empowerment in simply not caring."

"How old were you when you discovered Strattera?"

"Fairly recently. I had horrible nightmares about Ritalin, so thought that Strattera might be a good alternative. I'd already tried all the other medications, Ritalin, Adderall, all of them. They all had the same effect as Ritalin, but milder. Ritalin was just horrible. Strattera is different than the others. It's a serotonin or neurotonin reuptake inhibitor. It's not a stimulant like the others."

I asked what happened between the time he made the decision to stop taking the Ritalin type of drug and when he started taking Strattera.

"I went to college during that time period," he said, "and in college I was completely unmedicated. I drank a lot, and I also smoked marijuana because it helped alleviate the hyperactivity of ADHD. It helped calm my nerves and let me sit there and study. I would smoke a joint and sit in the same place and write an entire paper."

"So basically you self-medicated. Did that cause any problems for you?"

"Oh, of course!" he said. "The marijuana takes away motivation. And even now, you know, I'm around a lot of big shots with my work, and I feel so small compared to them. I would never mention drinking or marijuana around them, because they wouldn't understand. They came from an environment that was completely different."

"Would you say that even though self-medicating helped in some ways, it still ended up causing more problems than solutions?"

"Absolutely! The drinking caused more problems than the marijuana. I stopped marijuana, but I had to stop drinking, too. I've had a hard time keeping a job because I say things. For instance, I'll be in a meeting, even in my current job, and I'll just blurt stuff out. And I feel vulnerable because I'm constantly open to attack from other employees, especially in a corporate environment. You're vulnerable if you have ADHD. You reveal things about yourself that you shouldn't. You say things that you shouldn't. It's hard for me to sit at my desk and actually work. There are errors in my e-mails. I forget to do things. It's a constant battle. All my life, in high school and college, I've had to work 150 percent harder just to be 80 percent as good as the normal students."

"It sounds like you've had a series of jobs since leaving college."

"Yes. A series of jobs that I couldn't keep. They were good jobs in great companies. Now I'm about to start my own company, which is my solution to this problem. David Neeleman told me that when he got out of college, he was mortified because he believed he'd never be able to keep a job. And it's true! I'm always scared to death I'll lose a job. So my solution was to do what he did, which was start something on his own— because you know what? Even though ADHD has taken away my family, it's taken away my self-respect at certain times, my dignity, I also believe it has given me the gift of creativity. Because your brain is so overstimulated, it gives you the ability to create, and I think that ability is the most powerful thing of all. ADHD has also forced me to be humble, because I realize I'm not as good as others, and that has actually been a strength in my life. I am setting up a social networking website for entrepreneurs with ADD and ADHD called thescatteredbrain.com. There is a kinship among people with these disorders. We feel an affinity for each other because we know how it is. In many ways, in the corporate world, you are shunned if you have any form of LD. But I believe the world was built by creativity. It was built by people with ADHD and LD. Look at Einstein, look at Michelangelo, look at Da Vinci. They all had LD. The goal of thescatteredbrain.com is to harness the strength of a social network of people with ADHD and LD instead of always focusing on it as a debilitating weakness. People who have it start to feel it's a weakness if they hear that all the time, and the self-pity comes in and the self-defeating attitudes."

Turning the conversation back to medication, I asked if he noticed an immediate change after taking Strattera for the first time or if it was a gradual effect.

"Immediate. But I'm also supersensitive to drugs. Doctors tell me I'm not supposed to notice the effect of something for a few weeks, but I'll notice it the next day. That's why I had such a problem with alcohol and drugs. They affected me very quickly and strongly."

"What was the sensation you had when taking Strattera?"

"A focused feeling," he said. "I'm still taking Strattera, but the thing with ADHD is that I forget to take the medication sometimes! And for me the Strattera didn't cure the hyperactivity. I was just prescribed a different drug to calm the central nervous system down a little bit so I'm not fidgeting or going nuts."

"You still have the hyperactivity even when taking Strattera?"

"I do, yes."

"So if you're in a meeting at the office . . ."

"I can focus on what's being said because of the Strattera. Sometimes I hyperfocus where I get a staring-into-space look, or I might look like I'm staring at someone . . . and it bothers people. Bosses have gotten mad about it and asked if I was paying attention. The way I've learned to compensate for that is at meetings I take notes. I sit there and act as the transcriber of the meeting, because that way I can multitask and still hyperfocus, but in ways that don't bother anyone."

"So doing something physical helps with the hyperactivity part, but still allows you to focus."

"Exactly. The problem is that for people with that hyperactivity, even if they take Strattera they still have to take something for the central nervous system. I actually think Strattera makes the hyperactivity more obvious because now you're able to focus, but you're still hyper."

"You said you used to blurt out things at meetings. Does that still go on?"

"Yes, it does. And it does cause problems. It's really tough. In all honesty, *everything* is really tough. I think knowing when to speak or to say nothing can be one of the hardest things to learn in life. There have been times when I have walked out of meetings and gone into the bathroom and cried because I had just embarrassed myself so much. It still happens, at least once a month, where I just break down and cry away from everyone else."

"What type of situation causes the most difficulty for you?"

"Social situations, especially ones that are very formal and proper. I remember I was at a fundraising benefit and a woman asked me a simple question, and I just started going on and on and on about different things, and she was kind of just staring at me ... and then I raised my hand and knocked her wine over. I do that a lot, too. Knocking things over. One time I was having dinner with some really important people, and I said how cool it would be to be Alexander the Great, but the way I said it was like this: 'Yeah, it would be so cool to be Alexander the Great, because he could go into villages and order everyone to be killed.' Everyone sort of stared at me. Of course, I didn't mean it would be cool to kill people—I don't know *what* I meant, but I had just read a history book about Alexander and that was the first thing that popped into my mind. Even so, it was a crazy thing to say in that particular situation."

"Do you think you might be oversensitive to other people's reactions?" I asked. "Do you think people take things much worse than they actually do?"

"I do, yes, and that's gotten pretty bad. It's a sort of emotional defense or maybe it's simply a repercussion from all the times that I actually *do* say things that are pretty bad. I always assume that I'm offending everyone, and I always end up apologizing all the time."

"My daughter, Allegra, does the same thing," I said. "She apologizes for things she has nothing to do with. It's almost a built-in mechanism with her now."

"I think it becomes that way, yes. When I was in the foster-care system, I was eleven years old. I was put in a position where I had to survive by myself, with no one. When I look back and think of all the kids who were in the system, I would have to say that all of them had learning disabilities or ADHD. It's a huge problem in our society. It may be the biggest problem of all. It increases your chance of being a criminal. It increases your chance of engaging in risky behaviors. It increases all of these things. Even for me, when I was young, I always had this love of danger. I loved fighting, because when things were too calm, I needed stimulation, so I'd go and get into some trouble."

"Our prisons are full of people with LD or ADHD," I said. "The same with substance abuse. So much of it comes from self-esteem issues, from the time when they were children and it was hammered into them that they're 'not good enough.' After a while you need to escape from that constant hammering, and sometimes you do it in ways that might not be healthy."

"Even now, when I go out with friends . . . I don't drink anymore, but I go with them to bars after work, and whenever I do, I see that the bars in New York City are full of people with LD and ADHD. They stand out from the crowd, because you know how you act and you know how they act; and you identify it right away. And so many of them end up as heavy drinkers or doing drugs."

"And what now, Shawn?" I asked. "Are there other challenges you feel you need to work on?"

"Relationships," he said without hesitation. "Especially relationships with women. With ADHD, it can be hard. Maybe your wife or girlfriend asks you to do something, and you don't want to do the monotonous things . . . like you don't want to go see the freakin' opera with your girlfriend. You *can't stand* to sit and watch the opera, and so you don't go. But in a normal relationship you have to be unselfish and do those sorts of things. Some problems are caused just by saying the wrong thing to your girlfriend. It's just hard. And women have less ADHD than men. Women are more focused. Well, let's face it. Women are just straight-up better than men, I think."

I, of course, agreed with him wholeheartedly on that. "And what about disclosure?" I asked. "In relationship situations, do you suggest someone discloses early on the fact that they have ADHD or LD? For example, a lot of people advise against disclosure at the workplace, at least not in an interview. But in a relationship, when should someone disclose?"

"I'm not sure I'm the best person to answer that one!" he said. "But as far as the workplace goes, for an adult with ADHD who is having a hard time . . . in the words of my friend David Neeleman, 'find your area of hyperfocus.' That is probably going to be the only solution that will propel you to the place in life where you deserve to be, careerwise. What I'm doing now with my current job is project management, with multi-tasking and constantly moving, which is perfect for me. So project management, sales, art—those are all good jobs for someone with ADHD."

"What would you say to the parent of someone who is thirty years old and can't keep a job? Is there anything that parent might do to help the situation?"

"First of all, if you find out your child has LD, no matter how old they are, you should immediately go to your church or wherever you need to go to find solace and strength. You need to do that because you are going to have to prepare yourself to become an extremely patient person. For some people, patience is not in their personality. So prepare yourself, and know that you are going to have to be super-patient. Second, think of that hyperfocus. With that thirty-year-old who can't keep a job, you can go through their history with them, or work with them and a therapist to help that person find their hyperfocus. Educate yourself on the disability so that *you* are an expert and so that you know more about that learning disability than the average psychiatrist does."

24

The Fine Print

For those with severe LD, the need for academic success can sometimes take a back seat to the more critical need for life skills. We hear that term a lot—life skills—but what does it mean? Subtract everything we associate with employment and school and look at the issues left on the table, mostly involving day-to-day living. Now think of those day-to-day living skills that you take for granted such as paying a bill or taking a bus, and you're closing in on a definition of the life skills that often pose a problem for those with severe LD or ADHD. Some high schools help prepare young adults for life on their own, as do some special programs within a college setting. Most parents can come up with hundreds of situations in which LD or ADHD can have a negative impact, but I'd like to focus on a few that cause trouble in ways we might not expect, especially for young adults newly out on their own.

FINANCE AND DEBT

No matter how long we hold out, sooner or later we all succumb to the lure of technology. Our lives are surrounded by digital buzzes and beeps from the time our alarm clock wakes us up, through our daily routine involving transportation, banking, and restaurants, until we end up back at home, where our computer, phone, television, DVD player, and TiVo system await. These gadgets and services add to our enjoyment of life, but let's face it, they also add an element of frustration. How many times have you been on the phone, following an endless trail of "press two for customer service," only to end up back where you started, or being cut off, or reaching the wrong department. That sense of frustration and helplessness is magnified for those with LD and ADHD.

It's not uncommon to find young adults with severe learning disabilities who thrive on today's technology, particularly the computer and Internet. They are able to solve many of the small computer bugs that drive the rest of us crazy, while at the same time they find themselves unable to figure out how to pay their Internet-service bill.

This inability to handle everyday financial transactions often comes as a surprise or even a shock to parents. Your child has lived with you all his life and now, in his own apartment for the first time, finds himself unprepared for the simplest things—things we assume he should know. But why should he? He gets a credit card in the mail that tells him all he has to do is make a phone call to activate his new account, and off he goes to the mall, thrilled by the notion that he has just been "given" a credit limit of $8,000 with an interest rate of 22 percent for purchases and 29 percent for cash advances. He soon reaches his limit and can't figure out why the amount he owes doesn't go down even though he's been paying the minimum every month. But look! Another card has arrived in the mail, and this one has checks that the company claims can be used "just like a regular bank check" for anything he wants— iPods, computers, clothes, or even a cash advance up to a limit of $7,000. Now he has $13,000 in debt and two monthly minimum payments to make, and he still can't figure out why the balance isn't going down. And on it goes . . .

People *without* LD get into situations like this all the time, so it's not surprising to find a young man or woman with disabilities sinking lower and lower into debt. Parents can perform a huge service for their children by simply explaining the mechanics of credit cards and debt. Here's a quick way to do that:

Credit Cards vs. Debit Cards

There are several versions of the little plastic cards that can cause such havoc.

Credit cards such as VISA or Mastercard allow you to pay for items or services by borrowing against a line of credit and making monthly payments on the outstanding balance. The opportunities for getting in trouble are substantial with this type of card.

Charge cards like American Express look like a credit card and can be used like a credit card, but there is a difference. Instead of paying over time, a charge card requires total payment of the outstanding balance every month. In general, these are safer than credit cards because it's more difficult to pile up debt over time.

Debit cards, also called ATM cards, allow you to get cash directly from your bank account. You can also use these cards to make purchases, once again drawing the funds directly from your bank.

Store charge cards are credit cards specific to a store. These should be avoided whenever possible as the interest rates are usually well above average. There's also the hard sell to consider. Many retail sales representatives are given incentives to sign you up, so it's in their interest to offer a deal that sounds too good to be true.

My strong recommendation for young adults with LD is to stick with debit cards and charge cards, and whenever possible avoid the use of credit cards—especially those from a store.

Interest Rates

Turn a credit card bill over and take out your reading glasses along with a magnifying glass to look at the tiny, very fine light-gray print on the back. Credit card companies don't want you to read this. Much of it is legal language designed to confuse, and you shouldn't even try to explain it all to your son or daughter. You're really only looking for one thing at this point: the interest rate.

Anything approaching the 20 percent range is considered high. Cash advances nearly always have a higher rate than purchases.

If a card has a rate of 23.99 percent and someone charges $1,000 and only pays the minimum payment due each month, by the time they get it down to $0 they will have paid nearly $600 in interest (over half of what the purchased item cost!). It will also take over six years to pay it off. A card with a lower interest rate of 9.9 percent requires interest payments of $176 over the same six years, saving over $400.

If your son or daughter is in a financial hole, you can help sort through the tangled rules and penalties involving interest rates and late fees. It's tedious and sometimes complicated, but it pays to read the fine print!

Easy Targets

Many young people buy goods and services over the Internet, usually through the use of a credit card. The potential for identity theft is increased—we all know that—but rather than push for your adult child to end all online purchases, you can explain the dangers of identity theft and the benefits of countering it with a credit card with a maximum upper limit. Most online purchases are well below the $1,000 range, so a card that can only be used up to $1,000 allows for the freedom of buying online but also prevents enormous losses, should it be stolen.

Another very important warning for everyone is to never—*never*—give out the PIN number to your checking account. "Who would?" you might ask. A friend of mine showed me an e-mail he received from eBay, the online auction company. It was a form asking for information to update his profile. He started to fill it out, dutifully giving his name, address, the number of his checking account . . . but he hesitated before writing down his PIN number. He had never been asked that before. He wrote a letter to Ebay, and they responded with a letter telling him of a scam making the rounds. Those unfortunates who fell for it had their checking accounts wiped out. The trouble was, the form created was so well done it looked exactly like the forms used by Ebay. The return address was also listed as ebay.com.

My friend is very astute, yet he nearly gave the thieves the keys to his financial holdings. What would happen to those with LD in a similar situation? Do they have the wherewithal to notice the very subtle signs that something is wrong?

Most parents would agree when I say that our adult children with LD or ADHD are "easy targets." Many have a naiveté that is quite charming in most circumstances but can raise alarm bells for parents when they think of their children let loose in a world of predatory sharks.

How about phone solicitations, for instance? Most of us are pretty good about sifting through the calls we receive, and are quite adept at refusing the offered time-share in the Bahamas or the "way to save you money" from the phone company, which invariably costs more than what you're paying now. Can your son or daughter do the same? Are they equipped to say no to the pleasant person on the other end of the line who *assures* them that if they'll only agree to this pricing package, their phone bill or electric bill will go down, or that the magazine they've never once read in their lives is now somehow vital to their very existence?

Many states have Do Not Call lists. By putting your name and number (and your child's name and number) on the list, you are shielded from the majority of phone solicitations.

It's difficult to know when and how far to get involved in issues like phone or credit card bills, or even apartment leases; but if your child is willing, I strongly suggest taking the time to go over your child's finances with him or her. Small problems have a way of escalating into tremendous headaches. Arlyn Roffman, in her book *Meeting the Challenge of Learning Disabilities in Adulthood*, told of a young man who didn't understand that the letters CR on a bill meant Credit. He paid the CR amount over and over, without understanding why his bill kept going up each month. Before long he was spending all his money on that one bill while neglecting others.

A simple word of advice and explanation from a parent would have ended it all in less than a minute.

FROM HERE TO THERE: GETTING AROUND

Another daily activity that can cause a lot of trouble for those with LD or ADHD is the simple act of getting from here to there. We've already talked about the problem of time management and how much of it is wrapped up in the physical necessity of commuting to a job by car or on public transportation. If your son or daughter comes to you for advice, you can help them work out a timetable and suggest how to compensate for things such as traffic and weather.

Most of the time, this will be enough. For instance, if your son needs to take two buses to get to work, you can help him settle on that particular route and be fairly certain he'll follow it with little or no difficulty. The problems come when he has to go somewhere else and follow a different route.

Many young people with LD or ADHD thrive on a routine. By doing the same thing the same way day after day, they minimize uncertainty in their lives. Troubles can occur when they are confronted by a situation that forces them to break out of their routine.

An example: I know of a young man who travels the same way every day to work in New York City, by taking a certain subway that leaves from Grand Central Station. This works out fine at the beginning of his workday, but on most afternoons he is required to make deliveries in various parts of the city. Instead of looking at the subway map and figuring out a circular route that will take him from point A to point B to point

C, he creates his own route that looks more like the spokes of a wheel. He goes from his office to Grand Central, a route he knows well and which we'll call point A. From there he goes to point B, but instead of continuing on to point C, he returns to A and *then* goes to C. From there he goes back to A before finding his way to D, so instead of moving in a logical way from A to B to C, he goes from A to B to A to C to A to D, and adds anywhere from an hour to two hours to his delivery time.

If this happened only once a month or so, it wouldn't be an issue; but on a daily basis, the time wasted due to his inability to read the subway map not only increases his frustration but could eventually threaten his job. Bus maps and train schedules can be intimidating (just ask anyone trying to get around in an unfamiliar city), but taking a little time to help your son or daughter understand at least the main routes within their city can save them a great deal of trouble. They don't need to know every route—only the ones they are likely to take.

The same applies for those who drive. If they follow only one route day after day, that's fine—unless that one route brings them over the mountain and through the woods and adds twenty minutes to what should be only a ten-minute drive if they went another way.

The attachment of some with LD toward their own particular routine can be strong, so be forewarned! I have seen this firsthand. Not long ago, Allegra and I went to a restaurant in Boston. Her gym was across the street. I asked if we could go look at it, and instead of simply crossing the street, she insisted on going all the way down to the crosswalk she usually takes and then walking all the way back up to the place directly across from where we started.

I didn't say anything, because I knew the route she wanted to take was her usual one and the one that made most sense from her apartment. But if you see these kinds of obvious inconveniences in your child's daily life, help them fine-tune their routine to make things a little easier. I hesitated before including this chapter, especially as the issues seemed so trivial when compared to health problems or substance abuse or estate planning; but as the whole purpose of this book is to help our adult children make it in this world "on their own," we sometimes have to take a close look at the fine print.

25

Estate Planning

Sooner or later the subject of estate planning becomes one of the most important subjects of all, for it influences how our adult children live after we are no longer around to protect them. Those of us whose adult children have severe learning disabilities need to be able to answer the following questions:

> Do you know the difference between a will and a trust?
>
> Have you written a Letter of Intent?
>
> What is a Special Needs Trust?

If you had trouble answering any of these, read on.

OUR OLD FRIEND DENIAL

Few of us harbor the wholly irrational belief that we'll be around forever. We know we're not immortal, but you'd never know that from the way some of us refuse to plan for the future. The idea of leaving our child behind is such a painful subject that we simply tuck it away in the back of our minds.

This is denial's last stand in a parent's life. It first came when we discovered our child had LD. "It will go away," we said, or "She's just immature, she'll grow out of it." Denial stayed with us through our child's school years and told us she would be able to go on to the college we wanted her to attend, and denial followed us when she entered the workforce to tell us she could get a job far beyond her abilities. Now here it is again, telling us not to worry about the future because things will work out if we don't think about it.

You *do* need to think about it. Denial about your own mortality can have detrimental consequences that last long after you (whether you like it or not) have left this mortal sphere.

There is a great deal of sentiment and emotion wrapped up in this issue. They do have a place in this discussion, but let's set them aside for now and talk about the cold, unsentimental legalisms necessary to ensure a secure and comfortable life for your child.

To help me with this I spoke to John Langeler, a financial manager and father of a disabled son, who first explained to me the difference between a will and a Special Needs Trust.

THE DIFFERENCE BETWEEN A WILL AND A SPECIAL NEEDS TRUST

A will is a disbursement of your assets after you are gone. Sounds simple, right? You die, your estate is divided up according to your wishes, with your disabled son or daughter getting enough to live on (hopefully) for the remainder of their lives. Wills can be contested, which means another relative could block the disbursement of those assets until a court settles the matter. You can tell yourself that such a thing would never happen in your family; but even if you are right and no one would ever dream of contesting your will, there remains a much greater threat to your disabled child.

John Langeler explained it this way: "If you leave your disabled child more than $2,000 in assets, they can't get any government benefits like Supplemental Income or the more important medical benefits of Medicaid. There could be no need for the medical benefits, or there could someday be a bottomless pit of medical needs. We never know what kind of medical expenses will be needed down the road, no matter how healthy our adult children are today. With my son, I had to make sure we set up a trust that made sure we got through all the government issues. The child has to have less than $2,000 in assets. They are entitled to earn $500 a month, but they can't earn more than that."

John set up a Special Needs Trust for his son. True to its name, this type of trust is designed specifically for disabled relatives of the deceased. Unlike a will, it can and should be made irrevocable, which means that it can't be undone. It can't be contested or get all wrapped up in legal difficulties. The assets in the trust are technically not your disabled child's assets (thereby keeping their assets under that important figure of $2,000).

"Because he doesn't have the $2,000 in assets, he's eligible for all of the government benefits," John said. "If he gets to a point where he needs Assisted Living, the trust would supplement that. The trust can supplement whatever the government has available. Let's say you have a daughter with disabilities and she is currently a beneficiary of your estate. Whether you have five dollars or five million dollars in assets, your daughter has to *stop* being a beneficiary because she cannot directly have those assets. She has to have access to them through the trust. And you can put two dollars in the trust or fifty million dollars in the trust. There is no limit on how much it can hold. The trust can provide housing, it can provide all those things. Her lifestyle can be maintained quite handily; but regardless of the amount you leave behind in assets, you have got to make sure that your disabled child does not directly get any of it. The trust gets it. You also need to draft in something that stipulates what happens to the money when it is no longer needed. If you put a lot of money in the trust and the child lives a good long life and then there's still money left over, there has to be an indication of what happens to the money after the disabled person's death. I have it set up so that it all eventually reverts to my disabled son's siblings and all the nieces and nephews."

You can also set aside funds within the trust to benefit others in the family. For example, if the disabled child has a sibling still in school, his education and living expenses can be paid for by the trust until he leaves school or reaches a certain age. After that, you could set it up so that the funds once again revert back entirely for the benefit of the disabled child. These additional disbursements must be specified by you at the time you set up the trust.

SETTING UP A SPECIAL NEEDS TRUST

Parents can set up a Special Needs Trust in a number of ways. Nearly every major brokerage firm has Special Needs financial advisers, and most law firms will have a lawyer who can set one up for you. The legal work costs about $1,000 to $2,000. This amount may be out of range for some, but families without the means need not go through a brokerage firm. You can do something as simple as take out a life insurance policy and make the trust the beneficiary of that policy. The cost of these policies rises as you get older (a good reason to start the process as soon as possible!), but a couple in their twenties with a disabled child can buy a very large life insurance policy for a relatively low amount of money. And remember, even with the insurance policy, the beneficiary *must* be the trust or the disabled child has a problem because it puts them over the $2,000 limit.

I run the risk of irritating some of you by harping on that $2,000, but it may be the most important factor of all in estate planning for a disabled adult. Some experts go so far as to advise parents with a will to disinherit their disabled child completely, just to make sure they stay beneath that figure.

"Disinheriting a disabled child sounds so cold and dispassionate," John says, "but it isn't. You can leave the child something in a will as a token gesture, but if you leave them over $2,000 in *total* assets, they are out of luck. If you die and leave them even $3,000 in cash, they are automatically disqualified from government benefits. What could be colder than that? Even more, the government can look back. So let's say the adult child was given $10,000 through a will and they spent it, and now they're below $2,000 in assets. The government could theoretically go back, so if the child had those assets for two or three years, he could be disqualified until that time forward. It's retroactive. In other words, if you leave them $10,000, you remove their eligibility until they've spent that money, plus that time added on again because the government looked back."

These strict rules were created because too many people were playing games with trusts. For every IRS agent who is trying to get your money there are fifteen lawyers trying to make sure they don't. Lawyers are always inventing new schemes and then laws get passed to knock them out. John Langeler advises parents to have their Special Needs Trust reviewed every three to five years because every time a new law gets passed, things change. When creating the trust, you should also stipulate what happens to the money after the disabled person's death. At that point you can set it up so the money reverts to other family members or whomever else you wish to include.

Choosing the Trustees

The money in a Special Needs Trust is disbursed to the disabled individual by trustees. They can disburse it for lots of things—vacations, cars, whatever the disabled person needs—but it has to be disbursed by the trustees.

A sibling of the disabled person can act as a single trustee, but parents should be wary of this. Estate planning in general should not be set up as the moral obligation of a sibling. You might think that it's perfectly fine, and even preferable, to make out a will that leaves everything to a nondisabled child with the understanding they will look after their disabled sibling. We may be thoroughly convinced that this nondisabled sibling will gladly and without reservation take care of their disabled brother or sister; but if that sibling happens to die, you now have heirs in charge of the money—heirs who may or may not care one bit about their disabled uncle or aunt. The nondisabled sibling could get divorced, too, and a morally obligated responsibility is part of the marital estate, so the money intended for a disabled sibling could be lost in a divorce settlement.

With a Special Needs Trust, as mentioned, the money is far more protected than it is in a will. Anyone can be set up to act as trustee, such as a sibling, a family friend, or a lawyer. I've already suggested that parents should be wary of setting it up with a sibling as the single trustee . . . but note that word "single."

Ideally, there should be more than one trustee, in which case it is perfectly fine that one or even two of them are siblings of the disabled person. John Langeler suggests setting up the trust with three trustees. "Having only one trustee can cause problems," he says, "especially if that person is a family member. No matter how much they may love their brother or sister, if they fall into hard times, they'll find a way to get the money. You can easily imagine someone in a family who is a trustee saying to their disabled brother, 'You need to get around, so I'm going to buy a new Ferrari with this money and drive you everywhere you need to go.' The opposite of that situation can also occur with the trustee refusing to disburse the money based on a whim. That person can say to the disabled adult, 'No, you don't need that,' and there's nothing that can be done about it."

If you *do* decide to designate only one trustee, it should be someone who is not personally involved and whose focus is exclusively on the welfare of the child, like a bank trust department. By taking it out of the family, you take the emotion out of it.

John also cautioned against the use of only two trustees. "With two, there is always the potential for a fifty-fifty battle over various issues such as how and when the money should be disbursed, or what it's disbursed for. Three is best. One gives a single person too much freedom. Two gets you a fight. Three solves problems."

The trust takes care of everything the disabled adult child may need, and that includes things like vacations. If the disabled adult goes to the trustees and says they want to go to Florida for two weeks, the trustees can't say, "I'm sorry, that's not part of the deal." It *is* part of the deal. The trust can be used for anything the adult child needs to maintain a normal life, but at the same time the trustees can also use their judgment. For example, if the disabled person comes to them and says they want to vacation in Florida, that's fine—but if they also say they want to pay for airfare and all expenses for the four friends they just met last week, the trustees can decide together whether to release the money. The trust is a legal document, and the trustees are responsible for what happens to it. They have to sign on the last page, and their signature is witnessed and notarized.

You can also set up a clause in the Special Needs Trust that stipulates a successorship of trustees, thereby ensuring there will always be three. If one resigns or dies, the remaining two can settle on a successor.

Even with three trustees, parents may want to make sure that at least one of them is someone from outside the family. If all three trustees are siblings or other family members, we can envision a situation where one of them happens to get into severe financial constraints at some point in time, and goes to the other trustees and says, "Hey look, I know this is for our brother, but I really need . . ." and so on. You need at least one trustee who is dispassionate about the situation.

LETTER OF INTENT

Trustees—especially those all-important dispassionate ones—should know something more about your disabled adult than the fact that every once in a while they will need money. A Letter of Intent accomplishes this. It is a living document, written by the parent and revised from time to time while the parent is alive. Essentially it's a letter about your disabled child. It puts a human face on that person by answering questions like Who is this person? What do they like? What don't they like? It can list simple things like hobbies and favorite foods. It could also talk about known medical issues, and list the names and locations of their doctors and dentists.

The Letter of Intent lies halfway between the legal planning for a trust and the purely emotional side of estate planning and where we find the softer, human components often neglected in the bank or law office.

THE EMOTIONAL SIDE OF ESTATE PLANNING

A doctor once told me that the person who best takes the news that a long illness is probably terminal is the one who has that illness. The spouse and children and other family members take it the hardest. I think that's the case with parents of disabled children and adults. We don't worry so much about our own mortality, but we care deeply about our children's reaction to it. We wonder how in the world they will cope with the loss of the person who has always been there and done the most for them all their lives.

There's no getting away from it: they will be devastated, of course. What is not always so clear is how they will handle that grief and how they will manage their new life without you.

Many adults with LD are not able to fully comprehend the meaning and reality of death. What happens to Mom or Dad? Where do they go? They often ask such questions in hope of receiving a concrete answer, for that is what they deal with best. But how can we be concrete about what is unknowable?

Faith plays a large role in dealing with death. Not every family has it. Those who do, find comfort in their beliefs, but even those with no religious tradition should find comforting ways to talk about mortality with their disabled adult children. Focus on things that tell them they will not be abandoned. If talk about guardian angels does it, that's fine; but you need not go into the spirit realm to provide comfort. Simply letting young adults know that *someone* will be there for them after you have gone can be enough.

My daughter was abandoned by her father, but she was devastated when he recently died. Her way of dealing with it was to create the "perfect father" in her memories. She has put up pictures of him everywhere and is now making a collage of their life together—father and daughter. It helps her deal with the situation, so I'm all for it.

In years past, at the loss of others she cherished, she created a fantasy where that particular loved one would join the others for lunch in heaven. I think she got the image from a restaurant frequented by her grandmother. It may seem like an obvious fantasy, but I wouldn't dream of tarnishing it in any way. In fact, I first broached the subject of my own death by telling her how excited I'm going to be to sit down with my mother and order a salad and a glass of wine from the angel waiter...assuming they allow wine up there. "And everyone will be looking down at you and smiling," I told her, and that's what she latched on to.

Such simple images may change as your young adult gets older, but whether or not they still believe in angels, it will comfort them no end to know that you will still be there to take care of them, even after you've gone.

PART VI

Interviews: Advice for Parents from Prominent People with LD

Introduction

Betsy Morris

I first met Anne Ford at a dinner for the Lab School—a school for LD in Washington, D.C.—and though I barely knew her, I admired her drive. She too had an LD child, and she was pouring her energy into helping others grapple with the painful struggles I dealt with daily. She was then the chairman of the National Center for Learning Disabilities. I was a senior writer for *Fortune* magazine, there to meet John Chambers for a story I was doing on dyslexic business leaders. My story, "The Dyslexic CEO," ran on the cover of *Fortune* the following May. Anne would go on to write *Laughing Allegra* and begin work on her new book. It never occurred to me that our paths would cross again. Then, out of the blue, I was flattered by a call from her asking if I would write an introduction to a section of her new book. After reading my *Fortune* story, she said, she too had become fascinated with the success stories of Charles Schwab, John Chambers, Richard Branson, and others who had not only overcome their learning differences but had gone on to soar in their careers. She wanted to know what advice they could offer parents about how to help their own children overcome their learning challenges.

What follows is the advice of the very best experts. These men have not only lived with LD, they've learned how to make the most of it. Some, like Charles Schwab and JetBlue CEO David Neeleman, are also parenting their own kids through it. Their stories are breathtaking, especially when you consider all they've accomplished. Charles Schwab pioneered the discount brokerage business, making the world of investing accessible not just to the very wealthy, but to most Americans. John Chambers built one of the world's most successful and enduring tech giants on his unique ability to predict just how the Internet Age was

Journalist Betsy Morris won a Luce Award for Public Service for her article "The Dyslexic CEO," which appeared in the May 16, 2002, issue of *Fortune* magazine. She is currently a Senior Writer for *Condé Nast Portfolio*.

likely to unfold. The advice you will hear in the following pages is bet-ter than 100 lectures about how to parent an LD child. It can provide a road map. It can give you hope.

As I have become familiar with the following stories, I have become convinced that LD does not have to be the grim life sentence it first appears. In many of these cases and others, it can turn out to be just the opposite—a gift, bringing with it wisdom, compassion, and its own kind of brilliance. What I discovered in my own research and what I hear again in the following interviews has made me a true believer in—well, let's call it the silver lining of dyslexia. These business leaders succeed-ed not by doing things the easy and obvious way. Often they don't even see the easy and obvious. Rather, they take out-of-the-box approaches and invent creative solutions to problems. Because they'd struggled so much along the way, they are often unusually patient and empathetic—qualities that enable them to be especially effective with their customers and their employees.

In the following interviews, you will hear that self-esteem is critical. These business leaders will tell you firsthand how important it is for par-ents to believe—truly believe—in the worth and talents of a dyslexic child, even when nobody else does. That becomes so much easier as you read each of these interviews, because they reveal an end game that is so much more promising than most of us thought. In the stories of Charles Schwab, Richard Branson, and David Neeleman, the patterns became crystal clear. These kids are late bloomers. They follow their own timetables. They won't necessarily shine in school. As Gaston Caperton tells Anne: "I always graduated from every school I went to, though my mother said it was always a photo finish." He would go on to serve as the governor of West Virginia and is now the president of the College Board.

These kids gain momentum and confidence once they get past all those school requirements that weigh them down and are able to focus on the areas in which they excel. That's why these men are adamant that parents move heaven and earth to enable their LD offspring to pur-sue a passion—any passion. That passion often becomes a job, a career. And that career can lead to greatness. Often, Charles Schwab and oth-ers point out, this means a parent must let go of preconceived notions about getting top grades or pursuing a conventional career path. The point is not Harvard. The point is enabling your LD children to be the best they can be at whatever they choose. As David Neeleman tells Anne: "I keep telling [parents], 'Your kids are going to be more successful than you are, if you just get off their back."

Self-knowledge is absolutely critical to success. Each of these men succeeded because they were way smarter than most people about figuring out their strengths and weaknesses, accepting them, and organizing their lives accordingly. Because these guys have lived it, because they speak with authority, they can change the way you and your children think about LD, and that can change your lives. Truly. I know, because that's what happened in our household. Thanks to the stories that follow, our sixteen-year-old son no longer believes he has a "rotten brain." He knows he's dyslexic, which, to him, currently means he's really good at the violin but has tremendous headaches with math. It means he must work twice as hard and twice as long as most of his classmates. That's frustrating, even maddening, but it's better than being stupid. He'll work hard and he'll try anything. He believes that if he works hard enough, and if we help find the right teacher, eventually he'll get it. Self-knowledge, it seems, is the key to finding the silver lining in LD, and the stories that follow can help get you there.

Sir Richard Branson
Chairman and CEO, Virgin Group

For those who have somehow missed hearing about this "Rebel Billionaire," as he was known on a television show with the same title, Sir Richard Branson is the chairman and CEO of the Virgin Group. The company started with Virgin Records but has expanded to include international music Megastores, Virgin Atlantic Airlines, mobile, financial, retail, music, and Internet services, rail lines, hotels, and resorts, with over 200 companies in over 30 countries. Sir Richard is renowned as an adventurous businessman, but his taste for adventure doesn't stop there. He's also undertaken several record-breaking hot-air balloon voyages over oceans and continents, and orchestrated a nonstop balloon trip around the world.

We met in New York, where he had come to participate in a conference focusing on AIDS in Africa (charities and world health issues are another passion). I suppose part of me wondered if he might show up wearing a balloonist's helmet and goggles, so I was a bit surprised to be greeted by a tall, very handsome man wearing a blazer with the insignia of his investiture into knighthood on the lapel—an English gentleman, relaxed and confident, with nothing stuffy or formal about him, yet so soft-spoken he comes across as a little shy at first.

I first asked him about his reputation as a rebel and if he thought having LD had anything to do with it.

"My learning disabilities are rather mild," he said, "but I certainly didn't feel they were mild when I was in school. Back then, I would look at an exam paper and it might as well have been upside down. I struggled with everything in school—crosswords, IQ tests, everything. I was absolutely hopeless."

"Did you know something was wrong?"

"No, I just thought I was stupid. And I happen to have bad eyesight as well, and that was my other excuse. I had bad eyesight and I thought I was stupid, so quite early on I had to compensate for it."

Most people with LD learn to compensate, and I wondered how he did it.

"I would push myself into things I was good at," he said. "Fortunately, I excelled at sports and became the captain of all the sport teams. I was lucky also that I was physically capable of that. I really thought that sport would be my life, but one day I was on the football field and heard this almighty scream and then, when I found myself buckled up in agony on the ground, I realized it was *me*. That was the end of my sporting career. I was only nine or ten years old, and I was carried off the field. So now I had no academic career ahead of me, and I certainly didn't have a sporting career ahead of me.

"It was at that stage that I started looking at the way we're taught at school. And I started to question whether it was a matter of me being stupid or if there was actually a better way of motivating and teaching people than the conventional way. I decided that there was a better way. I noticed that people could spend years and years learning French at school, yet nobody ended up leaving school being able to speak French. Or why are we spending hours and hours on Latin when it would only be of use for a very few people?"

Most students with LD have occasional thoughts about the structure of education, but generally these thoughts are fleeting and short-lived attempts to explain their own difficulties. They are usually overwhelmed by a second, stronger thought that it's not the school's fault but their own. I asked Richard about his parents and if they backed him up in his questioning the manner of his schooling. "Did they help you by giving advice or pushing you in any way?"

"Encouragement, yes. I always had an extremely loving background, with tons of encouragement, and lots of praise and very little criticism. That was an extremely important part of my upbringing, I think."

"Did they back you up when you questioned the school?"

"They were certainly very supportive. And I felt strongly enough about it that in my later school years, while other people were playing games, I decided to start a magazine to deal with all these issues. Writing was difficult for me, so I decided the way to overcome it was for me to buy a couple of tape recorders and go and interview lots of eloquent people who could speak well. And then in the magazine, I could write down what they said word for word. I obviously had the power of persuasion because I used the telephone and rang up Vanessa Redgrave and Jean-Paul Sartre and people like that."

"Did they all agree to see you?"

"Maybe one out of nine, but I phoned a lot of people. Sometimes I used other methods. When someone like the writer James Baldwin arrived from America, rather than ring him up, I'd go bang on his hotel door." He pointed at my recorder on the table. "In those days we didn't have small tape recorders like this one. They were three-foot by three-foot reel-to-reel, and I lugged this enormous tape recorder up to his hotel room, and because the plugs were always different, I would have these two leads, and I'd have sparks flying everywhere as I was trying to get the plug in to get the interview going. My interview with James Baldwin ended up being a tirade against this particular white man rather than white people as a whole."

"How old were you when you started the magazine?"

"At first I was just pulling it together, so it was all talk, and I was getting lots of interviews together. And then, at about age fifteen, I went to the headmaster and told him I was going to leave school to start this magazine. I wanted to use the magazine to put the world right. It was the time of Vietnam, the time of Biafra and students marching in the streets. I already knew I was a hopeless case as far as school was concerned."

"What was his reaction?"

"I first asked him if I could run the magazine out of the school and he said, 'No, you've got to either do your schoolwork or the magazine. You can't do both.' And I said, 'Well, if that's really what you think, I'm going to leave and do the magazine.' His parting words were, 'Branson, you're either going to go to prison or become a millionaire.'"

FIND OUT WHAT YOU LOVE TO DO

Richard, at age fifteen, was already a rebel. I wondered about his parents and how they reacted to his leaving school. I know I would have reacted very badly and would have done everything I could to keep my children in school until graduation. But what happens if your son or daughter is determined, and backs up that determination with a strong passion?

"We walked around the garden quite a few times," Richard told me, "but in the end my dad said, 'Look, you already know what you want to do. Most people don't know what they want to do when they're in their twenties, so give it a go. And if it doesn't work out, we'll try to get you back into an education again.'"

"And how have the learning disabilities affected your life since that time?"

"As far as ways to compensate for being mildly dyslexic, any time I have a conversation with people, I take notes. I'm quite good at simplifying things, too, which has been very good for business. For example, when I do interviews on television or when I'm launching a new business, or we go into the financial services industry, we don't use jargon. We tell people clearly what we're talking about. Hopefully, we don't talk over people's heads. I've also found that in the real world, once I've found something that really interests me, I can grasp things pretty quickly. I think a lot of the problems people have is just the way they are taught at school. I really think it's disgraceful. I thought it when I was in school and I still think it today."

The importance of parental encouragement and of following your interests are common themes of every interview I've conducted. I pointed this out to him and said, "The problems come when kids are forced into something they don't like, either by the school or parents. I suppose that would be the case for anyone, but it seems particularly to be a problem for people with LD."

Richard agreed. "And you don't want to push people above what they are capable of," he said. "You can get enormous pleasure from being a nanny, if that's what you really like to do. You can get enormous pleasure from things that some people would look down on a bit. And if some people have trouble grasping certain things, you want to make sure they've still got something that really satisfies them."

"Exactly," I said. "And an unfortunate reality in much of today's society is that a lot of professional people do not realize that the very jobs they look down on are filled by people who happen to love their work. That's why I tell parents not to denigrate their child's desires—if your son really wants to be a motorcycle mechanic instead of a doctor, so what? That's fine. I've also met a lot of parents whose adult children have a hard time finding work, or once they get a job, they have a real hard time adjusting to it. Some just give up completely. They can't find a job and so they don't look for a job. They fall into a malaise of sorts. Do you have any words for somebody in that situation?"

He looked out the window, thinking. After a long pause, he said, "I don't think you have to be dyslexic or have a learning disability to dislike a job. There are lots and lots of people who are unhappy with their work. If you can't get satisfaction from one job, then try something different. As long as you've given it your best shot, you shouldn't be depressed about it. There are millions of people doing things they are not happy doing, and sometimes the brave thing to do is to break away and try something different. But obviously, if you're keeping on and on at something, and you are still unsatisfied, then maybe you have to ask yourself if you are making the best effort. Jobs are people. And how you deal with people and how you relate to people is the key."

"Yes, but one of the troubles is that sometimes people with learning disabilities have a hard time dealing with people."

"Yes, that's true."

This brought on another thoughtful pause, as though the realities of LD had somehow contradicted his set of optimistic beliefs.

"What about you?" I asked. "When did you realize that you weren't really stupid but that you had dyslexia?"

"I suppose I realized it when I noticed that when I was doing something that interested me, I had little trouble grasping it. But even then, I had difficulty with some things. I've told this story before, but right up until I was fifty years old and operating the biggest group of private companies in Europe, I had a complete blockage on the difference between the words *net* and *gross*. I could not work out the difference between the two, and for a long time nobody would dare admit that they knew I had no idea what they were talking about. Finally one or two people started saying, 'That's good news, Richard' or 'That's bad news, Richard.' Just after my fiftieth birthday, a friend of mine sat me down and said, 'Let's see if we can help you here. Let's say we're fishing, and you throw your net into the ocean and then you pull in the net. The fish that are left inside is the money we've got at the end of the year, or Net. All the rest is Gross.' And I finally got it."

I told him of a young businessman I know who has ADD. He runs five separate small companies and told me that he would find it impossible to focus on one company alone. I wondered if it was the same for Richard. "Do you like to be involved in all those different businesses, or is it the same situation as my friend, that one alone doesn't really hold your attention?"

"I just love learning about new things and love meeting new people. So if you look at most big brands...Ford specializes in cars, Nike in shoes, Coca-Cola in soft drinks, Microsoft in computers. Virgin is more a way-of-life brand, and that's because I'm fascinated by people and fascinated about learning about things. I've also never seen it as a business. I see it as exploring life and seeing if we can do things better than the way it's been done before, and creating things we can be proud of. If they pay the bills, so much the better. And of course, one thing leads on to another. I'm also terrible at saying no, so we've got new ideas and new projects all the time. In fact, my nickname at the office is 'Dr. Yes' because I say yes to everything."

"When did you decide to go public with having mild dyslexia?"

"I have friends whose kids are dyslexic, and it helped them to know that I had my own problems, and get my words wonderfully muddled up—sometimes on television. You never know when it's going to happen. It definitely encouraged my friend's kids, so I then thought I would go public with it. I know it has helped encourage other kids."

FIND THE RIGHT KIND OF PEOPLE TO WORK WITH

I believe that a great part of Richard's success is his genuine curiosity about people. In this next exchange, watch how he slowly shifts the focus of the interview away from him around toward me and my daughter. Unlike so many others in a similar situation, he didn't do this to avoid my questions, but because he was truly interested.

He started by saying, "I understand that there are different levels of dyslexia or LD. For instance, I'm sure your daughter has a very tough side of learning disabilities."

"Yes, she's got the worst side."

"But even then, she's got something she's good at?"

"She has figure skating. But right now she's going through a hard time trying to find a job. I think it's because she feels so inadequate."

"Can she afford not to work?"

"She can, and she knows that."

"Well, you know, work is not the be-all and end-all if you can afford not to work."

"But then do *something*. Take a part-time job. Volunteer somewhere. I tell her that I don't care what she does, but do something."

"Yes, that's true. So what could she do?"

"At the moment she's even given up her skating. At one time she taught young children how to skate. She's lucky in that she doesn't have much of a problem with social skills, which is the number-one problem for people at her level. She needs somebody—not me—but somebody to help her get out there and get going. I think that happens a lot. Parents may have a thirty-five-year-old son living at home who has no friends and can't keep a job."

"And if they haven't got any money, that's really tough, isn't it?"

"Of course, yes. Sometimes the parents can't support them and it's a very difficult situation. But at the same time, you have to have some motivation. You have to want to go out and get a job. The problem is, sometimes these adults with LD have been pounded again and again with defeat and failure, starting in school."

"Right. And at school, they just think they're stupid. This may not be right for your daughter, but for someone else, working at a hospital in Africa could be a wonderful experience. It's on my mind right now because I'm in New York attending a conference where we're trying to figure out a way to use entrepreneurial skills to help address the AIDS and malaria problem. In Africa, there are sixteen thousand people dying of AIDS every day, and it's growing. We need young people to help administer the tests. We need an army of people to help keep these people from dying. For some people—it could be, that if they could have a purpose in life where they could help other people, they might get enormous satisfaction from that."

"And that's what you would advise parents to focus on when they are trying to help their adult children with LD?"

"Yes. There's no point in doing something you're not equipped for, but if you can find the right kind of people you like to deal with or work with, it can make for a very satisfying life."

Gaston Caperton

President, College Board, former Governor of West Virginia

I first met Governor Caperton in the mid-1990s. He had just finished two terms as governor of West Virginia, where he built a reputation for aggressive reform and improvement of the education system. He then went to the John F. Kennedy School of Government and then to Columbia University, where, along with Governor Tom Kean of New Jersey, he founded and managed the Institute on Government and Education. While he was at Columbia, our paths crossed when he expressed an interest in working with the National Center for Learning Disabilities. He served on our board for many years. He is now the president of the College Board, a not-for-profit membership association best known for administering the SAT.

Gaston is a quintessential Southern gentleman. He is tall, with gray hair and a relaxed, languid manner that immediately puts one at ease. His accent too comes from the South, as does his choice of words—he says "my daddy" rather than "my father"—which made our discussion in his New York City office more like a casual conversation on a front porch.

My main purpose for visiting him was to talk about the SAT test as it relates to those with LD, but before the subject came up, our conversation veered off into his own personal story, and I found it so inspiring, I decided to let it stand on its own.

I started off by pointing out the unexpected irony that someone whose major challenges in life revolved around learning has ended up as the head of one of the largest educational associations in the country. It shows us how far someone with LD can go, and how even the most difficult barriers can be overcome, but it couldn't have been easy. "What was your experience growing up with LD?" I asked.

"I have a sister who is five years older than I am," he said. "She always got straight As, was Phi Beta Kappa; and when I was in the fourth grade my parents got a call from my teacher saying that I couldn't read. They didn't know what to do. My daddy was from a small coal town in West Virginia called Slab Fork, and fortunately, one of his closest friends became an eye doctor. He thought maybe there was something wrong with my eyes, so he took me to see this doctor. He's a brilliant guy who thought about a lot of things besides making sure people had the right-sized glasses. He gave me a lot of tests, and he told my father that I had 'reversal.' He'd have me look at *1 2 3* and I would say '3 2 1'; or *ABC* and I'd say 'CBA.'"

"Dyslexia," I said. "And he called it reversal?"

"Yes. So my daddy taught me to read. He got out a dictionary, and every day before I went to school he made me memorize a word and how to spell it and what it meant and how to read it. That's really how I learned how to read."

"It wasn't called a learning disability back then," I said. "Maybe they didn't realize there was such a thing. Did everyone think it was an eye problem?"

"No, I think everyone just thought that I had a hard time in school, and that's all. No one talked about it very much. Everyone tried to do everything they could—in other words, I was always being tutored by somebody. In the summers I had to go to summer school, and I had to be tutored. When I went to high school, I was the only person in my school who was doing remedial writing and remedial reading; and I was being tutored in math and English. But nobody ever talked about it much."

"How did all that make you feel about yourself?" I asked.

"Well, the unfortunate thing about being learning disabled is that it's hard for you to think you're smart. If you've got people who are your best friends, and they're getting 100 on the spelling test and you're getting a 50, it doesn't make you feel very smart. And if you're in the lowest end of your class, basically everyone says you're not very smart. Fortunately, I was a good athlete and I'd always been a pretty good leader, so I had enough things that I did outside of school that made me feel pretty good about myself. That was very helpful to me. It helped me keep my self-worth. And my mother used to tell me, 'You're just as smart as your sister but in a different way.' I'm not sure she totally believed that, but she knew it was a smart thing to say."

"And you believed it," I pointed out. "That's the most important thing."

"Well, I'm not sure I totally believed it either," he said, "but I certainly liked hearing it!"

"Would you advise parents to do that?"

"The most important thing you could say to a parent today is actually two things: one is that you say to a child, 'You are smart, but you're smart in a different way. Your brain works differently. So certain things are not as easy as other things.' Now for me, when I look back on this, I'd have to say that one of the most formative and important things in my life was the fact that I had this learning disability. It taught me to overcome adversity. It taught me to work hard. I think it made me much more intuitive. I'm a very intuitive person, and I think I'm more compassionate and understanding because of it. So even though there were a lot of really bad things about having LD, and even though it was really hard to have LD, in the long run it's also true that most of us don't learn anything from good times. We learn from hard times and things we've had to overcome.

"The second thing I would tell parents and students is that they need to realize that an awful lot of what you do in school is not what you do in life. You have to go through school and you have to be able to make it through school to open doors to opportunity, but once you get out into life . . . if you're producing a movie and you're a great movie producer, nobody is going to ask you whether you got a 92 or a 32 on your algebra test. People just don't ask that. I give speeches a lot, and I'm almost getting to a point where I'm comfortable reading a speech."

I reminded him of a speech that he gave at a fundraiser for NCLD. It was both heartfelt and memorable, particularly since he appeared to speak off the cuff, using only a few notes. He didn't read a word of it.

"No, I don't *ever* read speeches," he said. "But I'm almost comfortable reading one now, because I've learned how to do it. I still have to work very hard at it. I have to read it many times through, over and over. And now there are only one or two times in the speech when that little inner voice says to me, 'What are *you* doing reading this speech? You don't know how to read.' When that happens it makes me miss two or three words, and then I lose my confidence. So most of the time when I give speeches I speak from notes. The trouble is that when you're giving a speech that is complex and is something you want people to read as well as listen to, then you have to read it. I've almost gotten comfortable with it, but not 100 percent. I also think that I've convinced myself that its okay that I'm not as smart as some people."

"But you *are* smart!" I said.

"Well, I'm smart in certain things, but I have a lot of friends who can learn and memorize and understand things much more quickly and deeply than I can. Some people can play the piano better than other people. Some people can play tennis better than others. So yes, I'm smarter than a lot of people in certain things, and I'm certainly smart enough to be able to do anything in my life that I want to do. Could I be a nuclear physicist? No. I don't think I could have been a doctor, either. I don't think I could have gotten through the rigors of medical school, and I respect those people who can. But that doesn't mean there was no place in life where I couldn't be successful. And I can do a lot of things that a doctor could never do. I think we all have to be aware of that."

"It sounds like you're advocating not only realism for the parents, but for the LD students or adults, too. They need to understand their strengths as well as their challenges."

"That's right."

"Now getting back to reading a speech. Is the main problem that you still reverse letters or is it your own mind telling you that you can't do it? In other words, what matters most: the reality of your situation or your perception of it?"

He thought for a moment and then said, "I don't quite know. I think it's probably a combination of both. I may lose my concentration, and then I make a mistake, and then I lose my confidence. I can find my place again and regain my confidence, but it makes me feel bad when it happens. I'm embarrassed by it, and I feel a little inadequate. I'm a good public speaker, and so when I have to read something and I don't do it well, I really don't like that."

"And yet it's obvious that public speaking had to be part of your job as governor of West Virginia. How did you hit on the idea that you could do it better without reading?"

"I had to give a State of the State speech once. It was very long and very complex. I remember being about halfway through it, when the inner voice came to me and once again said, 'What are *you* doing up here reading this thing? You don't know how to read! You didn't have the nerve to stand up in third grade and read to the class, and here you are reading a televised speech to the people of West Virginia. What is *wrong* with you?' Now of course that voice didn't come through the whole speech, but it did come ... and that's when I'd mess up three or four things, a couple of sentences. I'm much more aware of messing them up than most other people might be. So after you do the first speech and you mess it up, then on the second you work a lot harder and practice a whole lot more until you have it memorized. And you begin to gain confidence."

"Now what about influences in your life? Was there anyone who really made a difference?"

"Yes. I had a teacher in the eleventh grade. His name was Mr. Ravenell. He was a magnificent teacher, an English teacher. It didn't matter whether it was Shakespeare or Hemingway, he really made literature come alive. That's when I fell in love with learning. I'm a great learner and I read more than most. I read all the time. I never go anywhere without a book. So I am a person who fell in love with learning, and that's one of the most important things that can ever happen to a person. I think that people with learning disabilities tend to view learning as an enemy rather than a friend. When I was a kid, we used to play touch football in the street where I lived, and I was the youngest kid in the neighborhood. When everyone got tired, they went over to one kid's house, and he had a great collection of comic books. Everybody but me loved reading those comic books. I just looked at the pictures, because I couldn't read very well. When I had to read for an assignment, that was not something I looked forward to. It was drudgery. But once you have a great teacher and you fall in love with the process of learning, then it gets a whole lot easier."

"The passion of the teacher makes the difference."

"Yes, because it then becomes your own passion for learning. You begin to understand what a valuable thing learning is."

"Don't you think every child has that passion for learning, or at least the capacity for it?"

"I think every person has it, whether they are a child or not," he said. "It doesn't matter what age we are. We all have it inside ourselves, but it gets killed or buried under what we see as the ordeal of school. A huge number of people never fall in love with learning."

"They need a teacher like Mr. Ravenell. He was someone you respected, and who taught you and respected you."

"Yes, and someone who brings joy to you, too."

"So when you read now, do you still have difficulty reading? Is it a slow process?"

"I read at a fairly fast pace," he said, "though I think there are a lot of people who can read faster than I can. I read novels, history; I read lots of things."

"So why can't you read a speech?"

"Because when you read to yourself, it doesn't make any difference if you mess up a few words. You read to understand. But with a speech you have to read it out loud, word for word, and it has to be exact."

"People who read a lot tend to be much better readers than those who don't at all. I would think the same applies for reading a speech, that the more you do it, the better you become. I would think that reading a speech would be easy for you now."

"Well, I'm totally comfortable getting up and talking about anything with notes," he said. "And there's another difference between reading a book on your own and giving a speech. When you read a novel and there's a character with a Spanish or French last name, you don't really read it. You see it but don't really read it. But when I have to publicly introduce someone with a last name I'm not familiar with, it's very hard for me. In a novel, I skim right over it. I know what it looks like and I move on. I don't have to say the very difficult names out loud. I've also learned that when I write a speech, it has to have a rhythm to it; and when I hit combinations of words that are too hard for me to put together and say out loud, then I just make it so that it isn't hard. I change it. Some words are hard to pronounce when I have to say them aloud, so I change those, too."

"So you went from fourth grade and remedial reading to becoming someone who reads a lot and enjoys it. Would you say that meeting that teacher was the tipping point?"

"In retrospect I see that as a big moment in my life, yes."

"A lot of people who had a terrible time with reading early on *never* enjoy it later in life. It's always a chore for them. I wonder if learning to enjoy reading could help them get through the difficulties of reading. Some people will always have difficulty with it, but if they like it well enough, they'll try it."

"That's true," he said. "It's also important to have goals that you want to accomplish. If that goal is important to you, then you'll deal with the problem of getting there. If the goal is not very important, then why go through the pain of it? My parents had high expectations for me. They never dreamed that I wouldn't go to college. My parents never dreamed that I might not have a successful life, and so getting through things that were difficult was just something I had to do."

"But are you born with that determination, or do you acquire it?" I asked. "Some kids don't have any goals and then they drop out."

"That's always the argument—is it an innate quality or is it something you develop? I think it's both. Some people are naturally driven to do things, but it is also something you can teach people. Maybe not at the same level, but you *can* teach it. For instance, you can teach almost anybody to hit a tennis ball, but you can't teach anybody to win the U.S. Open. At the very least, everyone can be taught the value of setting goals. Of course, there are some people who never get it."

"A lot of people don't," I said.

"Right. But if I were talking to parents, I would say that they've got to try to find something that makes it work. Something that says to the child, 'You know, if you really think it's important to go to the movies once a week, then one of the things you've got to do is this, which earns you the money to go.' That's setting a goal. It's not a goal of trying to be president of the United States, but certainly it is a goal. There's another thing that parents need to try. I was talking to the dean of a highly selective school, and he said that if you look at the bottom quarter of the students, that's where the geniuses are. It's oftentimes where the most successful people in the class are."

"At the bottom half?" I asked.

"Not even the bottom half—the bottom quarter. If you look at the one who graduated last in their class and the one who graduated at the top, you'll be amazed how often that bottom kid is the one who really does something very special in life. Sure, the top half will always do well. There will always be doctors and lawyers, but they're not going to be the Bill Gates or the famous artist or actor, or even a politician. So people shouldn't worry if their kids aren't at the top of their class. They shouldn't worry because their kid doesn't go to Harvard. They just have to want their kids to do as well as they can and to nurture the things that they do well and to look for those things they can be successful in. And it's amazing what they can do. I really believe that: no matter how learning disabled someone is, there is still some genius in everybody."

"And what about the issue of disclosure?" I asked. "What do you think about people being upfront and honest about having LD?"

"I didn't know much about it when I was young. I just got through it. People didn't know much about LD when I was in school. In some ways I think that was good. I think sometimes people allow this to be some excuse or a crutch that doesn't let people run as fast as they should."

"Who does that? The child or the parent?"

"Sometimes people make learning disabilities into too much of a handicap for a child. They create low expectations for what the child can do. They say, 'Well, my child is never going to be able to make it, and so I'm not going to worry about it.' I don't think it hurt me to have to do things that were a little hard. It was hard at the time, but I'm glad I did them."

"I wonder what would have happened if you had been labeled with something?" I said. "Did you go to college?"

"Yes. I graduated from the University of North Carolina. I always graduated from every school I went to, though my mother said it was always a photo finish. So as far as LD goes, I didn't think about having it. I never really thought about it at all until I spoke to Tom Kean. He had been governor of New Jersey for about six years when I became governor of West Virginia, and he was someone who I had observed and admired very much. I've always admired him tremendously. One day he said something about having a learning disability. He has dyslexia. I started talking to him about it, and he told me about the Lab School in Washington. He asked if I would help with their fundraising benefit."

"Did he know you had LD?"

"Yes, that day I told him I had dyslexia, too. It was really Tom Kean who got me to talk about it. When I saw him talking so openly about it, I thought it was important enough that I should start doing it, too. I soon realized it was helpful to others, especially kids. When I was governor I went to schools to talk about it. I used to say that if they liked me, the teachers could say to the kids, 'See? You too can be governor someday.' And if they didn't like me, they could say, 'See what happened?'"

"I've met some parents of adults who have LD and can't find work and have no friends. What would you say to a parent of an adult like that?"

"You have to be aware that there are different degrees of LD, and that it is coupled with the mental attitudes that are already a part of a person's makeup. I think the people who have the greatest difficulty are those people who are more susceptible to depression and more susceptible to feeling bad about themselves. Having LD only adds to that. My sense of it is that's when you need to get professional help. I'm certainly not somebody who knows enough to give out advice as it relates to that, but people do overcome those things. But you really have to get professional help. Today that professional help is much more available than in the past, and society is much more open to it. You don't have to feel bad about it. The only thing to feel bad about is if you don't seek help."

"Some parents," he continued, "have a difficult time trying to help their child. Maybe their child is thirty or forty years old, and resents what they see as an intrusion. I have a good friend who has an adult child who is bipolar, and the parents really can't do anything about it. All you can do in that case is to love them as much you can and support them as best you can, and just recognize that that's life. I don't know what else you can do. There are times when you just can't get the child beyond where they already are, except to love as much as you can and to hope as much as you can."

John Chambers
President and CEO, Cisco Systems

J ohn Chambers is the president and CEO of Cisco Systems, the fastest-growing company in the history of the computer industry and the world leader in networking for the Internet. In 2000, John was honored by the National Center for Learning Disabilities in New York City. He spoke so eloquently and with such emotion about his own experiences with dyslexia that he made a huge impact on the audience. When I decided to include this section of advice for parents, John Chambers was the first person I asked and the first who accepted. At the NCLD benefit, and at an earlier event at the Lab School in Washington, D.C., I was struck by how open he was about his own struggles with LD and wondered if he had any qualms about going public with it.

When we spoke by phone, it was the first topic that came up. "It's something I probably wouldn't have done several years ago," he said, "but I now realize that by sharing my experiences with children or young adults it can make a difference. I only learned to see that because I blundered into it. But I think it's the right thing to do, and secondly, I think it's an obligation."

John has an easy way with conversation, a charming Southern accent, and like so many Southerners, the ability to make us feel comfortable talking to him. At the same time, he's a very sharp businessman, and I wondered how someone with his skills could have "blundered" into a public admission of LD.

"It was an unusual scenario," he said. "I was at Bring Your Children to Work Day, where children come to the office so they can understand what their parents do. I got heavily involved with that years ago when President Reagan got shot and there was some talk of the vice president becoming president. My son was five or six years old at the time and said, 'Dad, I thought *you* would become president.' He had no idea what I did. So I've always been heavily involved in Bring Your Children to Work Day, and we do one general conversation on what it's like to be a

CEO and then we do a question-and-answer session. During the Q-and-A session quite a few years ago, a young girl about ten years old tried to ask me a question and she couldn't get it out. She started to cry and said she had a learning disability. She started to leave the room and there were four or five hundred people watching this, so of course it was pretty traumatic.

"I talked to her and said, 'I have a learning disability, too.' And I tried to veer my statements away from the audience and focus in on her. I said, 'I know the pain that you go through when that happens to you.' And that's true—I *do* know that pain. It's hard to describe to a parent or to someone who hasn't been through it, the embarrassment and how much your stomach tightens up. You just feel so inept. And so I said to her, 'Let's just sit down here and talk about it.' Of course the microphone was on, but I wasn't thinking about that, and I said to her, 'I'll walk you through what it was like for me.' I told her that I found that when you start to ask a question, you end up trying to memorize the question as opposed to sharing—and I said, 'Now, what is your question? Just take your time. There's no hurry.' And she did. And it was a really good question, and I gave a really good answer. And then I went on, not thinking anything about it.

"After that I had literally dozens of e-mails. Parents would come up to me, children would come up to me who were dealing with similar situations; and because I shared it, it allowed people to understand that this was not something that they needed to be embarrassed about. It's something that many of us will always have. And while on the one hand it absolutely is a weakness and you can't truly overcome it, on the other, you can learn to compensate for it, and in some ways that makes you become stronger.

"So it was that event that changed my thinking, and then Betsy Morris from *Fortune* called and asked that I be part of a major story on dyslexia. I told her I was uncomfortable with that, but she talked me into doing it because she said her child had a learning disability and she said parents just don't know how to deal with it. Our only agreement was that she would not put me on the cover, that she would put somebody else on the cover, because it still to this day—even right now, talking about it, my hands start sweating. That article had an enormous impact. You'd go into schools two years later, and they'd have that article from *Fortune* there and tell me how they shared it with the kids in school. So that's how I got into it, and today, even though it still makes me uncomfortable to talk about it, I'm not only very willing but very open to discuss it."

"What specific disability did you have? Was it in math, reading, or ...?"

"It was dyslexia. It manifested itself in reading, but at times I just misspelled things. I would read right to left. I'd get letters reversed. Looking up things in phone books was really hard for me. If I could visualize a map of how to get somewhere, I had it down cold; but if I only had written directions, no. If I couldn't visualize it, I couldn't execute on it."

"You said you understood the little girl's difficulties. How so? If you were asked to get up in front of your class to read something you wrote or something from a book, would that be the sort of thing that sent you into a cold sweat?"

"Oh, yes. I'd mess it up and the kids would laugh. I remember in about second or third grade when they came around the room and asked you to take turns reading. I could read to myself, because if I misspelled or didn't understand it, I could just go back and do it again. But reading out loud, I would lose my place or start to go right to left. This was traumatic, and so the fear when they'd come down the aisle for my turn or the fear that the teacher would call on me was tremendous. Also within that there was a feeling that, even though my parents said I was smart, and in certain topics I was pretty good, I always had the feeling that I was really dumb. Your parents can get you over that hurdle. I knew my teachers had doubts about me even going on to high school, much less to college; and yet with my parents, college was a given. I think the whole thing can be a traumatic time in a person's life."

"You said your parents said you were smart. First of all, did you know it was dyslexia at the time? If not, how long was it before you knew there was an actual name for it?"

"This was in a time when dyslexia was not understood, nor learning disabilities particularly. Both my parents were very well educated. They are both doctors. They were very tightly tied in to the education system, and they found a teacher who dealt with 'reading issues.' Her name was Mrs. Anderson. They sent me to her—it seems like every day, but it was after school for several years. She had a series of techniques that helped correct and compensate for my difficulties, and she made all the difference in my life. Now if my parents hadn't gotten me there, and if they hadn't been supportive of this approach, I don't know what would have happened."

"You also said they thought you were smart. So even if you had the reading problems, did they see beyond that and see that you had strengths in other areas? What makes you say that they thought you were smart?"

"Well, first of all, they tell you. And that's part of the problem. Your parents will always tell you you're smart. The problem is, on the one hand, it is important reinforcement, but on the other, you say, yes, but you're just saying that because you're my parents. But I was very good in math. In math I could really move fast. One of the things with dyslexia is that you often have skills in other areas. Also, and this is just something I realized after the fact, because the way your brain works, you often go A B C Z. That is not the way most people think, but if you learn how to focus it constructively, it can be a huge competitive advantage. I had a talk with a college student who had dyslexia, and he said for him, it was like finally understanding that life was going to throw him a curveball every day, and once he knew that, he could handle it. Understanding your limitations and how to compensate for them is a key element."

"Others we have talked to told us that their parents also told them they are smart," I said. "That really seems to help. Even if you think they're your parents so of course they're going to say it, I think it might be a very helpful thing. Did they have strategies that helped?"

"They tried multiple things. Without my family's love, and it was unconditional love from both of them, it would have been very difficult to get through. The first approach was practicing, and having me read to them in the evening, and trying to get through it just by practice. But it didn't work. In fact, it was the reverse of that. The harder I would try, the more uptight I got and the more frustrated I got. They also had an ability to realize when something wasn't working."

I asked him if his parents ever became frustrated.

"If so, they never showed it," he said. "They're both remarkable psychologists. Mom is a trained psychologist in internal medicine, and Dad was an OB-GYN; but he was also really good at psychology. They never showed me their frustration. They were very patient, and when one method wasn't working they—just like you would as a doctor, if one approach to solving an issue wasn't working—they would try another. And because they were tied in to the West Virginia education system, they were able to locate Mrs. Anderson and try that approach. Because of this, my reading difficulties were corrected somewhat while I was still in grade school. She taught me techniques on how to work by the fifth or sixth grade, and because I also understood my limitations, I was able to get through fine."

"And that was Mrs. Anderson who made the difference?"

"All the difference in the world. But to end this part of your question, was I ever going to get an A in English? No. But I could get a B, and it would require a lot of work. With almost any other topic, I could get an A. So with English, it was just a question of working hard enough to get the B. The capability was there. I think it's a tremendously humbling experience and one that teaches you to treat others with a level of sensitivity that I may not have gotten if I hadn't been through that."

ADVICE FOR PARENTS OF
A HIGH-SCHOOL STUDENT

"What advice would you give a parent who has a high-school student who is getting ready to graduate in a year or two and is having a really hard time?"

"The earlier you deal with this, the better off you are. It's like anything in life. The earlier you learn how to compensate for LD, the better off you are. Having said all the above, if I was to give advice to parents, it's always to give the child unconditional love and support. And even if the kid says, 'Oh, you're just saying that,' it is still important. The second issue is to try to identify what the problem is and see if there is a way to correct it or compensate for it, and to learn what you can do and not do. I was never going to be an English professor and I would never be super at reading, and I had to accept that. That doesn't mean you can't overcome elements of it. I'm a pretty good public speaker, but I speak differently. Most public speakers read beautiful speeches or they read it off a monitor. I can't. I lose my place in the speech. I lose my flow. I speak without notes or with just a slide in the background to remind me of the progress of the outline in my head. And so you take something that is a weakness and you develop it to the point where it becomes a strength. While others use notes and have to stay behind a podium or have the speech in their hands, I try to do it more like a conversation where I can look people in the eye. And so the other thing I tell people is, just because something is a weakness, that doesn't mean it will stop you from doing things. You have to understand that there are some things you won't be able to do as well as others, and you can learn how to compensate for that."

THE BENEFITS OF TECHNOLOGY

Cisco is such a high-tech company that I wondered if John saw a role for technology in helping an LD student compensate. I first asked him if he had any experience as to the benefits or drawbacks of technology in his own efforts to handle his dyslexia.

"I would say I had a little bit of help from technology in the beginning, because Mrs. Anderson had a machine that forced me to come down the page and keep on the right sentence. It prevented me from scrambling things up or going to the wrong place. It helped me go down the page line by line in a way that I couldn't until I learned the technique. I have some of these frustrations, even today. With my wife, who I've been married to for thirty years and dated for seven years before that, when we travel I ask her to describe my turns two or three turns ahead. That's very stressful for her, but if I try to make a turn by following written directions, I'll mess it up; and if I make the wrong turn, I'll make the wrong turn multiple times. Being able to visualize things is the way I approach directions, and once I visualize it, I've got it. So if someone describes it to me two or three turns ahead and I can draw the map in my mind, I'm fine. We now use a Global Positioning System, or GPS system." John laughed and said, "It has certainly helped our marriage!"

I mentioned that a lot of kids with learning disabilities use computers, and I wondered if it was the same for him, and if he felt he was drawn in some way to computer technology.

He surprised me a bit when he said, "No. In fact it was the reverse. I had very little interest in computers."

"Really? I would have thought that was something that attracted you right away."

"Not at all, but I was very drawn to sports. I was pretty good at sports. Like many areas in life, if you're not good in one area, you ask yourself what can you be good at? One thing for a parent is, not only to give unconditional love, but to say to your child: 'If you do the best you can do, that's all I'm ever going to ask of you.' The real message there is that all we want our children to do is do the best they can. I think that's a very delicate message to communicate."

"You're very lucky you had the parents you did," I said. "A lot of these kids are called stupid by their parents."

"It isn't just the love that's important. It's also the ability to lead them through this because, even if you have the love, you can still put pressure on them in ways that don't benefit them and that can backfire. If my Mom or Dad had forced me to try to read every night, it would have made me miserable. They recognized that, after a certain amount of time, it just wasn't working. And it wasn't. And forcing me to do it would have backfired."

FIGURE OUT WHAT YOU CAN DO
AND WHAT YOU CAN'T

I asked John to comment on a hypothetical yet all-too-common situation involving a young adult who is looking for work. "Let's say this young adult can't find a job," I said, "and let's also say the parents are not supportive. Do you have any advice for a young person in this situation?"

"Yes, I do. The advice is to figure out what you can do and what you can't. Don't waste a lot of time on what you're not as good at or don't like or know you can't do, and go do something that you can. There was not a prayer that I was going to be an English major, and even though I got a law degree, I hated reading. I went to college for engineering and then switched over to business, and then went to law school. This made me realize even more that even though I learned how to compensate for all the reading I had to do in law school, I really didn't like it at all. So the key is to find something that you enjoy and that you're good at. That's easy to say, but I really believe it: if you can't do something, don't continue to beat yourself up over not being able to do it. It doesn't help at all, and life is too short as it is."

I made the observation that some adults who can't find work fall into a depression and can't seem to find the motivation to look for work anymore.

"I think a lack of self-esteem and a lack of a job are very difficult for any person," John said. "If you add learning disabilities on top of all that, it's even worse. You can sit around and feel sorry for yourself, or you can say, 'I can overcome elements of this. Let me focus on those elements and let me keep trying.' It's like the young man who said to me, 'I'm going to get a curveball every time. As soon as I can accept that, I can hit it to right field every time and really become a good baseball player.' There is a governor, I don't remember his name, but he said, 'When I had to give a speech, I would often get to the middle of it and lose my place and couldn't pick it back up. I had to just laugh about it. I'd apologize and say it's dyslexia, and find my place in the speech and move on.' That openness about the issue allowed him to be pretty successful. So even though it wasn't something that absolutely affected him in a major way, he learned how to deal with it in that scenario. That's the toughest thing.

"And role models—well, maybe role model is the wrong choice of words, but I do think it's important for young people with LD to realize that there have been many people who have been able to overcome this. Part of it is hard work. Part of it is just understanding the issue. That's what it is for me. I will make the same wrong turn over and over. If I make it once, I will make the same wrong turn unless I refocus *every* time thereafter. I have to realize that about myself. The GPS system takes the strain off—not just off my wife, but for me as well. Or when I go someplace instead of writing out the directions, I can now print out a map on Yahoo.com and use that."

"What about the issue of divulging LD?" I asked. "This is also tied in to the idea of accepting LD. You first accept it in yourself, and then you may or may not divulge it to others. What are your thoughts on those two issues?"

"Well, accepting it at the right point in time is something I think you have to do. I've really thought hard about this one, because if I was told early on that I had a learning disability, I would have been linked to the 'disability.' And that word sticks to me. It's not a Red Badge of Courage. It's a symbol, depending on how and when it's presented, and it can last forever. This can be especially bad if it's a misdiagnosis!"

"So you're saying the term 'disability' can have a negative impact on somebody's self-esteem?"

"Yes. Or other issues. But with this one, I'm not sure there's an obvious answer. Understanding that you have a disability that affects your life is very important. If this is presented to you wrong or presented in a way that doesn't give you something else you can do in addition, that's a hard one to deal with. To answer your question, I think it has a lot to do with age, maturity, how severe it is, and how you get into it. Because once I got into it, and then I had the label, then I knew what I could do and couldn't do."

"It's easy to see someone using the word 'disability' about themselves and maybe not trying as hard as they might otherwise," I said. "In other words, using it to coast."

"Coast may be the wrong choice of words, but basically it can certainly make your challenge much more difficult. It's one thing to say, 'Math doesn't come easy to me.' For me it came very easy. But let's say it's reading. You already think you're having trouble enough with reading and now you're told you have a learning disability on top of it; that makes it even harder. For me, anyway, I think it might have been tougher. I think it really depends upon the degree and also upon understanding if there are parts of your capability that can become stronger. All of us understand that if you lose your sight, other senses of your body—touch, smell— become stronger. So when you have a disability in one area, sometimes your body or your mind is able to compensate for it differently."

"With this new book I am assuming that the audience will be parents who already know their kid has LD. But what about . . ."

"They may already know it," John said, "but it's always surprising to me how often people misdiagnose a problem. I always suggest a second opinion because the medical profession...and let me digress. My parents are both scientists and we have some medical professionals in the family, so when we receive a diagnosis we often look deeper into it, and it's surprising how often it's wrong. I think we tend to prescribe Ritalin or something else to 'fix' the disability a little bit too quickly, so I think we always want to make sure we get a second opinion."

"That's true," I said. "But back to divulging the issue. We know when someone is going to apply to college that it is helpful for them to divulge that they have LD because then they can apply for accommodations, but it's a little different in the workplace. You don't want to walk right in and announce to everyone that you have LD. I'm sure you can understand that. You said you had a difficult time coming forward, too."

"I never shared it," he said. "It's interesting, because after I did share it, I found out that my chairman had it, too."

"Oh, I've seen that happen so often. Once you divulge, you'll find yourself surrounded by people telling you they have it, too. But you always have to do it first."

"It's like a role model, I guess. I never understood why there might be any benefit to sharing it, so I didn't. It was only when I saw that it could make a difference in that young girl's life that I decided to share my experience. You can feel the pain. She was having so much trouble getting the words out, and you hurt so much for her. And it brings back feelings of what it felt like for you and all the frustration you went through, and so you'll do anything to help. And once you share the issue...for me it was a relief. Of course, there are certain disabilities you have to share. For example, if you have physical disabilities and you can't handle a certain type of work, or if you have a disability that they're going to find out about shortly thereafter, you better tell them. Because openness and honesty are a lot better, even if it costs you the job. And it's a lot better to have trust when you do get a job and for people to understand the issue. You might also be surprised how many people are willing to help you out if you ask for help. It's that way in college. People realize that there is a disability and that the person may need more time for the admissions test, and maybe some extra time in the classroom. The same is true for employers. People can have disabilities, and if you understand those disabilities, you can get them in the right job within the company. Don't ask them to do something they can't do."

THE BETTER PREPARED YOU ARE, THE LUCKIER YOU GET

"I have another hypothetical question for you," I said. "Assuming similar economic and social backgrounds, why are you a success and someone with the same background is not?"

"I never believe in labeling anybody a failure. I think that is just a terrible and unfair word. But if you talk about the degrees of success, I would say first it was my parents. Not only did they provide unconditional love and caring, but they were willing to work through this with me and try different approaches. When one didn't work, they tried a different one. The second is Mrs. Anderson. I don't know where I would have ended up...I sure wouldn't be CEO of a company without her help. So I had a professional who was able to help me through the difficulties. She never told me I had a disability. In fact, I don't think she ever used the word 'dyslexia.' She clearly knew that I had problems and fixed them without ever tagging me with a label. The third issue is preparedness. I found the better prepared you are, the luckier you get. Sometimes you just get more lucky cards than others, and I can't explain why that occurs. I think it's like the economy. There are five or seven different variables that have major effects on the economy, and even the best economists in the world can't tell you which ones to tweak in which sequence. Some people have success and some people have less degrees of success, and there are a lot of variables. I can't weigh what each one of them does; I just might identify what some of them are that have helped me and my friends who have similar issues."

"That's about all I have to ask for now. Thank you very much, John, you've been a great help. I'm going to include this interview in a section of advice to parents."

"Rather than advice, I like the words 'Lessons Learned.' It's so difficult to give advice on each person's particular situation. It's like me going into a company and telling the CEO, 'Here's my advice.' The only thing I can really say is, 'Here are some of the similarities, here are some of the challenges, here are some of the mistakes I've made, here's what works.' When I talk to people with dyslexia, we all seem to have had similar problems, and we all found similar ways to compensate for the problems. Sharing those lessons learned rather than have someone learn them on their own gives them a huge advantage. And it might not work for everyone, but if you can make a difference for people who read the book, that would be pretty darn good."

David Neeleman

Founder and CEO, JetBlue Airways

Air travel has become such a nightmare these days, with the long lines, the necessary airport security with its questionably necessary requirement to remove our shoes, and the overall feeling of being trapped in a herd of cattle. Then along comes JetBlue and an effort to make flying fun again. Some of you may be too young to imagine the words "fun" and "airline" together in the same sentence, but believe me, it truly was fun in its earlier years: fun and civilized, with an aura of adventure. JetBlue brings us back to that experience with attention to detail and an effort to get rid of the things that most annoy us about air travel. Much of this is due to its founder and CEO, David Neeleman, a man with tremendous energy and a sense of fun, who is completely open about the fact that he has LD and ADHD.

I first heard him speak about this during an interview on *60 Minutes* and hoped I might have a chance to meet him someday. That chance came in 2003, when he called to invite me to be the honoree of a fundraising event for Smart Kids with Learning Disabilities, a Connecticut-based organization dedicated to helping gifted children with LD. David serves as honorary chairman of Smart Kids.

I had already sent him a copy of *Laughing Allegra*, and most of our first telephone conversation centered on his difficulties in reading. That is not such a handicap in these days of audiobooks, and David was able to listen to my book on his daily commute.

Two years later, in 2005, I was asked to attend the Smart Kids benefit and present a lifetime achievement award to Dr. Fred Epstein, founding director of the Institute for Neurology and Neurosurgery at Beth Israel Hospital in New York City, and author of the book *If I Get to Five*. Dr. Epstein also has learning disabilities. I knew David Neeleman would be there, too, so I took the opportunity to meet with him to talk about his own experience with LD and to ask if he had any words of advice for parents.

We began by talking about Dr. Epstein's involvement with LD. "It was personal with him, too," David said. "He thought he was stupid his entire life, and thought that the only reason he got into medical school was because he worked harder than anyone else. But when his daughter had trouble in school, an education specialist tested her."

David opened his copy of *If I Get to Five* and read the following excerpt aloud: "When my daughter Ilana was tested, I'll never forget sitting there listening to the specialist describe her learning disability. They said she has problems with auditory processing, sequencing written commands and reading comprehensively. 'But you're describing me,' I blurted out."

While David read, I noticed his concentration as he focused on each word and occasionally stumbled. He could obviously read, but by his own admission, reading is not something that comes easily to him.

He continued reading Dr. Epstein's moment of discovery: "This was the most dramatic moment of self-evaluation I've ever experienced. I felt like the scarecrow at the end of the *Wizard of Oz* when the wizard awards him a diploma. I did have a brain. I wasn't stupid. My brain was simply wired to learn differently. So much of the shame I carried around with me, the mantle of a dumb kid in a smart family, the classroom dunce and the butt of cruel jokes fell away. In an instant I realized that I had been struggling all my life with a learning disability rather than limited intelligence. "

"Just like me," David said, closing the book. "Here you have an accomplished, brilliant man like Dr. Epstein still feeling stupid no matter how much he achieved. I felt the same way. I kept accomplishing things, but I felt stupid. I always felt stupid, and I believed that everyone else thought I was stupid."

"Who told you that?" I asked. "Your parents?"

"No. The interesting thing about this is that my mother and father thought I was really smart. I feel the same about my nine-year-old son. He's kind of brilliant in his own way, but he can't read. I sit down and try to get him to read, and it's a little frustrating because I can't help thinking, 'Oh, man, I *know* you're smarter than this.' I don't say that out loud, of course. I have a fairly deep understanding of these issues, so I know what's going on. My own parents didn't understand LD at all, but every parent wants the best for their kid, so they look on the good side. Another thing that helped was that I didn't grow up in a scholastic home. My parents didn't beat the crap out of me if I didn't get straight As. They had other ways of measuring what they thought was 'successful.'"

"What were those ways?"

"They looked at my ability to do other things beyond the classroom. I worked in my grandfather's grocery store from the time I was nine, and I could count money and do other things—visual things, like organize the shelves. But if I had to read a chapter in a book and write a composition on what I'd read, I couldn't do it. It was simply impossible for me to do something like that."

"So your parents were able to look beyond that. Is that something you would advise other parents to do?"

"Sure," he said. "The best advice I can give to a parent is also the simplest: focus on your child's strengths. Find something they are good at and promote it. Just yesterday, when we were driving into town, my wife said that we had to find some way to get our son to read more. I believe the best way to do that is to find something he enjoys. He'll spend hours setting up little army guys and then he'll create an entire battle. Hours! But he won't read a book for five minutes. I told my wife we needed to find a book that talks about armies, a book that talks about things that interest him.

"It was the same for my oldest daughter, who has ADD. She's twenty-three now and is a graduate of the Fashion Institute of Technology. That's what she was interested in—fashion. And so the best thing for a child or young adult is to help them discover their interests. And don't tell them what to do. Don't tell them to follow something that interests *you*. Find out what they like to do and give them all kinds of encouragement."

I asked David about his own experience as a young adult entering college, and I found out it wasn't so great—not at first. He went to a university for one year and did very poorly. He then left college and worked in Brazil as a missionary for the Church of Jesus Christ of Latter-Day Saints. "And that taught me structure," he said.

"More than school?" I asked.

"Oh, yes. Much more. I had to get up at six o'clock. I couldn't call home. I couldn't have a girlfriend. I was focused on the work, and when I finally went home, I had a lot of confidence. In the system we had in Brazil, the missionaries led themselves through a structure of district leaders. The highest position was assistant to the president of the Mission, and I made it to that position rather quickly because I was very successful. And so there I am meeting all these important people, and I'm just this dumb, stupid kid, and suddenly I'm feeling like a success. It was the first time in my life I ever felt like I succeeded at something. It was the first time I rose to the top. I found the environment to be easier than school. We were down there to share a message, so a lot of our work was oral. We talked, and no one was there to give me a test and grade me on it. I also had passion for my work, and I learned really quickly how to be successful in that environment. And if you're successful, then people say, 'Hey, you—go meet these people and teach them how you're doing it.'"

"So you had difficulty with the written tests."

"Yes," he said. "There is a school for kids with LD in Washington, D.C., called the Lab School. Everything there is visual and oral, and that's what Dr. Epstein said about his daughter, Ilana; that as long as teachers quizzed her orally and asked her questions or talked to her, she did really well. But when it came time to read something and then get tested on it, she couldn't do it."

THE BENEFITS (AND CONTROVERSIES) OF MEDICATION

I knew that David had caused a bit of a stir with his *60 Minutes* interview when he touched on the issue of medication and ADHD. "How did that come about?" I asked.

"Well, first of all, for some kids and adults, medication can be the answer to their problems. I know a young man who takes Strattera, which is a type of medication like Ritalin. He thinks it is a miracle drug. He couldn't function in life without it. He keeps saying that I should take it, but I keep saying, 'No, not yet, maybe someday...' When I was interviewed on 60 *Minutes*, I talked about having learning disabilities. I also talked about some of the drugs, and the way they put the show together made it sound like I was against Ritalin and similar drugs. I ended up getting hate mail from child psychologists all across the country saying, 'You destroyed our ability to prescribe.'"

"So you're not against the use of medication?"

"Not at all. When I was interviewed on another program, I had a little more time, so I took the opportunity to explain my position. I said that while I, personally, do not take the drugs, I know that some kids take them strategically, when they have to take a test or a final. They can focus and study when they take them. There is no way that I want to intimate that the fact that I don't take drugs means that I don't think other people should. For me, for my situation...I don't take drugs, and when I was thirty-four and found out I had ADD, I wasn't about to run out and start taking them. But I've talked to a lot of educators who say, 'If this kid doesn't have the medication, they do much worse.'"

THE LD ADULT IN THE WORKPLACE

We then moved on to the issue of employment, often the most difficult area in the life of an adult with LD or ADHD. I asked David what advice he would give young adults who are having trouble finding a job. He said, "I always tell people, if you just show up to work on time with a good attitude, you're better than 75 percent of everyone else. You are head and shoulders ahead if you can just come to work and have a great attitude and go to work. Now that sounds pretty simple, doesn't it? But it's true. Most people come to work, they drag in, they come in late, they have a bad attitude. It makes a huge difference if you come to work and say, 'Oh, man, this is a new day. I'm going to go out there and do my best.' So that's what I tell people. You don't need superhuman powers, just come in on time and have a good attitude."

"What about telling employers about LD?" I asked.

He thought for a moment and said, "I wouldn't right off the bat. I wouldn't come in and advertise it. It's only when you get into trouble because of it that you might want to consider disclosing it. I make public pronouncements about LD because I don't want kids to feel like having a learning disability automatically means they will fail. I want them to feel like they can succeed. But it's quite a different thing if the CEO of a company asks you to come in and the first thing you tell him is that you would like the job, but you have LD and you're disorganized and have a hard time focusing."

"Do you have employees with LD at JetBlue?"

"I don't know. That's not something we can ask. But I'm sure we have some. The statistics are too high not to have at least one person with LD in the company. As far as I'm concerned, the LD might not affect their job performance at all—in fact, it may make them better at what they do. It can be a plus. It was for me. I'm positive that if I didn't have LD, I wouldn't be where I'm at today."

I pointed out that some people seem to have a difficult time accepting LD. Some people completely reject the idea, whereas he seems to embrace it.

"People must be true to themselves," he said, "whether they shout it from the hilltops or not. At this stage my son probably wouldn't tell anyone he has it. I also have a daughter with LD, and she doesn't tell anyone at all. She's eleven and doesn't want people to think she's stupid. I don't spend a lot of time talking about it with them, either. When we were watching 60 Minutes and I spoke about it, my son stood up and looked at me and said: 'That's me! That sounds just like me!' I don't want them to use it as an excuse and say, 'I'm not going to try because I have LD.' But if they try their very hardest and they still don't do as well, then that's good enough. And that's all you can ask. The reason I became involved with the Smart Kids organization is that I didn't want parents to destroy a kid's self-esteem by saying, 'What's wrong with you?' It's often the case that the parents have it, too! Many parents take their own ambitions and try to put them into their children. I keep telling them, 'Your kids are going to be more successful than you are, if you just get off their back and not cause them to be miserable.'"

"There's also a lot of addictions that can come with this," I said, "and parents have to be careful of that. Sometimes young people with LD get into a cycle of losing a job, and getting depressed, and then giving up. They spiral down."

David agreed. "And very often the reason they lose their job is that they weren't in the right place to begin with. You have to figure out a place for them. One of the attributes of the type of ADD and LD that I have is that I have the ability to hyperfocus on that thing that I'm passionate about. It's like my son, when he can sit for hours and set up all these armies. That doesn't interest me, so I couldn't possibly do it, but it does interest him, so he sticks with it. So again, it's the same with adults looking for work as it is for kids. They need to figure out what they want to do and what they're good at. If they can work at what they're good at, then they can excel on that job, and they're not going to lose their job and they're not going to be miserable. They're not going to dread going to their job.

"I have a brother who has ADD. He's the reason I found out that I had it, too. He worked at the Gap. When he took his ADD medication, he'd go in to work and arrange things and fold things and get everything lined up. If he didn't take his medication, he was out in the mall saying, 'Come on, guys, come in! Let me show you some clothes!' And he could no more fold those clothes than he could fly to the moon. But he could sell. He was gregarious. He knew he needed the medication sometimes, but not all the time. He takes it when he needs to study or concentrate, but otherwise he doesn't take it, because he wants to be on the top of his game in a different way. That's how it works with my family, though I'm not sure that the pharmaceutical companies would recommend that."

"And so your advice to parents ..."

"My advice to parents is that they should try to help their adult children find something that excites them. Find the passion. When they find that passion, they're going to be a lot easier to deal with. And if they need some help, get them to try the medication. It's not just Ritalin. It's all over the board. Strattera and there's Adderall and other drugs, but don't ask me to spell them. I can't spell anything. I can't spell my own name."

Charles Schwab

Founder, Chairman, and CEO, Charles Schwab & Co.

Everyone knows Charles Schwab, at least by name. His company, Charles Schwab & Co., Inc., was launched in 1971 as a traditional brokerage company and in 1974 became a pioneer in the discount brokerage business. Today, the Charles Schwab Corporation is one of the nation's largest financial services firms engaged in providing securities brokerage and related financial services for nearly 7 million active accounts.

On his company's website the caption under his picture identifies him as founder, chairman, and CEO, but he is much more than that. Along with his wife, Helen, he founded the Charles & Helen Schwab Foundation, which operates Schwab Learning, a nonprofit program based in San Francisco dedicated to helping parents of children with learning and attention difficulties. The caption under his picture on the Schwab Learning website is different: it identifies him as dyslexic and father of a son with LD.

I met Helen years ago when Schwab Learning and the National Center for Learning Disabilities began the first of many collaborative efforts in the LD field, especially relating to public awareness. I was chairman of NCLD at the time, but for some reason I never was able to connect with Chuck. I really wanted to interview him for this book, as he had the perspective of being dyslexic himself, as well as the parent of a dyslexic child, now an adult.

We met in the elegant offices of U.S. Trust in New York City, with its polished marble floors and hushed aura of high finance. We talked in a small private dining room, and after a few pleasantries and talk of mutual acquaintances, he took off his jacket and draped it over the back of his chair, I took out my tape recorder, and off we went.

I started off as I always do by wondering aloud if he thought LD had anything to do with his success. I phrased it this way: "You were the first to come up with the idea of a discount brokerage firm. Because of this a lot of people think of you as a visionary and innovative. Do you think having dyslexia had anything to do with it?"

His reaction made me think I need to find a new first question whenever I conduct these interviews. Each time I ask whether LD had anything to do with a person's success, it causes an immediate pause, sometimes one so long that I wonder if I've made a mistake in asking. It doesn't matter whom I ask, the result is the same. Surely they must have considered the notion before and wondered if LD had any bearing on their career, but maybe the question asked aloud is too bold an invitation for them to talk about success in ways that might seem a little self-aggrandizing rather than encouraging, especially when their goal within these interviews is to try to give confidence to those who might be struggling in careers or jobs of their own.

Chuck put down his fork, looked at the table, and finally said, "Well . . . I think that's such a broad question about whether LD has anything to do with anything. I think it may have had to do with everything, or with nothing. I'm not sure."

I thought I'd better help out with this. "When I've interviewed other professionals with LD, they've told me that because they have to think around problems or come at them in an indirect way, they sometimes come up with solutions others might not think of."

"I've always thought that I had interesting ways to solve different problems," Chuck said. "And I always thought that I could solve any problem. Now that's a crazy thing to say, but I really did think that if I could think about a problem long enough, I could solve it. I don't mean to sound cocky or to lack humility, but I always loved to solve problems. So discovering discount brokerage and going on with it was more an accumulation of thirty-five years of doing things. All my collective thoughts and interests and passions that I had at the time, which were about investing and about how to do investing better and how to do it the right way . . . a lot of things went into it, so it wasn't a flash of light with me thinking, 'Oh my God, discount brokerage!' It wasn't like that at all."

I agreed that it is always hard to tell what impact LD has on a person's career, at least in a positive way (we all know the difficulties it can cause); but at the same time I pointed out to him that there were many other people who had the same years and experience he had who did not come up with the same innovations.

"When I was a child it was not identified," he said. "You didn't walk around with a big label on, saying you're this or that. In order to achieve, you had to work harder. I don't mean this in a competitive sense, but I probably did work harder than other people at the same subject. Particularly if it was English or English-related.

"Math came easy for you?"

"Yes. And I liked it."

"But with English, since you did have to work harder, what was your perception of your experience? Some people who go through a similar situation say they thought they were stupid."

"I had to struggle big-time on language-type things. I really struggled. I have a great rationale for the whole thing, which is that reading literacy has only been important for the human race for the last several hundred years. For at least one in seven of us, this new development called reading literacy presents a challenge because the part of the brain which deals with language doesn't work quite as proficiently. My own understanding of what I have relates to the fact that when I look at words, I have to remember that I'm looking at code. All language is code, whether it's Spanish or Japanese or Chinese . . . and for me, this code happened to be English. You take that code and you convert the code to sound, and from sound you create meaning. For me, it's that little conversion process in my brain that doesn't convert the code to sound very well, which then, of course, screws up meaning. And so I do that conversion process very slowly, especially with unfamiliar words. I have to really dissect that word or words, and it slows down the whole process. Meaning comes very slowly to me, particularly with new material or anything to do with abstract names. I have a difficult time retrieving sound. The worst thing in the world is to have the professor up there in college lecturing away, and you're converting sound to code, which is your notes, and then obviously into meaning. Well, my notes were always screwed up. I couldn't read my notes because I couldn't convert the sound into words. So for me, I was probably a classic dyslexic kid. And, like many people with dyslexia, I don't have any problem with spoken language. I can stand up and talk to a large group of people."

"With notes or without?"

"Oh, I'm much better without notes. I hate notes."

"That's a good point you made earlier about literacy. I've never thought of that. People have only been reading and writing for a couple of hundred years."

"Sure. The monks in the 1500s could write, but not the rest of us. In America, only two hundred years ago, literacy was only 5 or 10 percent."

"When you said you had trouble with 'abstract names,' what did you mean by that? Do you mean a foreign-sounding word?"

"No, I mean actual names. 'Smith' I can handle pretty easily. But a name like 'Schwab' would be a very difficult name for me, if I saw it quickly. And remembering names and the proper names of things—if I'm going to have to remember a bunch of names, I cannot seem to hear them well enough to retain them. I've got to look at them."

"So you have some processing difficulties?"

"I think so. It's a difficulty converting code to sound and then to meaning. People who are pretty good readers do that automatically, but I have to think about it. Sometimes you can see me mouthing out words, and things like that. I have to look at every word as a very discrete piece of code. Now, having said that, for familiar material that I've read a thousand times, like the financial section, I have no problem because it's repetition, repetition, repetition. But if you give me a new book today on a subject . . . "

"Do you read books?"

"Oh, I rarely read a novel. I've read them, yes . . . but would that be a very difficult situation? Yes. It's not pleasant to struggle. I'd much rather listen to a book on tape."

"It seems that you actually have to focus on the mechanics of read-ing instead of just reading. So there's probably a lot of energy going into it that most people wouldn't have to expend."

"Exactly."

I wondered, as I so often do, how students take the experience of struggling on a daily basis as a child and somehow gain enough confi-dence to get through it or go past it and become successful as an adult. "How do you get through with your self-esteem intact? Especially con-sidering that during the time you went to school, no one knew about dyslexia or LD. One thing I run into with a lot of adults is that low self-esteem becomes so strong that it keeps them down in so many other areas of their life, and it often seems to start in their school years when they were called names, sometimes by the teacher. What was it like for you? Were your parents understanding?"

"I grew up in a time, unlike today, when parents weren't totally engaged with children. There wasn't the same focus as today. Today kids have mothers and fathers who are equally engaged in all their activities from soccer games to reading to studies."

"That's true," I said, "but I wonder if there is a lot more expectation, too. Since they are so engaged, maybe they push their children in ways they didn't years ago. You have grandchildren, don't you?"

"I have ten!"

"Oh, then you know how it is today with parents. They get more involved and have high expectations. Some send their kids to programs starting at two years old."

"Somehow or other I just really lucked out in self-esteem."

"Then you did luck out. You also had dyslexia but you missed out on the low self-esteem."

"I was good in athletics and I was good in some other things. And I think the teachers liked me. I always worked extra hard, so teachers liked me."

"Richard Branson said the same thing about athletics, and so did John Chambers. Athletics really helped their self-esteem, too." I told him a story about a young woman I know who was fired from a job years ago. The experience was so traumatic she has simply never been able to work again. Her self-esteem spiraled down into the lowest depths, and she moved in with her mother, who still supports her after all these years.

Chuck nodded thoughtfully in response and then said: "Let me say something that just occurred to me. You're interviewing all these entrepreneurs, which is a whole interesting class of dyslexics. But I have to tell you, that in order to achieve self-esteem, we all need to seek different ways to do it. Certainly in my case, as a child, I spent all kinds of time thinking about ways I could make money. I used to be one of those kids picking up Coke bottles at a football game and turning them in for a nickel. I never saw a football game, but at the end of the game I'd end up with six or seven dollars in my pocket. In the Depression years, the post-Depression years, that was a great way to be measured. You'd get most of your self-esteem at that time through things like that. I did a lot of things like that.

"I'll bet if you talked to John Chambers, he probably did the same kinds of things I did. The same with Richard Branson or David Neeleman. I'll bet all of these guys didn't just wake up one day and say, 'Hey, I think I'll start an airline.' They've been doing this kind of thing for a long time."

"Since they were very young."

"Yes. I had chicken farms. I had a chicken operation. I did all kinds of things."

"Richard Branson left school to start his music business."

"But what did he do it for? Yes, because he loves music. But also, he was hopeful of making money."

"Sure, it's a goal, it's a passion," I said, and I pointed out that the need for adults with LD to find something that interests them is a thread that runs through all these conversations.

"Totally!"

"Another thread is about attitude," I said. "To learn to feel good about yourself. But what can we do as parents to help? What advice would you give to a parent whose child can't or won't work?"

"Are we talking about a child who is seventeen or eighteen?"

"Yes. Or older. The one I told you about earlier is in her late twenties."

"First of all, what interests them? Do they have an interest in anything? Is it taking pictures? Is it cooking? Find out what that might be, and then encourage them. If it's cooking, for example, there are a lot of things they could do. They could cook in a restaurant or work in a fast-food place—anything at all, just to get the social interaction going, and then you can begin the early stages of self-confidence, and hopefully you would move up from there. A fast-food place might lead to a higher-level restaurant experience. I saw this just the other night. The kid was not a great learner. I don't know if he had dyslexia or not, but he was so proud of himself. Twenty-five years old and the maitre d' in a restaurant here in New York. I knew this kid had probably never done well in school, but he sure found his way. He learned how to clear the table, seat people, all those things.

"And for the parents of these kids, it sometimes becomes a matter of disconnecting the idea of making a lot of money from the idea of doing something that fulfills them. It may be that the parents put too much pressure on them to be a doctor or a lawyer or whatever they want their son or daughter to be. And it can be difficult for the parent to say, no, don't worry about being a doctor or lawyer. Stick with what you really like to do. Parents who are nurturing, that helps to some degree . . . nurturing and letting the child feel good about themselves, in whatever work they may be doing. In my experience, as with everything, you have to start very small and work your way up. A career doesn't start out on day one at the very top. It becomes a matter of collective experiences over many years."

"But even so, it can still be difficult. You had no trouble in math but trouble in reading; but how do you start a business if it's difficult to read? Not everything is numbers in your business."

"I had trouble, but I could still read things. But I wouldn't become a lawyer, that's for sure, or anything else with a strong focus on reading. I actually went to law school and I knew immediately that it was really not for me. My dad was a lawyer and my grandfather was a lawyer, so there was some expectation there. I went to law school for two weeks . . . it was a transition period for me. This was in the late 1960s, early 1970s, and the financial world was collapsing, and I thought maybe I would go to law school, but it didn't work out."

Chuck is an advocate of the term "learning difference" rather than "learning disability." This is one of those controversies in the LD world that will never go away. It rarely if ever leads to heated discussions, but I also notice that those who hold one position rarely change sides. I prefer learning disability, in part because of my advocacy work in Washington, D.C. (the funding possibilities for a "disability" are nonexistent when it is called a "difference"). As for Chuck, he thinks that "disability" is a pejorative word. "The same with 'learning difficulty,'" he said. "What does that mean? You have difficulty learning everything?"

"So for someone with a learning difference, or learning disability . . . or to cover both bases and make it simple, someone with LD . . . how important is it for them to accept and understand what they have?"

"I don't think it's something you dwell on a lot," he said. "It's important to understand certain things, like the fact that it's better to get books on tape or take a tape recorder to a lecture class. And again, it's important to find work in an area that you like, that you really enjoy. Parents should let them develop their interests. If they like art, help them find the path they are looking for."

"You only found out you had dyslexia when your son was tested, is that right?"

"Yes. That's exactly right. I was forty-eight or so."

"Until then, you didn't know that anything was wrong. You just thought you had a hard time in school. Then your son goes to be tested . . . "

"Right. For me, I could out-think people on certain issues, but what I couldn't do was sit down and write a paper. I couldn't read the book as fast or comprehend as well as others."

"Did you see this in your son in the early years, from fourth grade on?"

"Yes. And I could see all the things that had occurred to me at that age."

"When did you decide to go public with your own dyslexia?"

"In 1988, at the same time that we started the Schwab Learning Center. Originally it was called the Parent Education Resource Center (PERC), and it was designed so that parents could go there for counseling and to find resources. We didn't work directly with kids. Our focus was on guiding and helping parents. We went through a terrible experience after we identified our son as having dyslexia, and we thought, 'Why should we make people reinvent the wheel every time? Why not create a resource center for them?'"

"Why did you change your operations from serving parents directly in your center to helping families online?"

"We began to change our model around 1998, because we were seeing several hundred local families each month, and a great many of them were repetitions. I had been thinking a lot about 'How can I make this

thing bigger and have more impact on more kids and more parents?'
That thinking led us to a more web-based organization. We began the
transition in 1998 with the new name Schwab Learning, and in 1999
launched our first website at SchwabLearning.org."

We then turned the conversation to problems with social skills and
words. "Apart from scholastics," I said, "I would say that most parents of
children with learning differences think the largest problem for their
adult children is their lack of social skills. No friends or an inability to
relate to people, even on a simple level. It goes for the workplace, too.
Most of the problems in the workplace stem from difficulties with social
skills. Speaking as a parent myself, I see Allegra's problems as an ongoing thing. There's a sense that it doesn't end. I think the problems when
they are older are much worse than when they are younger, because
they're out there in the world, and there are no rules and regulations
anymore. Every day I have some sort of issue with Allegra . . . not always
large, but something. Every day. Whereas when she was in school, I did-
n't get that."

"There was structure and routine there," he said.

"Right, so what do we say to parents who are going through these
difficult times with their son or daughter? I hoped we could tell readers
of the book that things will get better, and maybe things do get better,
but nothing seems to end."

"They change into other things, other situations," he said. "But at
the end of the day, it seems to me that self-esteem is pretty crucial, isn't
it?"

"For everybody."

"Yes, for everybody. Our school systems are starting to give children
some hope that their ways of learning are different from other people's,
and that it's okay, and that you can be an okay person and have a good
life."

"I've also been thinking a lot about this whole concept of special
education where kids are separated from the rest. Even the word 'special'
has come to mean something other than its intended use."

"That's why I think I was advantaged by the fact that there wasn't
any special education when I was a kid. I think, for the parents, if you
have a kid with these problems, you've got to help them find a way

through the system. They may not be the top student in the English composition class, but try to figure out a way to manage the system—but all the while bombing away with what they're good in. Make sure you take them to special art schools or classes on the weekend, or music, or whatever the heck they like to do. Just make sure you honor that and enhance that."

EPILOGUE
A Last Word

In writing this book, I've covered the most important issues that relate to the well-being of LD adults—not an easy task when you think of all the stumbling blocks they must go through. It's not easy to be parents of LD adults, either. Their lives are so different now from the days when their childhood was defined by parameters. There are no boundaries now. Their decisions are their own, and their lives are what they make of them—at least, that's the theory.

When it comes to dealing with adult children with LD, however, we parents know we can never fully step back from their lives. Even though the central theme of this book is the necessity of learning to let go, we know that challenges and problems do not end. We can learn to accept them and handle them, but we can never eliminate them. We search for a sense of finality, but we never find it.

Events from the past can return to haunt us with questions and worries and musings of "what if . . . ?" When I looked into the research on chromosomal abnormalities for the chapter on marriage and parenting, I felt transported back to a time now two decades past when I spent days and days trying to find the answer to why my daughter had LD. I sought the solace of a factual statement to tell me I wasn't to blame. I found those statements in abundance back then, and I know for certain that Allegra's LD is a matter of "it's just one of those things that happen sometimes." But all my knowledge and certainty do not prevent me from continuing to search for additional answers, or for clarification of the answers I already have.

It may be that the search for answers is part of our healing process and our unconscious way of showing ourselves and our child that we haven't given up and that we still have hope—not of a miraculous cure, for those dreams are over, but of a new idea, a different trail to follow, or a more effective way to ease the burdens in our adult child's life.

These burdens, or challenges, as I like to call them, are the things that truly do not end.

When I was writing about substance abuse, Alison, a young woman with LD, told me that in her AA group they strive for "progress, not perfection." That phrase should be embroidered and hung on the wall of every parent with a child with LD. Progress, not perfection.

We cannot reach perfection. Sure, we try, but it will always remain out of reach, for that is where perfection is. It stands before us as a goal we move toward, always progressing, little by little; and sometimes we cannot help but feel we're alone in our struggle to reach it.

You will not receive a blue ribbon for all you have done and still do for your child. You will not have a medal pinned to your lapel, nor will you stand and bask in the applause of family and friends who so admire the sacrifices you have made and the monumental efforts you have put forth on behalf of your disabled child. You *will*, however, hear about the things you did wrong—who you slighted because you had to take your son to a doctor's appointment, or how you should have pushed your daughter more and not coddled her so much.

Try not to take the lack of praise and abundance of criticism to heart. Unsung heroes don't let such things drag them down, and that truly is what you are—an unsung hero.

We live in a world where some parents cannot face the challenges of LD. For them, these challenges are burdens, and some parents we know have gone so far as to abandon their young children to the foster-care system, solely because they couldn't handle the burdens anymore. My guess is that no one reading this book has ever come close to doing such a thing or even thinking about it in idle moments. At the same time, I can easily imagine a parent of a child now in his thirties saying, "I have done enough. I can't do it any more. To hell with it."

The truth is, a short-term break from the constant demands can have a beneficial effect, the same as "tough love." It is difficult for everyone involved: the adult child may feel utterly lost and resentful, and the parent ... well, yes, you may feel your heart is being ripped out, but it's also possible that you may feel a sense of relief. You know the break is temporary. In your heart, no matter how angry you are, or how frustrated, no matter how great your sense of futility, you know that sooner or later you'll step back in the ring and go for another round.

Don't feel bad when you take those short breaks. Even the best boxer has to retreat from time to time to take care of his wounds.

I have had this experience several times in the last few years. A crisis will come up in Allegra's life. It may be a situation with a job or a friend. She'll make her rounds of phone calls, to me, to her friends, to relatives, to some of my friends; and often these friends and relatives will react in the way the crisis demands. They'll give advice. They'll worry. They'll call me to ask what I'm doing about it, quite certain I will comfort them by giving examples of my heroic actions. But what I often say when asked is: "Nothing."

Dead silence at the other end of the phone.

I could explain that I've been through this countless times before. I could tell them that I know Allegra's patterns and that she'll work through this as she always does. I could tell them that even if she doesn't work through it, this particular experience is going to help her in the long run with real life experience I could never give her over the phone. I could tell them all these things, but I don't. I simply say, "I'm not going to do anything."

And we wonder why we don't get any blue ribbons.

The truth is, we do know what works and doesn't work for our children. We even know when we are doing things that work against their best interests. Sure, I can agree on one level that I may have coddled Allegra a little too much at various times in her life. On another level, I can say, "So what? She's had a tough time. She's had to struggle to make the simple gains that most of us take for granted—friends, relationships, jobs. The fact that she is living on her own is a monumental achievement, so yes ... sometimes I do coddle her, and I imagine I'll continue to do so."

I allow others to help Allegra when they can. Sometimes I allow her to find ways to help herself. Sometimes I even allow her to fail. When the truly big things come up, she knows I am there. Her father died a month before I finished this book. They were not close, but she was devastated by his death. She asked to read a biblical passage at his funeral, and everyone—myself included—went into the church that day fully expecting her to stand at the pulpit and dissolve into tears. Still, I felt it was important to let her try. Alessandro felt so, too. Most of all, Allegra wanted to be a part of it.

She stood and walked to the front of the church. I sat back, perfectly calm, perfectly ready to see the display of tears, and perfectly unconcerned that anyone in the church might think badly of us for letting her do this. That is Allegra. She cries when she gives a speech. It's part of who she is. Expecting otherwise, or working myself into a worrying fit over it, would be a waste of time.

But guess what? She stood at the podium and read in a clear, strong voice without stumbling over a single word and without a single tear. I sat and listened to her, and I felt Alessandro beside me sit up a little straighter, and knew he was as proud of her as I was. I was the one who came close to bursting into tears, but I didn't. I watched her with an expression suitable to the occasion, and when she finished and came back and sat beside me, I didn't hug her and tell her what a great job she had done. I simply pressed her hand in mine, and that was enough.

Through good times and bad, we sit beside them, sometimes pressing their hand, sometimes laying it gently aside, all the time hoping we have done the right thing. Just remember—it's all progress, not perfection. We know our child better than anyone else, but we still have questions. That's why you bought this book and that's why I wrote it. We can't help it. The search for answers has become a part of our lives, and I expect that you will continue on from here, searching for more. I know I will.

Acknowledgments

While on the book tour for *Laughing Allegra*, we met so many of you wonderful parents whose questions and concerns for your adult children with learning disabilities became the genesis of this book. Most of you we do not know by name, but we remember your faces and the stories you shared with us, and we can never really thank you enough.

We met many of you at events hosted by good friends and leaders in the LD community. Foremost among them were the present and former members of the Board of Directors of the National Center for Learning Disabilities throughout the country: Rick and Diana Strauss, Shelley Mosley Stanzel, and Nicki and Tom Arnold in Dallas; John Ingram in Nashville; Drake and Shelley Duane and Chip and Daryl Weil in Phoenix; Anne Fisher in San Francisco; Barbara Keogh in Los Angeles; Sally Smith in Washington, D.C.; Tina and Steve McPherson in New York City; and Mark Griffin in Greenwich, Connecticut.

In addition, we'd like to thank the leaders of the many learning disabilities organizations who so welcomed us at their national and local meetings: Emerson Dickman, Tom Viall and Robb Hott of the International Dyslexia Association (IDA); and the many chapters of LDA (with a special thanks to Carol Calzoretta of LDA Illinois, Catherine Senn of LDA Kentucky, and Ann Kornblet); Gwen Bowlby and Dr. John Howe of Project Hope in Detroit; Barbara Whitwell and Amy Foster from The Achievement Center in Roanoke, Virginia; Ann O'Neill and Karen Dukatz-DeVitis of Ford Motor Company's FEDA program; Danny Frank of YAI/National Institute for People with Disabilities; Dr. John Fowler and Thomas Hussman of The Fowler Center; Ellen Kramer Lambert, Lisa Block, and Beth Levithan of The Healthcare Foundation of New Jersey; Davida Sherwood and Helen Thurston of The Gateway School; and Jane Ross, President of SmartKids with Learning Disabilities.

We also thank those who have done so much in the field of employment for those with disabilities: Ella Craanan of VESID; Lana Smart of Abilities, Inc.; Lynn Broder of the National Business and Disability

Council; and most especially, our friend Joan McGovern of JPMorgan Chase, whose commitment inspires us all.

We thank those who took the time from their busy schedules to talk about their own challenges with LD: Richard Branson, Governor Gaston Caperton, John Chambers, David Neeleman, and Charles Schwab; and those who were so helpful with scheduling, Jodelle Seagrave at Schwab Learning, Debbie Gross at Cisco, and Lori Levin and Debbie Dar at Virgin Atlantic. We also send a very special thank-you to Betsy Morris for her introduction to the interview section.

We spoke to several experts in a variety of fields, and their advice and expertise were invaluable, especially NCLD Board member Kristy Baxter, Head of Churchill School; Jim Rein, Founder of the VIP Program at the New York Institute of Technology; life coach Casey Dixon; John Langeler of Optima Fund; and Shawn Ames. Arlyn Roffman of Lesley University was a great inspiration. Her book *Meeting the Challenge of Learning Disabilities in Adulthood* is one of the best of its kind in the field of LD and was very helpful to us as we planned the structure of *On Their Own*. The staff at NCLD was, as usual, incredibly supportive and an invaluable resource, and we thank Jim Wendorf, Laura Kaloi, and Dr. Sheldon Horowitz for their generosity with their time and knowledge.

We thank our agents, Phyllis Wender and Susie Cohen, and Esther Margolis and her amazing team at Newmarket Press: Keith Hollaman, Harry Burton, Heidi Sachner, and especially Linda Carbone.

It is such an honor to have a Foreword written by Sally Shaywitz. Dr. Shaywitz is a Professor of Pediatrics at the Yale University School of Medicine, where she co-directs the Yale Center for the Study of Learning, Reading and Attention. She is the author of *Overcoming Dyslexia: A New and Complete Science-based Program for Reading Problems at Any Level*, and has been a member of the Professional Advisory Board of NCLD for many years. She has also been tremendously helpful on a personal level, in many ways as a mentor to me as I first tried to find my way in the field of LD and also as a caring and compassionate professional with Allegra.

John especially thanks Joan and Ed Thompson, his sister Karen, brother Jim, and their families.

And from Anne: "I send a special word of thanks to my son, Alessandro, and to Kimm for their love and acceptance; to my granddaughters, Eleanor and Olivia; and, of course, to my daughter, Allegra, who continues to be an inspiration for so many, especially me. I love you all. Mom."

Resource Guide

NATIONAL LEARNING DISABILITIES ORGANIZATIONS
SERVING ALL AGES

NATIONAL CENTER FOR LEARNING DISABILITIES (NCLD)

381 Park Avenue South, Suite 1401
New York, NY 10016
Telephone: 212-545-7510
Fax: 212-545-9665
Toll-free Information & Referral
Service: 888-575-7373
Website: www.ld.org

NCLD seeks to raise public awareness and understanding, furnish national information and referrals through their website, and arrange educational programs and legislative advocacy. NCLD provides educational tools to heighten understanding of learning disabilities, including the quarterly publications called "Our World," informative articles, specific state-by-state resource listings, and informative videos regarding learning disabilities.

COUNCIL FOR LEARNING DISABILITIES (CLD)

11184 Antioch Road
Box 405
Overland Park, KS 66210
Telephone: 913-491-1011
Fax: 913-491-1012
Website: www.cldinternational.org

National membership organization dedicated to assisting professionals who work with individuals with learning disabilities. The *Learning Disabilities Quarterly*, a professional publication, is available through CLD.

EDUCATIONAL RESOURCES INFORMATION CENTER (ERIC)

ERIC Project
c/o Computer Sciences Corporation
655 15th St. NW, Suite 500
Washington, DC 20005
Toll-free telephone in USA, Canada, and Puerto Rico: 800-LET-ERIC (800-538-3742)
Website: www.eric.ed.gov

ERIC—the Education Resources Information Center—is an Internet-based digital library of education research and information sponsored by the Institute of Education Services (IES) of the U.S. Department of Education. ERIC provides access to bibliographic records of journal and nonjournal literature indexed from 1966 to the present.

INTERNATIONAL DYSLEXIA ASSOCIATION
(formerly The Orton Dyslexia Society)

Chester Building, Suite 382
8600 LaSalle Road
Baltimore, MD 21286-2044
Telephone: 410-296-0232
Fax: 410-321-5069
Voice Message Requests for Information: 800-ABCD123
Website: www.interdys.org

International nonprofit membership organization that offers training in language programs and provides publications relating to dyslexia. Chapters are located in most states. The association has 42 branches across the country that offer informational meetings and support groups. Referrals are made for persons seeking resources; in addition, the association publishes journals and publications regarding dyslexia.

Some local branches host Adult Support Group events for adults with LD.

LD ONLINE
www.ldonline.com

Comprehensive online resource offering information on learning disabilities for parents and educators, as well as children and adults with learning disabilities. Features include basic and in-depth information, national events calendar, bulletin boards, audio clips from LD experts, and extensive resource listings with hyperlinks. Their articles on Adult Issues, including College and Transition from High School, are particularly helpful.

LEARNING DISABILITIES ASSO-CIATION OF AMERICA (LDA)

4156 Library Road
Pittsburgh, PA 15234
Telephone: 412-341-1515
Fax: 412-344-0224
Website: www.ldaamerica.org

National nonprofit membership organization, with state and local chapters, that conducts an annual conference and offers information and various publications. The LDA website contains a wealth of articles of interest to adults

with LD and their parents. Call the national headquarters to receive a free information packet. State chapters may host events for adults with LD.

LEARNING DISABILITIES ASSO-CIATION OF CANADA (LDAC)

City Centre Avenue, Suite 616
Ottawa, Ontario, Canada
K1R 6K7
Telephone: 613-238-5721
E-mail: information@ldac-taac.ca
Website: www.ldac-taac.ca

Nonprofit membership organization with provincial and territorial offices that conducts programs and provides information for LD children and adults. Resources include books, pamphlets, and website articles that may be useful to U.S. residents.

NATIONAL ASSOCIATION OF ADULTS WITH SPECIAL LEARN-ING NEEDS (NAASLN)

1444 I St. NW, Suite 700
Washington, DC 20005
Telephone: 202-216-9623
E-mail: NAASLN@BostromDC.com
Website: www.naasln.org

Nonprofit organization comprised of professionals, advocates, and consumers, whose purpose is to educate adults with special learning needs. Publishes a newsletter and holds annual conferences.

NATIONAL DISSEMINATION CENTER FOR YOUTH AND CHILDREN WITH DISABILITIES (NICHCY)

P.O. Box 1492
Washington, DC 20013-1492
Telephone: 202-884-8200
Toll-free: 800-695-0285
Website: www.nichcy.org

NICHCY is an information clearing-house that provides free information on disabilities and related issues, focusing on children and youth (birth to age 25). Free services include personal responses, referrals, technical assistance, and information searches.

NONVERBAL LEARNING DISORDERS ASSOCIATION (NLDA)

507 Hopmeadow Street
Simsbury, CT 06070
Telephone: 860-658-5522
Fax: 860-658-6688
Website: www.nlda.org

NLDA is a nonprofit corporation dedicated to research, education, and advocacy for nonverbal learning disorders.

NLDline

Website: www.nldline.com
NLD Hotline: 831-624-3542
E-mail: NLDline@aol.com

A website developed to increase awareness among parents and professionals about non-verbal learning disorders.

SCHWAB LEARNING

1650 South Amphlett Boulevard, Suite 300
San Mateo, CA 94402
Telephone: 650-655-2410
Fax: 650-655-2411

Website: www.schwablearning.org

Schwab Learning, a program area of the Charles and Helen Schwab Foundation, is dedicated to helping those with learning differences be successful in learning and life. The Schwab Learning website provides reliable, research-based information and guidance. Developed especially for parents of children who are newly identified as having a learning difference, it is designed to be a parent's guide through the new and unfamiliar landscape of LD.

SMART KIDS WITH LEARNING DISABILITIES

38 Kings Highway North
Westport, CT 06880
Telephone: 203-226-6831
E-mail: Info@SmartKidswithLD.org
Website: www.SmartKidswithLD.org

Smart Kids with Learning Disabilities is a nonprofit organization providing information, practical support, and encouragement to parents of children with learning disabilities and attention deficit disorders. Its national newsletter, website, and educational programs promote parents' critical role as advocates, while also highlighting the significant strengths of people with LD and ADHD. The *Smart Kids with LD* newsletter regularly publishes profiles of high-achieving adults with LD and ADHD, and the organization presents an annual Youth Achievement Award in recognition of outstanding accomplishment.

GOVERNMENT DEPARTMENTS/AGENCIES

OFFICE OF SPECIAL EDUCA-TION AND REHABILITATIVE SERVICES (OSERS)

U.S. Department of Education
400 Maryland Avenue, SW
Washington, DC 20202
Telephone: 800-872-5327
Website: www.ed.gov/about/offices/list/osers/index.html

Provides information about special education programs, vocational rehabilitation programs, and information about national and international research regarding disabilities and rehabilitation.

STATE DEPARTMENTS OF EDUCATION

State Departments of Education can provide information about Individuals with Disabilities Education Act (IDEA) implementation requirements and regulations. Contact directory assistance in your state capital for further information.

OFFICE OF CIVIL RIGHTS (OCR) OF THE U.S. DEPARTMENT OF EDUCATION

400 Maryland Avenue, SW
Washington, DC 20202
Telephone: 800-872-5327
Website: www.ed.gov/about/offices/list/ocr/index.html

Contact OCR to file a formal civil rights complaint.

RESOURCES FOR ADULTS
ATTENTION DEFICIT DISORDER (ADD/ADHD)

CHILDREN AND ADULTS WITH ATTENTION DEFICIT HYPER-ACTIVITY DISORDER (CH.A.D.D.)

8181 Professional Place, Suite 150
Landover, MD 20785
Telephone: 301-306-7070
Fax: 301-306-7090
Website: www.chadd.org

National nonprofit membership organization that provides information, sponsors conferences, and encourages scientific research. Local chapters hold regular meetings providing support and information.

THE ATTENTION DEFICIT DIS-ORDER ASSOCIATION (ADDA)

15000 Commerce Parkway, Suite C
Mount Laurel, NJ 08054
Telephone: 856-439-9099
Fax: 856-439-0525
Website: www.add.org

National membership organization that provides referrals to local support groups, holds national conferences and symposiums, and offers materials on ADD and related issues. Website contains excellent articles of use for adults, especially workplace issues.

ASSISTIVE TECHNOLOGY

ABLE DATA
8630 Fenton Street, Suite 930
Silver Spring, MD 20910
Telephone: 800-227-0216
Fax: 301-608-8958
E-mail: abledata@macroint.com
Website: www.abledata.com

Sponsored by the National Institute on Disability and Rehabilitation Research (NIDRR) of the U.S. Department of Education; provides information on more than 27,000 assistive technology products, including detailed descriptions of each product, price, and company information.

ALLIANCE FOR TECHNOLOGY ACCESS
2175 East Francisco Boulevard, Suite L
San Rafael, CA 94901
Telephone: 415-455-4575
or 800-455-7970
Fax: 415-455-0654
E-mail: atainfo@ATAccess.org
Website: www.ataccess.org

A network of community-based resource centers; provides information and support services to children and adults with disabilities and helps to increase their use of standard, assistive, and information technologies.

CENTER FOR ACCESSIBLE TECHNOLOGY
2547 8th Street, 12A
Berkeley, CA 94710-2568
Telephone: 510-841-3224
Fax: 510-841-7956
E-mail: info@cforat.org
Website: www.cforat.org

Provides information and services supporting technology use and assessment of hardware and software for persons with disabilities; also builds the community's capacity to support the assistive technology user.

CENTER FOR APPLIED SPECIAL TECHNOLOGY (CAST)
40 Harvard Mill Square, Suite 3
Wakefield, MA 01880-3233
Telephone: 781-245-2212
Fax: 781-245-5212
TTY: 781-245-9320
E-mail: cast@cast.org
Website: www.cast.org

An educational, not-for-profit organization that uses technology to expand opportunities for all people, including those with disabilities; develops learning models, approaches, and tools usable by a wide range of learners.

CLOSING THE GAP
Computer Technology in Special Education and Rehabilitation
P.O. Box 68
526 Main Street
Henderson, MN 56044
Telephone: 507-248-3294
Fax: 507-248-3810
E-mail: info@closingthegap.com
Website: www.closingthegap.com

Provides information about the use of computer-related technology by and for persons with disabilities; provides referrals for students with disabilities; conducts annual conference on the use of technology to support students with disabilities.

REHABILITATION ENGINEER-ING AND ASSISTIVE TECHNOL-OGY SOCIETY OF NORTH AMERICA (RESNA)
1700 North Moore Street, Suite 1540
Arlington, VA 22209-1903
Telephone: 703-524-6686

Dedicated to improving the potential of people with disabilities to achieve their goals through the use of technology; maintains listing of State Assistive Technology Programs. Services include an annual conference and publications.

COLLEGE
SCHOOL TESTING

THE COLLEGE BOARD
45 Columbus Avenue
New York, NY 10023-6992
Telephone: 212-713-8000
Website: www.collegeboard.com

Each year, the College Board serves 7 million students and their parents, 23,000 high schools, and 3,500 colleges through major programs and services in college admissions, guidance, assessment, financial aid, enrollment, and teaching and learning. Among its best-known programs are the SAT, the PSAT/NMSQT, and the Advanced Placement Program. The College Board website has an excellent section for students with disabilities.

ACT UNIVERSAL TESTING
500 ACT Drive
P.O. Box 168
Iowa City, IA 52243-0168

Telephone: 319-337-1332
Website: www.act.org

ACT is an independent, not-for-profit organization that provides more than a hundred assessment, research, information, and program management services in the broad areas of education and workforce development. Students with documented learning disabilities can apply for test accommodations as appropriate. Contact ACT for more information.

EDUCATIONAL TESTING SER-VICE (ETS)
Rosedale Road
Princeton, NJ 08541
Telephone: 609-921-9000
Website: www.ets.org

Tests administered include: SAT, GRE, and GMAT.

GED

THE GENERAL EDUCATIONAL DEVELOPMENT TESTING SER-VICE (GEDTS)
1 Dupont Circle, Suite 250
Washington, DC 20036
Telephone: 202-939-9490
Website: www.acenet.edu

Administers the GED exam and publishes information on disability-related accommodations. Operates the GED Hotline at 800-626-9433, a 24-hour service that provides information on local GED classes and testing services. An accommodations guide for people

CONTINUING EDUCATION RESOURCES

ASSOCIATION ON HIGHER EDUCATION AND DISABILITY (AHEAD)
107 Commerce Center Dr., Suite 204
Huntersville, NC 28078
Telephone: 704-947-7779
Fax: 704-948-7779
Website: www.ahead.org

International organization that provides training programs, workshops, conferences, and publications.

HEATH RESOURCE CENTER
(Higher Education and Adult Training for People with Disabilities)
The George Washington University
2134 G Street NW
Washington, DC 20023-0001
Phone/TTY: 202-973-0904
Toll-free: 800-544-3284
Fax: 202-994-3365
E-mail: askheath@gwu.edu
Website: www.heath.gwu.edu

National clearinghouse that provides free information on postsecondary education and related issues. Publishes newsletter.

THE HIGHER EDUCATION CONSORTIUM FOR SPECIAL EDUCATION (HECSE)
Department of Special Education
Room 100 Whitehead Hall
Johns Hopkins University
Baltimore, MD 21218

Telephone: 410-516-8273

Nonprofit membership organization for colleges and universities that promotes the improvement of special education–training programs.

AMERICAN ASSOCIATION FOR VOCATIONAL INSTRUCTIONAL MATERIALS (ASVIM)
220 Smithonia Road
Winterville, GA 30683
Telephone: 800-228-4689

Provides information on educational materials, including a Performance Based Teacher Education catalog.

LEARNING RESOURCES NETWORK (LERN)
P.O. Box 9
River Falls, WI 54022
Telephone: 800-678-5376
Website: www.lern.com

International association in lifelong learning, offering information and consulting resources to providers of lifelong learning programs.

VIRGINIA COLLEGE QUEST
Website: www.vacollegequest.org

Listed as "A Guide to College Success for Students with Disabilities," this website contains a wealth of valuable information and resources for the college-bound student with LD or ADHD.

COLLEGE-RELATED WEBSITES

CAMPUS TOURS
www.campustours.com
Provides links to web pages of hundreds of colleges and universities.

College NET
www.collegenet.com
Provides descriptions, homepages, and applications for numerous colleges and universities.

Common Application

www.commonapp.org

Offers an online application form that is accepted by over 200 colleges in the U.S.

Embark.com

www.embark.com

Contains articles and tools to help students select a college.

FINANCIAL AID

The following sources provide information about financial assistance. Additional sources may be available at local libraries.
www.finaid.org/otheraid/ld.phtml

SOCIAL SECURITY ADMINISTRATION

6402 Security Boulevard
Baltimore, MD 21235
Telephone: 800-772-1213
Website: www.ssa.gov

Provides financial assistance to those with disabilities who meet eligibility requirements.

FEDERAL STUDENT AID INFORMATION CENTER

P.O. Box 84
Washington, DC 20044
Telephone: 800-433-3243
Website: www.studentaid.ed.gov
Free application for Federal Student Aid (FAFSA): www.fafsa.ed.gov

Answers questions and produces several publications about financial aid.

HEATH RESOURCE CENTER

The George Washington University
2134 G Street NW
Washington, DC 20023-0001
Phone/TTY: 202-973-0904
Toll-free: 800-544-3284
Fax: 202-994-3365

E-mail: askheath@gwu.edu
Website: www.heath.gwu.edu

National clearinghouse that provides free information on financial aid available to students with disabilities.

THE FOUNDATION CENTER

79 Fifth Avenue
New York, NY 10003
Telephone: 800-424-9836
Website: www.fdncenter.org

Provides referrals to local centers for information regarding scholarships and grants.

DISABILITY FUNDING NEWS

8202 Fenton Street
Silver Spring, MD 20910
Telephone: 301-588-6380
Toll-free: 800-666-6380
Fax: 301-588-6385
Website: www.cdpublications.com/ pubs/disabilityfunding.php

Offers a comprehensive listing of federal grants, detailed listing of foundations, legal news, grant-seeking techniques, and more.

DISABILITY RIGHTS AND LEGAL ASSISTANCE

ADA INFORMATION LINE

U.S. Department of Justice
P.O. Box 66738
Washington, DC 20035-6738
Telephone: 202-514-0301
Toll-free: 800-514-0301

Answers questions about Title II (public services) and Title III (public accommodations) of the Americans with Disabilities Act (ADA). Provides materials and technical assistance on the provisions of the ADA.

ADA TECHNICAL ASSISTANCE PROGRAMS

U.S. Department of Justice
950 Pennsylvania Avenue, NW
Washington, DC 20530
Telephone: 800-949-4232
Website: www.usdoj.gov/crt/ada/taprog.htm

Federally funded regional resource centers that provide information and referral, technical assistance, public awareness, and training on all aspects of the Americans with Disabilities Act (ADA). Calls to the 800 number will be automatically routed to the technical assistance center in the caller's region. Also provides information about the Americans with Disabilities Act (ADA) through a toll-free ADA Information Line: 800-514-0301 (voice); 800-514-0383 (TDD) www.usdoj.gov/crt/ada/infoline.htm

DICKMAN CONSULTING ALLIANCE

25 E. Spring Valley Ave.
Maywood, NJ 07607
Phone: 201-909-0404
Website: www.dickmanalliance.com
E-mail: info@emersondickman.org

Provides services to parents, educa-tors, practitioners, and advocates/attorneys, such as Child Advocacy, Planning for Individuals with special needs (including estate planning), and Educational Staff Development.

DISABILITY RIGHTS EDUCATION AND DEFENSE FUND (DREDF)

2212 6th Street
Berkeley, CA 94710-2219
Telephone: 510-644-2555
Fax: 510-841-8645
E-mail: dredf@dredf.org
Website: www.dredf.org

A national law and policy center dedicated to protecting and advancing the civil rights of people with disabilities through legislation, litigation, advocacy, technical assistance, and education and training of attorneys, advocates, persons with disabilities, and parents of children with disabilities.

EQUAL EMPLOYMENT OPPORTUNITY COMMISSION (EEOC)

1801 L Street, NW
Washington, DC 20507-0001
Telephone: 800-669-4000
TD: 800-669-6820
Website: www.eeoc.gov

Federal agency that provides assistance with discrimination complaints about employment.

WRIGHTS LAW

Website: www.wrightslaw.com

Parents, advocates, educators, and attorneys come to Wrightslaw for accurate, up-to-date information about advocacy for children with disabilities. You will find hundreds of articles, cases, newsletters, and resources about special education law and advocacy in their Advocacy Libraries and Law Libraries. Of particular interest to parents looking for information about the Individuals with Disabilities Educaton Act (IDEA).

NATIONAL ASSOCIATION OF PROTECTION AND ADVOCACY SYSTEMS

900 Second Street, NE, Suite 211
Washington, DC 20002
Telephone: 202-408-9514
Fax: 202-408-9520
E-mail: napas@earthlink.net
Website: www.napas.org

Protection and Advocacy (P&A) and Client Assistance Program (CAP) make up a nationwide network of disability rights agencies that provide literature on legal issues and referrals to programs that advocate for the right of people with disabilities. P&A agencies provide legal representation and other advocacy services to persons with disabilities. CAP provides information and assistance to individuals seeking or receiving vocational rehabilitation services under the Rehabilitation Act. Callers to the above number will be referred to P&A and CAP programs in their area.

EMPLOYMENT

JOB ACCOMMODATION NETWORK (JAN)

West Virginia University
P.O. Box 6080
Morgantown, WV 26506-6080
Telephone: 800-526-7234 (U.S.)
800-526-2262 (Canada)
Fax: 304-293-5407
E-mail: jan@jan.icdi.wvu.edu
Website: www.jan.wvu.edu

Job Accommodation Network (JAN) has a free consulting service that provides information on equipment, methods, and modifications for disabled persons to improve their work environment. All information is specific to the disability, including LD.

NATIONAL EMPLOYMENT COUNCIL

2020 Pennsylvania Avenue, NW, #940
Washington, DC 20006
Telephone: 800-299-9039

Matches individuals who have disabilities with prospective employers.

EQUAL EMPLOYMENT OPPORTUNITY COMMISSION (EEOC)

1801 L Street NW
Washington, DC 20507
Telephone: 800-663-4900
Website: www.eeoc.gov

Key federal agency for the implementation of Title I (employment) of the Americans with Disabilities Act (ADA).

OFFICE OF DISABILITY EMPLOYMENT POLICY U.S. DEPARTMENT OF LABOR

Telephone: 866-487-2365 (Department of Labor, toll-free)

877-889-5627 (Department of Labor, TTY)

Website: www.dol.gov/odep

The Office of Disability Employment Policy provides information, training, and technical assistance to America's business leaders, organized labor, rehabilitation and other service providers, advocacy organizations, families, and individuals with disabilities. ODEP's mission is to facilitate the communication, coordination, and promotion of public and private efforts to empower Americans with disabilities through employment.

NATIONAL COLLABORATIVE ON WORKFORCE AND DISABILITY FOR YOUTH (NCWD/Youth)

NCWD/Youth
c/o Institute for Educational Leadership
4455 Connecticut Avenue NW, Suite 310
Washington, DC 20008
Telephone: 877-871-0744 (toll-free)
TTY: 877-871-0665 (toll-free)
Website: www.ncwd-youth.info

NCWD/Youth assists state and local workforce development systems to better serve youth with disabilities. The organization is composed of partners with expertise in disability, education, employment, and workforce development issues. Its online information is organized in categories for administrators of a workforce development program, employers, service practitioners, policy makers, and family members of young adults with disabilities.

NATIONAL CENTER ON SECONDARY EDUCATION AND TRANSITION (NCSET)

Institute on Community Integration
University of Minnesota
6 Pattee Hall
150 Pillsbury Drive SE
Minneapolis, MN 55455
Telephone: 612-624-2097
Fax: 612-624-9344
E-mail: ncset@umn.edu
Website: www.ncset.org

The National Center on Secondary Education and Transition (NCSET) coordinates national resources, offers technical assistance, and disseminates information related to secondary education and transition for youth with disabilities in order to create opportunities for youth to achieve successful futures. NCSET also hosts Youthhood.org, an exciting resource to help young adults with disabilities plan for the future. It covers such topics as Apartment Living and Job Hunting.

Website: www.youthhood.org/youthhood/index.asp

PACER CENTER: EMPLOYMENT STRATEGIES FOR YOUTH AND YOUNG ADULTS WITH DISABILITIES

8161 Normandale Blvd.

Minneapolis, MN 55437
Telephone: 952-838-9000
TTY: 952-838-0190
Website: www.pacer.org/swift/index.htm

The PACER Center offers families and students with disabilities an array of resources to help them get ready and get out there. Their online resources include information on transition from high school to employment, and understanding the ADA.

THE NATIONAL CENTER ON WORKFORCE AND DISABILITY/ADULT (NCWD)

Institute for Community Inclusion
University of Massachusetts, Boston
100 Morrissey Blvd.
Boston, MA 02125
Telephone/TTY: 888-886-9898
Website: www.onestops.info

Provides training, technical assistance, policy analysis, and information to improve access for all in the workforce development system. Areas of expertise include: accommodations and assistive technology, relationships with employers, helping clients with disabilities find jobs, and advising employers on how to provide job-related supports.

JOB TRAINING

VOCATIONAL REHABILITATION AGENCIES

U.S. Department of Education
Office of Special Education and
Rehabilitative Services (OSERS)
Switzer Building
330 C Street SW
Washington, DC 20202

Telephone: 202-205-5465
Website: www.jan.wvu.edu/SBSES/
VOCREHAB.HTM

These agencies can provide job training, counseling, financial assistance, and employment placement to individuals who meet eligibility criteria.

EMPLOYMENT WEBSITES

AMERICA'S JOB BANK
www.ajb.dni.us

Useful both for job seekers and employers; offers job announcements, talent banks, and information about getting a job.

CAREER CONNECTIONS
www.career.com

Posts job announcements and an online application form; hosts cyber job fairs.

MARRIOTT FOUNDATION
www.MarriottFoundation.org

Provides information on job opportunities for teenagers and young adults with disabilities.

ONLINE CAREER RESOURCES
www.jobhunt.org/slocareers/
resources.html

Contains assessment tools, tutorials, labor market information, etc.

O*NET: THE DEPARTMENT OF LABOR'S OCCUPATIONAL INFORMATION NETWORK

www.doleta.gov/programs/onet

Useful for job seekers, employers, and teachers; has career information and links to government resources.

PETERSON'S EDUCATION AND CAREER CENTER

www.petersons.com

Contains postings for full- and part-time jobs, as well as summer job opportunities.

INDEPENDENT LIVING

LIVING RESEARCH UTILIZATION PROGRAM (LRU)

2323 South Shepherd, Suite 1000
Houston, TX 77019
Telephone: 713-520-0232
Website: www.bcm.tmc.edu/ilru

National resource center that produces materials, develops and conducts training programs, and publishes a monthly newsletter.

NATIONAL COUNCIL OF INDEPENDENT LIVING (NCIL)

1710 Rhode Island Ave. NW, 5th floor
Washington, DC 20036
Telephone: 202-207-0334
TTY: 202-207-0340
Toll-free: 877-525-3400
Website: www.ncil.org

Cross-disability grassroots national organization that provides referrals to independent living facilities around the nation.

LITERACY PROGRAMS

LITERACY VOLUNTEERS OF AMERICA (LVA)

1320 Jamesville Ave.
Syracuse, NY 13210
Telephone: 315-422-9121 ext. 353
Fax: 315-422-6369
Website: www.literacyvolunteers.org

National nonprofit organization that provides literacy opportunities for adults.

INTERNATIONAL READING ASSOCIATION (IRA)

800 Barksdale Road
P.O. Box 8139
Newark, DE 19714-8139
Telephone: 302-731-1600
Website: www.reading.org

Nonprofit membership organization that publishes journals for teachers, researchers, and professionals. A catalog of books, videos, and other materials is available.

NATIONAL INSTITUTE FOR LITERACY (NIFL)

1775 I Street NW, Suite 730
Washington, DC 20006
Telephone: 202-233-2025
Website: www.nifl.gov

Federal agency that provides leadership through advocacy, information sharing, and collaboration.

NATIONAL CLEARINGHOUSE ON ESL LITERACY EDUCATION (NCLE)

Center for Applied Linguistics
4646 40th St. NW
Washington, DC 20016-1859
Telephone: 202-362-0700
Fax: 202-362-3740
E-mail: info@cal.org
Website: www.cal.org

Provides literacy education for adults and out-of-school youth who are learning English as a second language.

NATIONAL LINCS LITERACY & LEARNING DISABILITIES SPECIAL COLLECTION

1775 I Street NW, Suite 730
Washington, DC 20006
Telephone: 202-233-2025

A collection of web-based and other resources on issues affecting adults with learning disabilities and their families, as well as literacy practitioners and other human resource service providers who work with these persons.

BOOKS ON TAPE

RECORDING FOR THE BLIND AND DYSLEXIC (RFB&D)

20 Roszel Road
Princeton, NJ 08540
Telephone: 609-452-0606
Toll-free: 800-221-4792
Website: www.rfbd.org

International nonprofit organization that lends recorded and computerized books at all academic levels to people who cannot read standard print.

NATIONAL LIBRARY SERVICE FOR THE BLIND AND PHYSICALLY HANDICAPPED (NLSBPH)

Library of Congress
1291 Taylor Street NW
Washington, DC 20542
Telephone: 800-424-8567
Website: www.loc.gov/nls

Provides books on tape to children and adults with learning disabilities. Contact your local library for further information.

SUPPORT NETWORKS AND LIFE COACHING

AMERICAN COACHING ASSOCIATION

P.O. Box 353
Lafayette Hill, PA 19444
Telephone and Fax: 610-825-4505
Website: www.americoach.org
Links people who want coaching with people who do coaching; coaches help individuals to set goals, accept limitations and acknowledge strengths, develop social skills, and create strategies that enable them to be more effective in managing their day-to-day lives.

INTERNATIONAL COACH FEDERATION

2365 Harrodsburg Rd, Suite A325
Lexington, KY 40504
Telephone: 888-423-3131 (toll-free) or 859-219-3580
Fax: 859-226-4411
Website: www.coachfederation.com
E-mail: icfoffice@coachfederation.org

ADHD COACHES ORGANIZATION (ACO)

Website: www.adhdcoaches.org

CASEY DIXON, MSEd, CTACC
311 Front Street
Lititz, PA 17543

Telephone: 717-431-8396
Website: www.caseydixon.com

SUPPORT NETWORKS WEBSITES

LD PRIDE
www.ldpride.net

Provides information about learning disabilities and offers support through bulletin boards and chat services.

PEER ASSISTANCE LEADERSHIP (PAL)
www.palusa.org
Outreach program for elementary, intermediate, and high school students.

PEER RESOURCES NETWORK
www.peer.ca/peer.html

A Canadian organization that offers training, educational resources, and consultation to those interested in peer helping and education. Their resources section has information on books, articles, and videos.

TEENS HELPING TEENS
www.ldteens.org

A resource site for teens operated by students with dyslexia; provides information about the disability, study tips and a support network.

These resources are listed with special thanks to the National Center for Learning Disabilities (www.ld.org) and the National Information Center for Youth and Children with Disabilities (NICHY—www.nichcy.org).

Index

About the Authors

Anne Ford is a woman of many accomplishments, but the one she's proudest of is her role as mother of her son, Alessandro, and her daughter, Allegra—and her new role as grandmother to Eleanor and Olivia.

Anne Ford served as Chairman of the Board of the National Center for Learning Disabilities (NCLD) from 1989 to 2001. During her term as Chair, she led the reorganization and broad expansion of NCLD, including establishing a presence in Washington, D.C., and organizing educational summits on learning disabilities in several regions of the United States. She has received many honors for her work in the field of learning disabilities, including the Lizette H. Sarnoff Award for Volunteer Service from the Albert Einstein College of Medicine. Leslie University has conferred upon her an Honorary Degree, Doctor of Humane Letters, for advocacy for people with learning disabilities.

Anne Ford is the author of the popular and inspirational book *Laughing Allegra*, about her experiences as the mother of a daughter with a learning disability. She continues to work on behalf of people with LD, appearing as a keynote speaker at conferences and corporations, including JPMorgan Chase and Ford Motor Company.

John-Richard Thompson is an award-winning playwright and novelist living in New York City. He is co-author of Anne Ford's *Laughing Allegra*. For more information, visit his website www.j-rt.com.

Also by Anne Ford
LAUGHING ALLEGRA
The Inspiring Story of a Mother's Struggle and Triumph Raising a Daughter with Learning Disabilities

"A must read for every mother and father, not just those of us with a 'special' child. Anne Ford shares the heartbreaking lows, the glorious highs, and lonely in-betweens of raising a daughter with a severe learning disability, at a time when few people, and few schools, knew what to do to help, or even tried. You will never look at a child with special needs the same way after knowing what even a parent of great privilege had to endure."
—Judy Woodruff and Al Hunt

"This smart and welcome book is a gift for all parents, not just those with children with learning disabilities.... An insightful guide through the challenges and rewards of parenting." —Tom Brokaw

"This poignant, intimate portrait opens an often hidden world and illuminates the many ways learning disabilities shape the lives of entire families."
—*Publishers Weekly*

"Unforgettable insights into the miracles of mothering and fathering fortified with the empowering knowledge of how a parent and a child can enrich and validate each other's lives." —Mel Levine, M.D.

"This book gave voice to my own feelings of raising and teaching a daughter with learning disabilities. In my journey with my daughter I have always felt very alone and isolated. *Laughing Allegra* mirrored my own experiences and emotions, and comforted me." —A mother, via e-mail

"I read *Laughing Allegra* in two days as I could not stop. The book helps me to describe my child when asking for services, understand her needs, and not be so afraid anymore." —A parent, Falls Church, VA

LAUGHING ALLEGRA by Anne Ford with John-Richard Thompson
272 pages. 6" x 9". 22 photos. Includes answers to most commonly asked questions, legal rights, resource guide, index. Foreword by Mel Levine, M.D.
ISBN: 978-1-55704-622-2. $16.95. pb. • 978-1-55704-564-5. $24.95. hc.

Our books are available from your local bookseller or from Newmarket Press, 18 East 48th Street, New York, NY 10017; phone 212-832-3575 or 800-669-3903; fax 212-832-3629; e-mail info@newmarketpress.com. Prices and availability are subject to change. Catalogs and information on quantity order discounts are available upon request.

www.newmarketpress.com   www.laughingallegra.com